Entering History

German Life and Civilization
Vol. 40

Jost Hermand
General Editor

Advisory Board

Helen Fehervary
Ohio State University

Peter Uwe Hohendahl
Cornell University

Robert C. Holub
University of California at Berkeley

Klaus Scherpe
Humboldt University, Berlin

Frank Trommler
University of Pennsylvania

PETER LANG
Oxford • Bern • Berlin • Bruxelles • Frankfurt/M. • New York • Wien

dresses a number of questions: What constitutes the fragment, when the fragment can only be defined *a posteriori*? Does the fragment begin on its own, or is it begun by others, writers and critics? Does it acquire a name of its own, or is it labelled by others? All these questions revolve around issues of agency, and they are best discussed in terms of performativity, which means seeing fragments as acts: acts of literature, acts of reading, acts of writing. The book demonstrates how a poetics of the genre can be created as literature and a modern criticis philosophy, art *Contents:* The C sual Fragmen Resolute Fra – The Epigr atic Fragment.

Silke von der Emde
Entering History
Feminist Dialogues in Irmtraud Morgner's Prose

Oxford, Bern, Berlin, Bruxelles, Frankfurt am Main, New York, Wien, 2004. 260 pp. German Life and Civilization. Vol. 40
General Editor: Jost Hermand

ISBN 3-03910-158-7 / US-ISBN 0-8204-6968-8 pb.

sFr. 67.– / €* 45.80 / €** 42.80 / £ 30.– / US-$ 50.95

This book offers a thorough examination of the novels of Irmtraud Morgner (1933-1990), one of the most talented, compelling and overlooked writers within East German feminist and avant-garde circles. Using a combination of theoretical approaches – including Adorno's aesthetic theories and Bakhtinian analyses of dialogism and the carnivalesque – the author traces Morgner's engagement with postmodernist aesthetic strategies back to her efforts, beginning in the early 1970s, to pose questions about effective political practices. Morgner's work sheds new light on the fraught relationship between GDR intellectuals and the state, a hotly debated topic that marks most recent attempts to understand literary culture in the German Democratic Republic. Situating Morgner's fiction at the intersection of postmodern and feminist theory, this study also offers new evidence for viewing literature from the GDR as significantly more complex and aesthetically interesting than has been previously assumed.

Contents: Biographical Details – The Cultural Debates of the 1960s – The Reception of *Life and Adventures of Trobadora Beatrice* in East and West – Dissenting Voices in the GDR – FRG Criticism (1974-76) – FRG Criticism (1985-90) – U.S. German Studies (1976-83) – Morgner's Novel Today: «Kein Ort, Nirgends?» – Morgner's Use of History and Myth – Morgner's Concept of Author – Subjectivity, and Representation – Woman as Author – The Historicity of Adorno's Aesthetic Theory – Feminism in the Early Seventies – Morgner's Postmodern Feminism – Intertextual Games – The Postmodernism Debate – Antipodean Artists and Tightrope Walkers – The Antipodean Artist Mikhail Bakhtin – Creating a «Legendary Historical Consciousness» – The Montage Novel – Carnival: Representing the Body.

The Author: Silke von der Emde is associate professor in the Department of German Studies at Vassar College. She has published articles on GDR literature, feminist theory, and German film. In addition to her cultural studies research, her interests in the intersection of teaching, learning, and computer technology have led to several publications in leading journals in the field.

* inkl. MWSt. – nur gültig für Deutschland und Österreich   ** exkl. MWSt.
* comprend la TVA – uniquement valable pour l'Allemagne et l'Autriche   ** ne comprend pas la TVA
* includes VAT – only valid for Germany and Austria   ** does not include VAT

Zeitschrift für Germanistik

Zeitschrift für

GERMANISTIK

Neue Folge

Peter Lang AG
Europäischer Verlag der Wissenschaften

Herausgegeben von der Philosophischen Fakultät II / Germanistische Institute der Humboldt-Universität zu Berlin

Die «Zeitschrift für Germanistik» versteht sich als breites Forum der Internationalen Germanistik. Sie diskutiert u.a. Probleme der Geschichte der deutschsprachigen Literatur und der Gegenwartsliteratur, geht neuen Theorieansätzen nach und verfolgt die Wechselbeziehungen zwischen Sprach- und Literaturwissenschaft. Sie beteiligt sich aktiv an den Diskussionen um die Perspektiven des Faches.

Neben Abhandlungen, Diskussions- und Forschungsbeiträgen, Konferenzberichten, neuen Materialien und Miszellen enthält jede Ausgabe einen ausführlichen Rezensionsteil.

Neue Folge 1/2005

Silke von der Emde

Entering History

Feminist Dialogues in
Irmtraud Morgner's Prose

PETER LANG

Oxford · Bern · Berlin · Bruxelles · Frankfurt/M. · New York · Wien

Bibliographic information published by Die Deutsche Bibliothek
Die Deutsche Bibliothek lists this publication in the Deutsche National-
bibliografie; detailed bibliographic data is available on the Internet at
‹http://dnb.ddb.de›.

British Library and Library of Congress Cataloguing-in-Publication Data:
A catalogue record for this book is available from *The British Library,*
Great Britain, and from *The Library of Congress,* USA

ISSN 0899-9899
ISBN 3-03910-158-7
US-ISBN 0-8204-6968-8

© Peter Lang AG, European Academic Publishers, Bern 2004
Hochfeldstrasse 32, Postfach 746, CH-3000 Bern 9, Switzerland
info@peterlang.com, www.peterlang.com, www.peterlang.net

Printed in Germany

Contents

Acknowledgements

This book argues that we must understand the work of Irmtraud Morgner as one of ruptures, displacements, and imaginative detours. It is impossible to appreciate this author's work as linear or unified. Although written under very different historical circumstances, the story of this book mirrors in some sense the fractured qualities of Morgner's work. *Entering History* began as a PhD thesis completed at Indiana University in 1994, in the tumultuous times after the *Wende*. In the years that followed, the book underwent many turns, trials, and revisions as I sought to rethink Morgner's work in light of our evolving understanding of the GDR.

I am indebted to many people for intellectual stimulation. I would like to take this opportunity to thank my parents for letting me grow up in a house full of books. I would also like to express my gratitude to former professors at Indiana University for guiding me in my journeys to explore new intellectual terrain and for allowing me to experiment with different approaches. In particular, I am happy finally to be able to thank Ingeborg Hoesterey for years of friendship, support, and intellectual exchange. Many friends and colleagues, especially Jeannette Clausen, Mark Weiner, and David Bathrick, were invaluable in helping me sharpen arguments, revise immature interpretations, and gain new insights. I am also grateful to my colleagues at Vassar College, especially Michael Joyce and Rachel Kitzinger for their mentoring and intellectual stimulation. Many thanks go to Günter Klabes for his support and above all to Jeffrey Schneider for his continuing encouragement and friendship. Finally, I am thankful to Linda Lincoln, who sharpened my prose and patiently persevered in weeding Germanisms from my text.

Vassar College provided me with many of the resources I needed to conduct research and carry out the writing. A research grant helped with the preparations for publication. I am grateful for having had the opportunity to test some of the ideas and interpretations put forward in this book in various lectures and conference papers over the years.

Drafts of certain chapters were presented at Dartmouth College, the Middlebury Summer School, the Kentucky Foreign Language Conference, the German Studies Association and the Modern Language Association. An earlier version of chapter 3 first appeared in *Women in German Yearbook* 10 (1994) published by the University of Nebraska Press.

This book would not have been possible without the support and encouragement of Bert Wachsmuth. Our two daughters, Leah and Lulu, were both born during the years I spent researching and writing *Entering History*. For grounding my thoughts throughout the writing process and beyond, I dedicate this book with gratitude to these three "anchors" in my life.

Introduction

Schreiben mit Engagement heißt Fragen stellen. [To write with commitment means to ask questions.][1]

Irmtraud Morgner, "Apropos Eisenbahn"

Irmtraud Morgner's novel *Rumba auf einen Herbst* (Rumba for an autumn) is one of the most prominent unpublished books ever written in the former German Democratic Republic. While readers were never able to view the original text, the existence of the novel, written in the early 1960s, was well known to Morgner's readers.[2] *Rumba* was listed in bibliographies, it appeared in 1975 in *Schriftsteller der DDR,* the official GDR writers' encyclopaedia, it was mentioned in interviews and scholarly articles, and Morgner incorporated parts of it into a 1974 novel, *Leben und Abenteuer der Trobadora Beatriz (Life and Adventures of Trobadora Beatrice).*[3] Only after the demise of the GDR, when Rudolf Bussmann published the reconstructed novel from Morgner's literary estate in 1992 (two years after the author's death), did readers see how the novel had looked when its permission to be published had been withdrawn in December 1965.[4] Bussmann writes in his postscript: "A piece of prose that goes around without being physically available to readers. It's as if we can hear Morgner's mocking laughter!" (331)

1   Unless otherwise stated, all translations from German in this volume are mine.
2   In a 1984 interview with Eva Kaufmann published in *Weimarer Beiträge*, Morgner said that after her two earlier texts, *Das Signal steht auf Fahrt* (1959) and *Ein Haus am Rande der Stadt* (1962), which had been praised by GDR critics, *Rumba auf einen Herbst* was the first book she *had* to write. In a covering letter to the publisher in 1965, she said: "I think of *Rumba for an Autumn* as my first novel," the exact sentence with which she later, after her manuscript had been rejected, designated her book *Hochzeit in Konstantinopel* (Wedding in Constantinople) (1968) in her essay "Apropos Eisenbahn" of 1973.
3   *Life and Adventures* was published in the GDR in 1974 and the FRG in 1976. Jeannette Clausen published her English translation of the novel in 2000 with the University of Nebraska Press.
4   In 1995, dtv published a paperback edition.

Rereading Morgner's novels at the turn of the twenty-first century after the demise of the GDR sheds new light on Irmtraud Morgner as a writer and feminist thinker and on her importance for the development of literature in the GDR. The fate of Morgner's novels in the GDR gives us insights into censorship practices and the strategies writers used to avoid them. *Rumba*, for example, which skilfully connects popular music, jazz, blues, and the rumba with Morgner's feminist agenda, offers new perspectives on the debate over popular culture in the GDR in the fifties and early sixties. In fact, taking a closer look at the debate and the way it was carried out in the arts is especially promising, since East Germany has largely been a desert for cultural studies. With the newly available sources from East Germany, such as the "forbidden films" of 1965 and manuscripts such as Morgner's *Rumba*, we learn more about the complex connections between the reconstitution of gender and the (re)construction of Germanness in the fifties and sixties on the other side of the iron curtain. Morgner's later novels participated in similar cultural conflicts, such as the debate over the new women's movement, which officially never existed in the GDR, and the discussion over the role of science and technology in the socialist state. In each case, Irmtraud Morgner was among those artists who pushed the debates forward and forced her readers and GDR cultural officials to take gender into account.

Irmtraud Morgner's *Rumba auf einen Herbst* was among the many texts, mainly films, that disappeared entirely after the Eleventh Plenum of the Socialist Unity Party of Germany (Sozialistische Einheitspartei Deutschlands) (SED) in December 1965 or managed to reach the public eye only in truncated or otherwise disfigured form. Yet even when it was finally published in reconstructed form, the novel received little attention. Reviewers characterized the novel as a product of its time, and therefore of little interest to readers in the nineties.[5] While there were enthusiastic voices, some admirers of Morgner's work, such as Doris Janhsen and Monika Meyer, complained that Morgner seemed to have been forgotten in the debates

---

5   Sabine Brandt, for example, talks in the *Frankfurter Allgemeine Zeitung* (8 May 1990) about "ein Hauch von Muff der ummauerten Provinz" (the bad smell of the fenced-in Republic), which supposedly sticks to the novel.

over GDR literature following the fall of the wall in 1989. Although Morgner's novels have been immensely popular with readers and although she belonged to the generation of writers who shaped the literary character of the East German state, her work is seldom mentioned in the debate over the quality and specific character of GDR literature. Janhsen and Meyer maintain that one of the reasons for this neglect might be that Morgner – unlike other GDR writers – was rarely an obvious player in the public debates over cultural policy in the GDR. Instead, she articulated her position between dissent and affirmation in her novels and narrative texts, which in their provoking complexity were hardly suited to be position statements ("Trobadora passé?").

This book traces Morgner's place between dissent and affirmation as she articulated it in her novels. In these texts Morgner's increasing joy in aesthetic experimentation can be seen as an attempt to open up alternative spaces for thought and creativity against the dogmatic prescriptions of cultural officials in the GDR. Morgner's texts are analyzed as countertexts that try to break open the official discursive code to make room for questions, dialogue, and dissent. This does not mean, however, that there can always be a clear-cut distinction between an official master discourse dictated by functionaries and other officials on the one hand and a clearly recognizable counter-discourse of dissidents on the other. Instead, as David Bathrick rightly points out, "the struggle to rewrite and reinscribe the master plot is precisely a process by which one as writer is textually engaged in stretching or realigning cultural political mappings."[6] In the case of Morgner, who up until her death in March 1990 had never denied her firm commitment to socialism (at least not to what Bathrick calls a "rhetorical terrain," within which she could generate a position of critique and change), the forms of her opposition were similar to those of the best writers of her generation: they attempted to rewrite the master code from within the code itself. Yet in her efforts to rewrite and reinscribe the master code, Morgner was one of the most daring and radical aestheticians of her generation, creating some of the most avant-garde texts of her time.

6   David Bathrick, *The Powers of Speech*, 19.

The connection between the political convictions of GDR authors and the quality of their literary texts – the question of conformity versus complicity – has been at the center of the debates over GDR literature since the fall of the wall; in fact, the field of East German scholarship is still adjusting to the dramatic collapse of the German Democratic Republic. Together with the stunning metamorphosis of the political, cultural, and geographic entity known as the GDR into the five new states of a unified Germany, many of the reference points that scholars used to approach GDR literature and culture have become insecure. The enormous challenges the people of the new Germany have faced, such as the high costs of unification, problems with economic development, relatively high unemployment together with lower wages in the East, environmental cleanups, and social and political reorganization, as well as "the wall in the heads" of Germans, are paralleled by the challenges fundamentally to rethink ideological positions in the scholarship on GDR literature and culture.[7]

Before the fall of the wall, many scholars of GDR literature and cultural politics tended to favor content-oriented analyses. GDR literature was often detached from other literatures and cultures and the texts' artistic dimensions neglected. It is important to note, as Bathrick points out, that scholars who occupied themselves with GDR literature in the West in the early seventies had to do so by positioning themselves against the norms and methodological assumptions of their new critical predecessors.[8] The move toward a radical historicizing of

7   Andreas Huyssen speaks of a "fundamental paradigm shift" in the "patterns of intellectual and political discourse in the new unified Germany." He argues that the "innumerable feuilleton and magazine essays, books, and conference proceedings, lecture series and round table discussions of the past year and a half [1990–early 1991] reveal a far-reaching crisis in the self-understanding and public role of German intellectuals" ("After the Wall: The Failure of German Intellectuals," *New German Critique*, 52 (Winter 1991), 109). This crisis is far from resolved today. Instead, David Bathrick's prediction in the conclusion to *Powers of Speech* has proven to be correct: "Like language itself, this system will release its hold not through a single act of revolutionary rupture or conscious renewal but by means of a gradual working through of its forty-year experience over time" (242).

8   David Bathrick, "The End of the Wall before the End of the Wall," *German Studies Review*, 14:2 (1991), 297–311.

literature by some liberal American Germanists in what Bathrick calls the second period of GDR scholarship (beginning in the early 1970s) brought with it a number of significant developments: GDR literature was for the first time taken seriously, and interdisciplinary, Marxist, sociological, and later feminist modes of literary criticism developed hand in hand with the study of GDR literature and culture. Nevertheless, the emphasis of these GDR scholars on history and contexts often tended to neglect GDR writings as literary and aesthetic entities. "The paradoxical result," says Bathrick,

> was that although coming from very different starting points, their focus upon theme, politics, and history to the exclusion of point of view, narrativity, and imagery seemed implicitly to affirm the very stereotypes that had prevailed in the 1950s concerning GDR literature being politics rather than art (308).

Since the end of 1989, therefore, there have been many voices that have called for a rethinking of the field of GDR scholarship.[9]

During the existence of the German Democratic Republic, West German and American scholars of GDR literature shared a confidence in the mimetic capacity of literature, which allowed them to regard literature as an *Ersatzöffentlichkeit* (substitute public sphere). Patricia Herminghouse explains that the focus was often on literature's function as a window onto the workings of an otherwise closed society, as a locus for the articulation of popular sentiment and the airing of political discontent, as a sort of repository of information about the life and experiences of citizens.[10] In addition, Germanists in the United States who embarked on the study of GDR literature in the 1970s were often personally invested in the study of the GDR. In fact,

9   A number of critics have pointed to the need to rethink our former biases and blind spots. Wolfgang Emmerich, for example, calls for a rewriting of GDR literary history and criticizes his own former approach for its tendency to read literature as a derivative of social and political conditions. "Do We Need to Rewrite German Literary History since 1945? A German Perspective," Peter C. Pfeiffer (trans.), in Friederike Eigler and Peter C. Pfeiffer (eds), *Cultural Transformations in the New Germany: American and German Perspectives* (Columbia, SC: Camden House, 1993), 119–20.

10   Patricia Herminghouse, "New Contexts for GDR Literature," in Eigler and Pfeiffer op. cit., 96.

American scholars tended to see the GDR as the potentially utopian alternative to "American discontents and disillusionments," as Herminghouse puts it (94). This was similarly true for West German leftist intellectuals, as Andreas Huyssen argues:

> The abstract need for a potentially utopian space, an 'other' of capitalist Germany, led to a continued hold of the official GDR on the West German left's imagination, however sublimated it may have been.[11]

Moreover, Angelika Bammer has traced persuasively the way the rapid development of contemporary Western feminist theory and scholarship coincided with the sudden emergence of a "proto-feminist" body of women's literature in the GDR, which for many feminists seemed to contain utopian potential with regard to the position of women.[12] In this sense, the feminist connection to the study of GDR literature represents just one of the ways in which the positionality of the scholars conditioned their relationship to their subject.

Aside from GDR scholars' critical rethinking of their own positionality after 1989, there has also been a major and far more problematic shift in the evaluation of GDR literature in German feuilletons. While Western critics before the *Wende* tended to view the East German author as a hero, as an agent of socialist opposition, critics who have taken part in the fierce battles in the feuilletons after the unification of Germany have emphasized the codependency of GDR author and state. Whereas earlier, West German critics had considered the GDR author as trying to hold the SED accountable to its own ideology while struggling for more openness, critics after the *Wende* have underscored the privileges, prizes, and pensions of authors, claiming that GDR artists provided a bankrupt state with legitimacy and even respectability. The different cultural debates that have accompanied the process of unification are places where a new German identity is being negotiated. The first of these *Literaturdebatten* started in 1990 with the heated and often polemic discussions of Christa Wolf's *Was bleibt* (*What Remains*) and they flared up again

11   Huyssen, "After the Wall," 116.
12   Angelika Bammer, "The American Feminist Reception of GDR Literature (With a Glance at West Germany)," *GDR Bulletin*, 16:2 (1990), 18–24.

14

in January 1993 after the disclosure of Wolf's brief involvement with the Stasi, East Germany's secret police. These heated debates, which tended to oversimplify the complex question of aesthetics and politics, presented scholars of the GDR with a need to negotiate a suddenly unstable terrain of confrontation and verbal violence.[13] To the extent that both paradigms – that which sees the GDR authors as dissidents and that which sees them as opportunists – primarily focus on the function of GDR writers as representatives, reformers, or revolutionaries, they fail to look at GDR texts as literature and preclude more productive models of studying literature's transgressive capacities.

More differentiated comments from critics such as poet Wolf Biermann, who called the writers of the former GDR *tapfer-feig* (brave-cowardly), have emphasized that neither of the paradigms is convincing. Instead, more thoughtful voices question the comfortable oppositions we use to label authors as either dissident or nondissident, "exiled" or adjusted, intellectual or party functionary, Left or Right. One of these more sensitive studies is David Bathrick's *The Power of Speech: The Politics of Culture in the GDR* (1995). Bathrick analyzes the evolving institutional and discursive framework of literary and cultural life within East Germany and its relation to the struggles on the part of a number of literary and cultural intellectuals to open up alternative spaces for public speech from within that framework. Bathrick maintains that it was precisely their function on both sides of the power divide, as official and nonofficial voices within the whole, that defined a particular kind of intellectual in the GDR. Julia Hell similarly questions easy dichotomies at work in GDR scholarship in her book *Post-Fascist Fantasies* (1997). She examines the cultural function of the novels of Communist authors in East Germany from a psychoanalytic angle, questioning the traditional literary historical narratives about the East, which have been guided by a relatively

---

13 For documentation of the different phases of the *Literaturdebatte*, see Thomas Anz (ed.), *"Es geht nicht um Christa Wolf": Der Literaturstreit im vereinten Deutschland* (Munich: edition spangenberg, 1991); Karl Deiritz and Hannes Krauss (eds), *Der deutsch-deutsche Literaturstreit oder "Freunde, es spricht sich schlecht mit gebundener Zunge": Analysen und Materialien* (Hamburg: Luchterhand, 1991); Herrmann Vinke (ed.), *Akteneinsicht Christa Wolf. Zerrspiegel und Dialog: Eine Dokumentation* (Hamburg: Luchterhand, 1993).

simple dichotomy of realism versus modernism. Both of these more recent studies represent the type of multicultural textual and intertextual studies that transcend what Herminghouse has called "the binary German-German paradigm" by opening up the former content-oriented focus of GDR scholarship and addressing larger questions of theory. With the amazing amount of new material that has become available since the fall of the wall, both the GDR itself and East German cultural studies are still in the process of reconceptualization. Yet, despite what Huyssen calls the "far-reaching crisis in the self-understanding and public role of German intellectuals" caused by the dramatic events of 1989, the call for self-examination among scholars of GDR literature presents a great chance to expand approaches to GDR literature.[14] By recognizing former blind spots and biases and by including an analysis of each scholar's own positionality in his or her investigations, the field of GDR scholarship is gaining unique insights into the function of literature and art in a socialist system, as well as into academic and scholarly discursive practices. We now have the chance to investigate former paradigms, to rethink our own positions, and to broaden our perspectives on the study of GDR literature. This study of one GDR author's work contributes to this process of rethinking. It originated exactly at a time when many scholars of GDR literature and culture began to examine and redefine GDR scholarship and is therefore deeply influenced by these events.

Rereading Morgner's work from today's perspective adds important dimensions to the critical discussion of GDR literature. In fact, Morgner's texts help us understand how GDR literature reflected and responded to the changing cultural and political landscape of the socialist state. Together with Christa Wolf and Heiner Müller, Irmtraud Morgner was one of the most important writers of the former GDR. Her radical feminism and her commitment to aesthetic experimentation have

---

14   Huyssen, "After the Wall," 109. Cf. among others: Emmerich, "Do We Need to Rewrite German Literary History since 1945?"; Herminghouse, "New Contexts for GDR Literature"; Bathrick, "The End of the Wall"; Marc Silberman, "German Studies and the GDR: Too Near, Too Far," Editorial Introduction, *Monatshefte*, 85:3 (1993), 265–74; and Thomas Fox, "Germanistik and GDR Studies: (Re)Reading a Censored Literature," *Monatshefte*, 85:3 (1993), 284–94.

provoked keen interest beyond the borders of Germany. Morgner's ulti-mate goal was to help women "enter history." The path toward this goal, however, led her to break definitively with the discursive para-digm operative in the GDR at that time. The emancipatory qualities of Morgner's texts rest in their form: the mobilization of fantasy as a counterforce to an abstract rationality; the creation of new narrative perspectives to achieve critical distance; the employment of fragmented story lines that question the production of meaning; and the parody of a multiplicity of intertexts. The subversiveness of her prose is apparent in the way that Morgner's aesthetic experimentation prevented any one critical school (Marxist critics in the GDR, neo-Marxist and leftist scholars in the West, feminists in the two Germanies and in the United States) from appropriating her ideas for their cause. In this sense, Morgner's novels are prime examples of how aesthetic innovation can take on direct political meaning. Fascinating contributions to theoretical discussions and literary, as well as cultural, controversies in Morgner's texts show how fully this author belonged to the intellectual avant-garde in her country.

In more than one sense, Morgner's biography can be regarded as a "model" biography in the context of the GDR, and her oeuvre spans the entire development of literature in the GDR. Morgner's lifelong loyalty to the GDR, her gratitude for the opportunities that socialism afforded her, and the discomfort with a "real existing socialism," which Morgner soon perceived as limiting her creativity and critical capacities (*Wider-spruchsgeist*), are very common in a writer of her generation. Yet, while Morgner's biography is typical for GDR authors, many aspects of her writing render her novels unique among GDR texts of the sixties, seventies, and early eighties. Morgner's overt and playful feminism, with its characteristic radicalness and humour, the extensive use of textual experimentation, the recourse to and discussion of postmodernist aesthetic theories and techniques, and the introduction of laughter into women's literature all make Morgner one of the most talented and interesting writers of the GDR.

Biographical Details

Born in 1933 in Chemnitz, Irmtraud Morgner grew up under National Socialism and subsequently belonged to the first generation to be educated in the newly founded socialist state.[15] In her autobiographical essay, "Apropos Eisenbahn" (Speaking of railways), Morgner mentions the following milestones: the opportunity to attend *Oberschule* (she received her *Abitur* in 1952); a university degree in *Germanistik* (1956) after studying language and literature in Leipzig with Hans Mayer; her job as assistant editor with the literary journal *Neue deutsche Literatur* (1956–58); and eventually her independence as a freelance writer in 1958.[16] Morgner emphasizes how extraordinary this educational development was for the daughter of a railroad engineer, saying, "I grew up in a household without books. My parents cultivated the phenomena of their world not with words but with tools."[17] With a father who regarded people who used many words as *Babelliesen* [wagging-tongues] or *Quatschköpfe* [blabbermouths], Morgner had no idea "that the secrets of this world could be expressed in words" (11) until she reached the age of thirteen. Thus, Morgner's entrance into the world of words after 1945 coincided with her entrance into high school in the young socialist state. Morgner

15 Christa Wolf writes about this kind of "split" education (first fascism then antifascism) in her novel *Kindheitsmuster*.

16 "Apropos Eisenbahn" was written in 1973 and first published in Gerhard Schneider (ed.), *Eröffnungen; Schriftsteller über ihr Erstlingswerk* (Berlin: Aufbau, 1974), 204–10. I am quoting from the reprinted version in Marlis Gerhardt, *Irmtraud Morgner. Texte, Daten, Bilder* (Frankfurt a. M.: Luchterhand, 1990), 17–23.

17 "Der Koffer oder Faust in der Küche" (A suitcase or Faust in the kitchen) is part of the second book of Morgner's *Salman* trilogy, *Amanda. Ein Hexenroman* (Amanda: A witch novel), ch. 32. I am quoting from the reprinted version in Gerhardt, *Irmtraud Morgner*, 9–16. Morgner describes her father's way of communicating with his family as follows: "Johann Salman preferred tools over words. At home he preferred interjections. For the communication with his wife and daughter he only needed eight of them: hm, na, ha, bh, nu, ah, ach, pst. With 'pst' meaning not only silence but also the choice of a different type of nail or 'attention'" ("Der Koffer," 10).

describes her escape from the speechless world of her childhood and her growth into a writer as a series of "recoveries from different educational shocks" [*Bildungsschocks*] that were only possible in the GDR at that time. Morgner's account makes clear that – given her anti-intellectual family environment – she was only able to overcome the intimidation in her first encounters with literature because of a socialist ideology that empowered her to "appropriate" a "cultural heritage" and an intellectual tradition that otherwise would have remained radically foreign and remote.[18] The socialist educational system that taught its young people to change the world and build a new society from the ground up provided Morgner with the self-confidence and courage to begin to write.[19]

The next big milestone, Morgner's break with Lukács's concept of *Widerspiegelung*, part of the official doctrine of socialist realism in the mid-sixties, came about not so much because of political occurrences and disillusionment, but because of "literary" encounters and events. Morgner experienced no problems publishing her first three texts in the GDR, *Das Signal steht auf Fahrt* (The signal is on "go") (1959), *Ein Haus am Rande der Stadt* (A house at the edge of town) (1962), and "Notturno" (1964).[20] Yet, like many writers of her generation who tended to renounce their early work as their thinking changed during the seventies, she later rejected these three early texts because of their schematic realism and "unliterary character." Morgner explains:

> I constructed my first book in exemplary fashion. In its production I voluntarily, automatically, and as much as I was able to, took into account all the advice

18 Morgner gives many examples for this empowerment in "Apropos Eisenbahn." She says, for example: "Because our amateur theatre group [in high school] could not use the old bourgeois plays by Goethe, Schiller, and others, we began to write our own plays. Collectively: Every member of the collective wrote a piece of the piece. We thought that people who believed that literature was something that only few people could produce were disciples of reactionary theories of gifted people. We believed that all people could do everything" ("Apropos Eisenbahn," 18).

19 Morgner writes about this in *Life and Adventures*, bk 1, ch. 11.

20 "Notturno" was an early version of a story that later became a chapter in *Rumba auf einen Herbst*.

circulating in the country at that time [...]. My first story is no story, because it did not treat subjects, about which I had to write. It was not vitally important to me. It did not treat a topic with which I had to come to terms, not for literary reasons, and not out of existential necessity. And because in this sense it was not important for me, it was also unimportant for my readers. Radio, TV, newspapers daily flood the public with information. Literature becomes redundant if it does not exhibit what is the specifically literary: the medium. That mirrors the world. The curiosity of reading is above all the curiosity for the medium, a capricious, unmistakable person. And in the understanding and disagreement with this medium that is in search of herself, her individuality, the readers are in search of themselves. Self-knowledge. World-knowledge. Since for lack of self-confidence I did not dare to step into my first book, neither directly nor indirectly, it did not develop into a book. In contrast to my other books it received a prize. I count *Wedding in Constantinople* as my first book" ("Apropos Eisenbahn," 21–3).

While socialism had first provided her with the creativity and confidence to begin to write, the socialist realist aesthetic doctrine now seemed to limit these same qualities. The author's reaction to the battles over the publication of *Rumba auf einen Herbst* shows even more clearly that Morgner's decision to change her narrative strategies radically came about because of her growing understanding of the inner contradictions in the artistic doctrine of a "real existing socialism."

The break in Morgner's oeuvre in the mid-sixties was more than a reaction to political or cultural-political occurrences in the GDR, such as the 1959 *Bitterfeld* movement, the building of the Wall in 1961, or the *Neues ökonomisches System* of the 1960s. To be sure, Morgner also began to tackle themes and topics that were taboo in the GDR at that time, most importantly her criticism of the GDR state in which women theoretically possessed legal equality, but in practice still did not have a voice. But more fundamentally, her break with the official GDR cultural policy came about through a growing realization of the contradictory and authoritarian nature of the monosemic master discourse in the GDR.[21] We can observe the break in Morgner's reaction to the criticisms of the different versions of *Rumba auf einen Herbst* at a time when GDR officials were desperately struggling to take control of an emerging public sphere in East Germany. With its

---

21   For an excellent analysis of the developing public sphere in the GDR, see Bathrick's *The Powers of Speech*.

radical use of modernist techniques and its thematization of jazz music, *Rumba's* form and topic contributed to the rejection of the novel in the GDR.

Rumba and the Cultural Debates of the 1960s

Morgner's book is built according to a four-part sonata with its four stories, "Blues," "Schalmeientwist," "Nottumo," and "Cantus Firmus." In between Morgner inserts a six-part frame story with the mythological couple Persephone and Orpheus. Morgner refuses to present a linear narrative or provide a reassuring totality through the authority of an omniscient narrator. Multiple perspectives, inner monologues, montage techniques, and her efforts to cross the borderline between fantasy and reality all ran counter to GDR aesthetic orthodoxy. In fact, in the early sixties, a time when GDR officials tried to repress the influences of a Western popular culture, the milieu of a youthful subculture, with its preference for popular (Western) music and the playful life of dreamers, represented an uneasiness with socialist culture that was more threatening to cultural officials than any direct political criticism.

In 1965, the GDR publishing house Mitteldeutscher Verlag announced the publication of Morgner's novel *Rumba auf einen Herbst* for spring 1965. However, after the Eleventh Plenum of the Central Committee of the SED in December 1965, permission to publish *Rumba* was withdrawn and the manuscript was never returned to the author. With the Eleventh Plenum, the attempts to attack and repress American popular culture in the GDR reached their culmination. In December 1965, party officials launched an unprecedented and carefully orchestrated attack against writers, musicians, and filmmakers in the GDR. At that party meeting, GDR officials attacked the reception of popular (Western) culture, especially popular music in the GDR. The conclusion was drawn that rock music, jazz, and other forms of popular culture were not and could not be in accordance with the goals of a socialist society. Couched in the familiar jargon of cultural functionaries, the critique was furthermore a defensive ideological assault aimed at "skepticism," the "superficial reflection" of reality, and the "unconvincing resolution" of contradictions in literature, the theater, and especially the cinema. East German authorities claimed that American imports destroyed the German cultural heritage and "barbarized" adolescents, making them prone to fascist seduction. The new popular music was indicted as "decadent" and this rejection was supported with references to jazz's allegedly sexualizing effects. The open dancing style, the new jeans fashion for young women, and the long hair for men were all examples of the allegedly "dangerous" effects of the new popular music, which turned proper gender roles on their heads. Connections were drawn between the consumption of mass culture, the "oversexualization" of women, and the feminization of men. Historians such as Uta Poiger have shown how East German authorities perceived American popular culture as a threat to established gender norms.[22] Since cultural officials relied on the image of the asexual female caretaker and the controlling and controlled male protector in their construction of ideal gender roles, youth culture – and the youthful taste for the latest US imports – became one battleground for struggles over German identities. Morgner's skillful connection of popular music and women in *Rumba* was in fact the main reason for the almost hysterical reaction of critics to her novel.

As the title of Morgner's book suggests, music is her major metaphor. The novel includes allusions to the rumba, the sonata, classical music, and, most important, jazz, blues, and swing. Music serves at least three functions in the text. In a first, most obvious sense, a preference for Western music, during a time when GDR authorities were attempting to suppress it, signaled political opposition. In fact, Morgner recreates most of the official arguments against popular music in her texts, as they could be later heard at the Eleventh Plenum, to show their contradictory and ideologically motivated nature. Second, music represents a utopian moment that contrasts with an ossified reality and the degraded language that both constitutes and mirrors that

---

22 Cf. Uta G. Poiger, "Rock 'n' Roll, Female Sexuality, and the Cold War Battle over German Identities," in Robert G. Moeller (ed.), *West Germany under Construction: Politics, Society, and Culture in the Adenauer Era* (Ann Arbor: University of Michigan Press, 1990), 373–410.

reality. Morgner draws brilliant portraits of those people, mostly men, who, stuck in their firm belief in the official ideology, betray their dogmatism and lack of creativity in their language. Finally, music is closely connected with women, and serves as an opportunity for Ev, Karla, and dissidents such as Kai to express their emotional energy in all its manifestations. Music encourages and supports women to leave prescribed gender roles behind and struggle for creative independence.

Not surprisingly it is precisely the ambivalence and multivalence of blues and jazz music – something that was unacceptable to officials interested in tight control of the public sphere – that Morgner emphasizes in her descriptions of the blues. In the first story of *Rumba*, it is the female character Ev who is most closely associated with this music, while the male character Lutz rejects jazz and blues as "anarchical" and "decadent." While Ev's favourite pronoun is "I," linguistically marking her individuality, Lutz almost always speaks of "we" when he tries to argue a point. Just like Lutz, GDR officials used different terms to condemn jazz, blues, and rock 'n' roll as "anarchical," "decadent," "nihilistic," and "amoral." At the same time, jazz and rock 'n' roll are associated with unbridled sexuality, with "primitiveness" and implicitly with blackness. The professor in *Rumba*, for example, designates jazz as "musical animalism" (46) and argues: "Well yes. But this music is foreign to us. It has to be foreign because it originates in a foreign, if not to say hostile world."[23] The racism apparent in East German charges of "decadence," "animalism," and "primitivism" was clearly at odds with East Germany's public stance against racism in the United States. Although jazz and blues were rooted in the culture of African Americans, whom Communists recognized as an oppressed group, East German authorities did not refrain from attacks on American music, dances, and especially rock 'n' roll. It is Lutz's repeated use of the word *enthemmt* (out of control, having lost all inhibitions) that interests me in this context. "A book of an uninhibited/out-of-control individualism" (*Ein Buch des enthemmten Individualismus*) was also one of the criticisms levelled at Morgner's book. In fact, the debates about popular

---

23 All translations from *Rumba* are my own. "Na schön. Aber diese Musik ist uns doch fremd. Sie muss doch fremd sein, schon weil sie in einer uns fremden, um nicht zu sagen, feindlichen Welt geboren wurde" (45).

culture were characterized by an emotional passion that is revealing in and of itself. Morgner knew that the moral tone of these attacks on popular music masked GDR officials' fears of the breakdown of established gender norms. In a letter to a friend she says:

> There is a pogrom in the newspapers, a new campaign against writers, even the new texts which I gave you are already censored by God himself; love in literary texts only if it complies with the recently passed marriage law. Unfortunately, I don't exaggerate, unfortunately I'm still not able to recognize this madness as reality. [...] I don't see many possibilities for my book, I don't even see many possibilities for myself in this country (Letter to a friend, printed in Bussmann's edition of *Rumba*, 346).

In fact, Rumba seems to have been so dangerous to cultural officials because it connected women, music, and the call for individual freedom.

Finding a Voice

Rereading *Rumba* today shows the amazing modernity of Morgner's prose even in the early sixties. Many of the stylistic characteristics of her texts are already in place. In addition, Morgner had found her most important topic: the criticism of traditional gender roles in a state that claimed to have emancipated all of its citizens, men and women. While music remained one of Morgner's favourite metaphors in her later books, it is remarkable how artfully she deconstructs the official debates over popular culture to show what is really at stake in these struggles. In *Rumba,* the skilful connection of women and popular music is evidence of this writer's clear sense of the burning issues of her time and of her sensibility to language and discourse.

The experience of not being allowed to publish this first book, which was truly important to her, had profound consequences for Morgner's development as a writer. Far from caving in to the demands of the censors, Morgner incorporated large sections of *Rumba* into her 1974 novel, *Life and Adventures*. In addition, Morgner decided to change her writing style, making it even more radical than it had been in *Rumba*. Her most important goal, she now said, was to write *literature*. To ensure that her texts would not be misunderstood as political pamphlets, Morgner began to use the textual experiment as her most important technique:

> To write means to think something through to the end. It is an adventurous process. A kind of research project. A turn that was not planned in the exposé is caused by the inner logic of the story. A scientist experiences a similar turn when he suddenly encounters a fact that can no longer be reconciled with his theory. These findings are inconvenient, but basically auspicious moments. Because they give the impulse for new theories. A true scientist longs for these moments. A poet, too ("Apropos Eisenbahn," 21).

The GDR critic Eva Kaufmann rightly pointed out that as a result of Morgner's experience with *Rumba*, she turned to comic and fantastic means of representation and developed a laconic style, which allowed her to express her ideas more indirectly.[24] In fact, Morgner radically changed her narrative strategies: she began to use intertextual quotations, montage techniques, direct and hidden allusions, pluralization of narrative voices, and masquerade.

Her explicit goal became "the absolute experiment," which she defined as the attempt to help women "enter history."[25] Her attempt to reach this goal, however, led to a radical break with the discursive patterns operative in the GDR at that time. The nature of this break is similar to that seen in the writings of such authors as Christa Wolf, whose *Nachdenken über Christa T* (*The Quest for Christa T.*) was published in the same year (1968) as Morgner's *Hochzeit in Konstantinopel* (Wedding in Constantinople). David Bathrick has argued that

> with the publication of this remarkable book [Wolf's *Christa T.*], we find not only a move inward – a break with a discursive paradigm based upon a

---

24   Eva Kaufmann: "Die Erfahrung, das Manuskript von *Rumba auf einen Herbst* nach ursprünglicher Zustimmung nicht gedruckt zu sehen, ist für Irmtraud Morgner äußerst folgenreich, zum Beispiel auch darin, dass sie sich viel stärker komischen und phantastischen Gestaltungsmitteln zuwendet, dass sie einen Lakonismus entwickelt, der vieles indirekt auszusprechen erlaubt" ("Der Hölle die Zunge herausstrecken," 174). The essay was first printed in *Weimarer Beiträge* in 1984. I am quoting from the reprinted version in Gerhardt, *Irmtraud Morgner*.

25   *Die wundersamen Reisen Gustavs des Weltfahrers*, 157.

dialectical materialist, i.e. an objectivist epistemology – but beyond that a problematizing of all the categories which had heretofore been accepted notions of socialist discourse: of history, of science, of one's political role, of the private sphere, of the situation and nature of the individual subject.[26]

Each of Bathrick's points apply to *Hochzeit in Konstantinopel* as well; in fact, in some ways, Morgner's break with acceptable ways of writing and speaking is more radical than that of any other GDR author at the time. In this sense, Morgner's texts become countertexts.

Like Wolf's *Christa T.*, Morgner's *Hochzeit in Konstantinopel* was not occupied with GDR concerns only, but spoke to Germany as a whole. It was the first book Morgner published in the West (by Hanser in 1969), and it introduced West German readers to her work. Together with her next two novels, *Hochzeit in Konstantinopel* was highly praised in East and West Germany. GDR critic Annemarie Auer, for example, wrote:

> With these relaxed erotic stories in *Wedding in Constantinople*, which Morgner's secure talent for form combined into an indestructible narrative texture, the author has written herself free. [...] Here, at last, somebody dared to switch from the position of an object to that of a subject ("Trobadora unterwegs oder Schulung in Realismus," 1068–71).

Morgner's reputation as a talented and extraordinarily skillful narrator was established with *Hochzeit in Konstantinopel; Gauklerlegende. Eine Spielfrauengeschichte* (A trickster's legend. A story of a female minstrel) (GDR 1970/FRG 1971); and *Die wundersamen Reisen Gustavs des Weltfahrers. Lügenhafter Roman mit Kommentaren* (The wondrous journeys of Gustav the world traveler. Mendacious novel with commentaries) (GDR 1972/FRG 1973). However, these texts were also perceived as "uncomfortable" and subversive in both East and West Germany because some critics judged the new form to be excessive and lacking in discipline.

In fact, as Annemarie Auer points out, Morgner's texts began to break with discursive patterns operative not only in the GDR, but in the West. Morgner's new narrative strategy was based on the realization that the female author's attempt to speak from the position of a subject

---

26   David Bathrick, "Productive Mis-Reading," *GDR Bulletin*, 16:2 (1990), 5.

meant breaking with a patriarchal discursive system that reserves for women the position of the object. It meant a search for a new language. In her typically ironic way, Morgner described her first experience with literature and her realization that she needed to find a new language that would allow her to speak as a woman as an encounter in the form of a suitcase full of high school editions of classical literature found in the attic of a relative's house. These texts opened a new world of words for her, she claimed. Although in school she was officially encouraged to make this world her own, she later learned that this was only partially true: only "half" of the words – those put into the mouths of the female characters by their male authors – were supposed to be appropriated by her. The "voice lessons" – which the teacher recommended in order to stop the young girl from wanting to act out the male roles of Don Carlos, Karl Moor, and Faust – encouraged Morgner to realize that the voice of the cultural tradition was a gendered voice, and therefore not her own. Morgner says:

> But I took the teacher's advice to heart, which allowed me to think of myself as diligent and not crazy. Whenever I was alone at home, I put on my mother's bathrobe, stepped to the kitchen table and, in a phony Bavarian accent, recited *Faust*, Act One, Scene One ("Der Koffer," 16).

The teacher's unwitting encouragement to engage in voice lessons was helpful in a double sense: it allowed her to step into a male cultural tradition, and in doing so, it helped her to realize that she needed to "disguise her voice." For this reason, the "excavation of women's vocal range" as Morgner defines her project in *Life and Adventures,* became her prime focus from the mid-sixties on. The break in Morgner's oeuvre was thus also a break with the discourse of the "fathers." In the last interview before her death in 1989, she emphasized that while she never wanted to leave the GDR, she had always been aware of the fact that, because she was a woman, the GDR was not "her" country. Instead, Morgner said, she regarded it as her "father-land" and not her home, since "home" (*Heimat*) was some-thing different for her.[27]

27 "Die große Trauerarbeit wegen der politischen und materiellen Herabwirtschaf-tung meines Vater-Landes (Heimat ist was anderes), aber auch wegen Mitschuld mußte ich tatenlos bewältigen" (Alice Schwarzer, "Jetzt oder nie! Die Frauen sind

Morgner developed her project of finding a new language, different from the "father-tongue" of "tenor, baritone, and bass," most directly in *Life and Adventures of Trobadora Beatrice as Chronicled by her Minstrel Laura*, published after some delay in 1974 in the GDR. *Life and Adventures* is the story of Beatrice de Dia, a female troubadour in twelfth-century Provence who wakes from a sleep of 810 years to the France of 1968. With the help of Persephone's magic sleeping potion, Beatrice had left the Middle Ages to wait for conditions that would be liveable for women. A bridge to the present is provided by her sister-in-law, the Beautiful Melusine, who acts as an informant during her sleep and an ally through space and time, a dragon-Pegasus for Beatrice's travels. Having been awakened prematurely, Beatrice progresses with picaresque naïveté and spontaneity through a series of exploits, from the 1968 Paris student uprisings to the GDR of the 1970s, which had been recommended to her as an ideal state where women were free and emancipated. Beatrice finds in Laura Salman, a socialist trolley-car driver, writer, and mother, her modern-day minstrel and apprentice. Yet, soon enough Beatrice realizes that even in the GDR, little has changed: although women are guaranteed legal equality, in practice they have gained only the burden of a second shift at home, while "eroticism is still the last domain of men" (114).

Life and Adventures was an immediate success with readers, especially women. In the GDR, the first edition of 15,000 sold out immediately, and the novel was reprinted twice, despite its length (close to 700 pages). Morgner was invited to give readings and talks in both East and West Germany, even before the Luchterhand edition was available in the West in 1976. The author received innumerable letters from readers in both states, and Nikolaus Marggraph (i.e. Wolfram Schütte) stated in 1975 that Morgner was one of the most discussed authors at the time.[28] In the GDR, Morgner was awarded the

die Hälfte des Volkes," *Emma*, 2 (1990), 32). I will disregard the complexities of the discussion on "Heimat" here, since I am most interested in Morgner's emphasis on gender in this context.

28   Marggraf says: "Die DDR-Autorin Irmtraud Morgner gehört augenblicklich zum offenen Geheimtip unter linken und liberalen Frauengruppen. Das verdankt sie einem Buch, das gar nicht in einem westdeutschen Verlag erschienen und in der DDR-Ausgabe bei Aufbau schon längst vergriffen ist: dem 'Leben

prestigious Heinrich Mann Prize for *Life and Adventures*, and in the FRG, she was the first woman to receive the Prize for Grotesque Humor of the City of Kassel in 1989. Despite its great popularity with readers, *Life and Adventures* was – except for two positive reviews in the *Frankfurter Rundschau* and *konkret* – vehemently criticized by West German critics, who perceived the new form as willful and out of control. "Official" East German critics took great pains to defend the novel in order to justify its publication.

This pattern of reception – the great popularity of Morgner's texts with readers and the great reservations and even confusion on the part of critics in both East and West – continued after the publication of the eagerly awaited second part of the *Salman* trilogy, *Amanda. Ein Hexen-roman* in 1983 (simultaneously in East and West Germany). In 1987, Morgner developed cancer. After her first surgery in East Berlin in 1988, she continued to work on the third part of the *Salman* trilogy, which she was unable to complete. More operations followed in 1989; Irmtraud Morgner died in May 1990 at the age of fifty-seven. Rudolf Bussmann, the administrator of Morgner's literary estate, published the novel in fragmented form in 1998 with the title *Das Heroische Testament* (The heroic testament). A short part of it had already been published posthumously in 1991 as *Der Schöne und das Tier* (The [male] beauty and the beast).

The Reception of Morgner's Work

Because of its unique blend of feminist theories and Marxist politics, Morgner's work continues to generate keen interest beyond the borders of her country, not least among American feminists, who consider her the most important feminist author of the GDR. Patricia Herminghouse praised *Life and Adventures* as "a Dr. Faustus for feminists," and Karen and Friedrich Achberger maintained that the novel "is without a doubt

und Abenteuer der Trobadora Beatriz und ihrer Spielfrau Laura'" (*Frankfurter Rundschau*, 24 May 1975).

the most important work of GDR literature to deal with women's emancipation." Angelika Bammer has pointed out that Morgner's

> importance rests in the sensational and sustaining impact of her work for both, the American reception of GDR literature and the development of feminist literary theory in Germany.[29]

Yet, it is not only the feminist take and the political force of Morgner's work that have fascinated readers. In fact, the prominent German scholar Walter Jens has compared Morgner's aesthetics to those of James Joyce, Thomas Mann, and Franz Kafka.[30] Morgner's insistence on the disruptive force of aesthetic creativity carries the texts beyond the borders of their historical location (the GDR of the sixties, seventies, and eighties). The power of the novels rests in their poetic strategy of constantly revisioning fixed meanings. A multiplicity of perspectives challenges any kind of closed discourse and prevents the texts from remaining in a specific historical situation.

In this study I treat Morgner's novels above all as aesthetic entities in order to search for textual codes as signifiers for historical points of change. In the current climate, between the poles of growing indifference and increasingly adversarial attitudes toward everything connected with the GDR, I attempt to read Morgner's work as a medium of subversive articulation of crises of meaning, as texts that disengage themselves from official GDR discourse and cast themselves as "countertexts." By this I mean that Morgner's novels do not refer only to themes that were taboo in the GDR. Instead, the emancipatory qualities of her texts rest in the power of their daring aesthetic experimentation. I therefore focus here on

29 Patricia Herminghouse, "Die Frau und das Phantastische in der neueren DDR-Literatur: Der Fall Irmtraud Morgner," in Wolfgang Paulsen (ed.), *Die Frau als Heldin und Autorin: Neue kritische Ansätze zur deutschen Literatur* (Bern: Francke, 1979), 248; Karen Achberger and Friedrich Achberger (trans.), "Life and Adventures of Trobadora Beatrice as Chronicled by Her Minstrel Laura: Twelfth Book," *New German Critique* 15 (Fall 1978), 121; and Angelika Bammer, "Trobadora in Amerika," in Marlis Gerhardt (ed.), *Irmtraud Morgner: Texte, Daten, Bilder* (Frankfurt a. M.: Luchterhand, 1990), 205.

30 Walter Jens, "Die Tausendsassa Irmtraud Morgner," in Marlis Gerhardt (ed.), *Irmtraud Morgner: Texte, Daten, Bilder* (Frankfurt a. M.: Luchterhand, 1990), 100–8.

the aesthetic and formal innovations of Morgner's texts as their outstanding features. Doris Janhsen and Monika Meier have rightly pointed out that the political reading of Morgner's work has often stood in the way of investigating those aspects of Morgner's novels that transgress a simplistic assignment of meaning to her texts.[31] Janhsen and Meier remind us that Morgner's novels – especially *Life and Adventures* – have advanced to the status of classics on the basis of a majority of content-based readings, which very often left Morgner's complex writing strategies unexamined. However, rather than providing unambiguous statements of political ideas, Morgner's texts subvert any kind of fixed meaning by insisting on the mediality of the poetic, as well as on the constant revisioning of seemingly stable concepts. In the current climate in which GDR literature – judged by the behavior of its authors – is denounced in West Germany as "conformist," "cowardice," "simplistic," "opportunistic," and a "state literature," Irmtraud Morgner's novels prove that the literature that came out of the socialist state was far more interesting, heterogeneous, and multifaceted than one might have thought.

Although Irmtraud Morgner was one of the best-known authors in the GDR and the two completed novels of the *Salman* trilogy were best sellers in East and West Germany, critical studies of her work are rare. After the initial celebration of her work by readers and critics, discussion of Morgner's novels died down and after the early eighties, her texts were hardly discussed at all. Although Morgner was often cited as one of the most important authors for the development of a new GDR literature, there were scarcely any detailed analyses of her texts. Only in the nineties can a renewed interest in her work be observed. In 1990, the first book with materials on Irmtraud Morgner's oeuvre was published, followed in 1991 by a volume with review articles and essays on Morgner's work with the title "Zeitmontage." The first book-length study of the development of Morgner's narrative techniques also appeared in Germany in 1991. In 1995, Alison Lewis published the first

31   Doris Janhsen and Monika Meier, "Spiel-Räume der Phantasie. Irmtraud Morgner: *Leben und Abenteuer der Trobadora Beatriz nach Zeugnissen ihrer Spielfrau Laura*," in Karl Deiritz and Hannes Krauss (eds), *Verrat an der Kunst? Rückblicke auf die DDR-Literatur* (Berlin: Aufbau Taschenbuch, 1993), 209–14.

book-length study of Morgner's works in English, which investigates the use of the fantastic in Morgner's novels.[32]

The present study examines Irmtraud Morgner's novels, especially her *Salman* trilogy, in the context of the different literary theories and debates about literature that were either conducted at the time of Morgner's writing or that Morgner anticipated in her texts. This study discusses Morgner's aesthetic strategies in the context of Frankfurt School critical theory, feminist debates in the early seventies about "female identity" and the possibility of "feminist aesthetics," postmodernist ideas about representation and the subject, and Bakhtinian theories about masquerade and the carnivalesque. The dialogue between theory and fiction that Morgner sets into motion in her novels renders her texts unique among feminist works from the seventies in East and West Germany. At the same time, a reading that takes the texts' aesthetic strategies seriously and places them in the context of other debates about literary and cultural movements reveals aspects of the texts that readers were unable to see before.

To provide the literary critical context of Morgner's work, I analyze the reception of the first part of her *Salman* trilogy, *Life and Adventures of Trobadora Beatrice*, in chapter 1. What interests me is not so much "correcting" certain "mis"-interpretations of the text, but analyzing the reasons for its radically divergent evaluation by different critical groups during different periods of reception. I ask what "horizon of expectations" critics brought to the text, and what discursive contexts shaped their criticism. The early seventies were not only a time when an increasing number of GDR authors began to voice their doubts about the political reality in their country; in West Germany, the second women's movement also began to gain momentum, and a debate about the so-called new subjectivity ensued. Discussions in West Germany about the need for German literature to catch up with literary modernism (most clearly in the debates and the reaction to the

---

32   Marlis Gerhardt (ed.), *Irmtraud Morgner: Texte, Daten, Bilder* (Frankfurt a. M.: Luchterhand, 1990); Kristine von Soden (ed.), *Irmtraud Morgner's hexische Weltfahrt. Eine Zeitmontage* (Berlin: Elefanten Press, 1991); Gabriele Scherer, *Zwischen "Bitterfeld" und "Orplid" Zum literarischen Werk Irmtraud Morgners* (Bern: Peter Lang, 1992); Alison Lewis, *Subverting Patriarchy: Feminism and Fantasy in the Works of Irmtraud Morgner* (Washington: Berg, 1995).

debates in the "Gruppe 47"), and the attempts to repress modernist aesthetic practices in the GDR shaped the responses to Morgner's novel and led to radically different readings. Analysis of the reception of *Life and Adventures* allows readers to gain insights into the workings of the "literary industry" in East and West Germany. Only since the 1990s have critics read *Life and Adventures* as a text that discusses and experiments with postmodernist textual strategies. These more recent interpretations seem better equipped to deal with contradictions and textual tensions that were criticized in earlier approaches to the novel. Among feminists, the contradictory reactions to the novel were caused by debates about the usefulness or danger of incorporating postmodernist aesthetic practices into feminist theory. These reactions suggest that Morgner's text can be placed in the center of debates about the intersections of postmodernist and feminist theories. Significant changes in the expectations of critics occurred in conjunction with broader discussions about the function of GDR literature, feminist literature, and postmodern texts. In addition, the critics' aesthetic and political affiliations shaped their assessment of the text. In other words, the evaluation of the reception of Morgner's text demonstrates how important it is to analyze each critic's positionality. We see how a critic's investment in particular literary debates always shapes her or his reaction to a literary text.

Chapters 2 through 4 center on the concept of intertextuality. Morgner uses intertextual citations to suggest how contemporary literature can function as a social and political intervention. More specifically, the novel uses intertextuality to participate in a debate about the political nature of feminist concepts of "female identity" and political agency. By using different intertexts as masks that her characters – and with them, the author and the reader – can put on, the author appropriates an historical and literary tradition and yet keeps a distance from it. This technique allows the female character to speak without succumbing to a tradition in which Woman is always already spoken for. As Helen Fehervary explains in an analysis of Christa Wolf's texts, the mask allows one literary self to expand and multiply into many and can thus help to redefine traditional notions of authorship. By thus creating a relational concept of authorship, the mask is the subversive underside of a patriarchal tradition and "an alternative to mankind's progressive journey toward perfection."[33] By using intertextual quotations as masks in a textual experiment, Morgner lets her character "exit (male) history" in order to "reenter it as subject."[34] This technique of intertextual masquerade allows the author to work through and experiment with key concepts and ideas, from theories of female or feminist aesthetics, to the political nature of postmodernist texts, to the competing models used to represent "difference" and "alterity" in literature. Morgner's use of intertextuality allows her to experiment with models of political intervention in literature.

One of the debates Morgner follows in her work concerns the possibility of a direct political application of Frankfurt School critical theory as it was discussed in West Germany in the late sixties and early seventies. With the beginning of the student movement there was a growing dispute in West Germany over literature's possible political impact, as well as critical theory's ability to provide positive models for political action. While the Frankfurt School had just begun to receive some attention in the GDR in the early seventies, official GDR doctrine still decried as decadent Adorno's defense of high modernism.[35] In chapter 2, I demonstrate that Morgner uses a line of argumentation similar to Horkheimer and Adorno's analysis in the *Dialectic of Enlightenment,* but goes beyond it in her own aesthetic strategies. Positing a feminist aesthetic and a new definition of woman, Morgner also uses what we would today call postmodernist textual strategies. Morgner's inclusion of Adorno's philosophical and sociological arguments in her fiction highlights the tension in different political movements – and especially in the feminist movement – between a negative critical impulse on the one hand, which is related to Adorno's negative critical theory, and the need to find positive models of political practice on the

---

33   Helen Fehervary, "Christa Wolf's Prose: A Landscape of Masks," in Marilyn Sibley Fries (ed.), *Responses to Christa Wolf: Critical Essays* (Detroit: Wayne State University Press, 1989), 74.

34   Morgner first uses this formulation in *Hochzeit in Konstantinopel*; she has Beatrice repeat it in *Life and Adventures.*

35   Cf. Peter Uwe Hohendahl, "Ästhetik und Sozialismus: Zur neueren Literaturtheorie der DDR," in Peter Uwe Hohendahl and Patricia Herminghouse (eds), *Literatur und Literaturtheorie in der DDR* (Frankfurt a. M.: Suhrkamp, 1976), 100–62.

other. In fact, Morgner antedates by almost ten years the discussions about the tension between the critical role of feminist theory and its positive political practices, which became important in the early eighties.

In chapter 3, I therefore place Morgner's text within the context of feminist debates about "female identity" and possibilities of "feminist aesthetics" in order to explore her unique blend of feminist and postmodernist ideas more fully. Irmtraud Morgner's aesthetics depart not only from Adorno's normative demands for high modernism, but from the majority of other texts produced by feminist authors in East and West Germany and the United States in the early seventies. Patricia Herminghouse has pointed out that the critique of scientific rationality, which was enacted in the texts of some GDR women writers of the 1970s (Morgner serves as her prime example), was almost a decade ahead of the theoretical critiques that have been developed by Anglo-American feminists since the mid-1980s.[36] Morgner did not participate in the cultural feminist discourse of woman's fundamental difference from man, which prevailed in Western feminist circles at the time. Instead, her explorations of various definitions of the author, of possibilities of representation, and of the construction of difference went beyond most other feminist approaches in the early seventies. The extraordinary features of Morgner's novels are their open form; the obvious attempts to rewrite, rethink, and expand genre definitions; the texts' investigations of theoretical questions; and their intertextual games, which lead the reader into a labyrinth of intertexts from many different literary periods, from the Middle Ages to the Renaissance, to the classical period and romanticism (especially Goethe, E. T. A. Hoffmann, Jean Paul), to modernist texts such as *Orlando* by Virginia Woolf and to contemporary GDR literature. As early as 1974, Morgner anticipated key questions that didn't surface until the feminist debates of the late eighties: How can feminists find a definition of female subjectivity that does not exclude differences among individual

---

36   Patricia Herminghouse, "Phantasie oder Fanatismus? Zur feministischen Wissenschaftskritik in der Literatur der DDR," in Ute Brandes (ed.), *Zwischen gestern und morgen: Schriftstellerinnen der DDR aus amerikanischer Sicht* (Berlin: Peter Lang, 1992), 69–94.

women? How is it possible to develop a theory of feminist agency and feminist political practice if the "autonomous subject" is supposed to have disappeared? How is it possible to ensure responsibility and accountability if the individual author seems to merge with a web of texts and intertexts? How can feminists use postmodernist textual strategies to deconstruct patriarchal traditions without having to give up any kind of positive identification? Much more than portraying the lives of women in the former GDR or providing "authentic" representations of women's experiences, as other feminist texts of the time do, Morgner's novels raise questions of representation and definition(s) of subjective identity and political agency. They articulate the tension within feminist theory that Teresa de Lauretis has defined as the two-fold pull in contrary directions: the critical negativity of its theory and the affirmative positivity of its politics.[37] Reading Morgner's work today, we find ideas that are in close proximity to those of other feminist scholars like Judith Butler and Donna Haraway, who have begun to think about new, plurally structured definitions of female identity and feminist agency. While postmodernist aesthetic strategies allowed Morgner to escape the dogmatism of the official doctrine of "socialist realism" in the GDR and catered to her inborn talent for playful irony, her strong political beliefs as a feminist and a Marxist guarded her against the dangers of political relativism, one of the main charges against postmodernism. In this sense, Morgner's fiction proves that postmodern texts can be politically responsible and relevant.

Morgner's continual struggle with questions of agency and the possibilities of political action, which makes her work so important today, can be seen in her engagement with Mikhail Bakhtin's theories of the dialogic and the carnivalesque. It is significant that Morgner discussed Bakhtin's theories of language and cultural symbolization as early as the 1970s. In addition to employing Bakhtin's ideas of dialogism and the carnivalesque to criticize an official patriarchal discourse in the GDR by unmasking it as authoritarian, restrictive, and contradictory, Morgner insists on exploring Bakhtin's ideas from a feminist perspective. In *Amanda. Ein Hexenroman,* she quotes long

---

37   Teresa De Lauretis, *Technologies of Gender: Essays on Theory, Film, and Fiction* (Bloomington: Indiana University Press, 1987), 26.

parts from Bakhtin's *Rabelais and His World*, examining his ideas on carnival as a survival strategy for women. In chapter 4 I analyze Morgner's attempt to experiment with concrete aesthetic and political strategies for women by using Bakhtin's theories as an explicit foil for testing various models for thinking "difference" differently. Morgner creates a complex play of masquerade in her novels, allowing her to manufacture a distance between women and their image as it is produced in patriarchy. As Mary Ann Doane has pointed out for film theory in her famous essay "Film and Masquerade: Theorizing the Female Spectator" (1982), "By destabilising the image, the masquerade confounds this masculine structure of the look. It effects a defamiliarisation of female iconography."[38] Morgner's plea for a dialogic text that could incorporate different positive definitions in a nondogmatic and nonprescriptive way is an attempt to think of difference not in terms of binary oppositions, but as a "simultaneous-with."

During the painful process of unification of the two German states, the West German press provided an increasingly critical, if not hostile image of major East German writers. This trend tends to deny East German literature any place in a common canon of German-speaking literature by denouncing GDR texts as opportunistic and aesthetically simplistic. A rereading of Morgner's novels challenges this revisionist movement and reveals that GDR literature was much more heterogeneous and complex than we might think today. Because of her premature death in May 1990, Morgner was not able to participate in the revolutionary developments in Germany. In a last interview before her death, Morgner talked about her labour of mourning in the face of the devastation of her fatherland and about the need to reflect critically upon her own complicity in the forty-year survival of the socialist state. She said, "[I]f this should be my last interview, don't take it as my last word, dear *Emma* readers: maybe *that* is somewhere in my books." *Entering History* is the search for Morgner's last words in her books. It is the attempt to follow Morgner's lifelong quest to help women "enter history," it is the search for Morgner's place in the literary history of the GDR, and it is

---

38 Mary Anne Doane, "Film and Masquerade: Theorising the Female Spectator," *Screen*, 23 (September–October 1982), 82.

a contribution to the critical evaluation of GDR literature within the context of German literary history in the twentieth century.

CHAPTER I

Discourse Displacements and *Ungleichzeitigkeiten*: The Reception of *Life and Adventures of Trobadora Beatrice as Chronicled by her Minstrel Laura* in East and West

The appearance in 1974 of Irmtraud Morgner's novel, *Life and Adventures of Trobadora Beatrice as Chronicled by Her Minstrel Laura*, sparked controversy in both East and West Germany. From the beginning, critical responses to the work were bewilderingly varied. Neither in the East nor in the West did critics wish to reject the novel completely, emphasizing Morgner's great narrative talent. But a storm of objections underscored the uncertainty of many critics as they were confronted with the complex and extraordinary structure of this novel. While the attempts to de-emphasize or ignore all elements of the text that challenged the official aesthetic doctrine of the GDR at the time – especially feminist topics and what I will define as postmodern tendencies – were to be expected from the "official" Marxist critics of the GDR, the strong reaction to certain formal elements in Morgner's novel by Western critics came as somewhat of a surprise. Martin Gregor-Dellin expressed "deep disappointment in the novel," which he called a "disaster," and an "epic monster"; Fritz Raddatz denounced the text's "downpour of horror and wit" and its "inflation of ideas" "based on a misunderstanding of the picaresque novel." In view of these attempts to force the novel into predetermined patterns, Morgner rightly complained about the critics' refusal to accept the book on its own terms:

> Most critics do not look for the inner laws of new works (the search for them should be the critic's main task, how else do we arrive at new standards?), but they instead apply the laws for traditional works to new ones and judge them to be: lawless, lacking discipline, confused.[1]

---

1   Eva Kaufmann, "Interview with Irmtraud Morgner," *Weimarer Beiträge* 9 (1984), 1511.

Although writers' complaints that they are misunderstood are nothing new, Morgner's statement makes it clear that she saw one of her most important tasks as a writer to be the development of different writing standards and new textual forms. Morgner was convinced that women had to find their own "voice ranges" to write and speak, since the available literary forms represented the male voices of "tenor, baritone, and bass."

Among feminists, too, the reaction to Morgner's novel was mixed, even contradictory. After an initially enthusiastic reception, the debate focused on the tension in the text between a feminist and a Marxist discourse. Critics, disappointed by Morgner's refusal to define the feminist discourse in her novel as the most important one, dismissed her intention as failed, closing the debate for some time. Biddy Martin, for example, argued that Morgner's text could be read "as a textual field of struggle between oppositional knowledge and the theoretical and unitary discourse of traditional Marxism."[2] She maintained, however, that the text does not keep its promises: it "constrains the emancipatory possibilities which it opens up" by giving in to "the discursive limitations of orthodox Marxist rhetoric and by the supposed historical necessities that govern the development of GDR society" (61). Martin criticized the novel's "final domesticity," arguing that the author refuses "to conceptualize the body and sexuality as privileged bases of political power" (73). By the time Morgner died in May 1990, the lively discussion among feminist critics from the early phases of reception had almost come to a stop. Although there was some general praise of Morgner's works as important for the development of a feminist literature, the earlier debate about the tensions in her text between supposedly contradictory political tendencies was not continued.[3] A renewed interest in Morgner's texts can only be

2   Biddy Martin, "Socialist Patriarchy and the Limits of Reform: A Reading of Irmtraud Morgner's *Life and Adventures of Troubadora Beatriz as Chronicled by her Minstrel Laura,*" *Studies in Twentieth Century Literature*, 5:1 (Fall 1980), 60.

3   Angelika Bammer discusses the reception of *Life and Adventures* in the United States in her 1990 article, "Trobadora in Amerika." At that time, Bammer still noted the lack of any more detailed studies of Morgner's work. She stated, however, that this situation might be changing at the beginning of the '90s, a prediction that proved to be true.

observed in the 1990s. A book edited by Marlies Gerhardt, *Irmtraud Morgner. Texte, Daten, Bilder*, appeared in 1990 followed by several articles that analyzed specific aspects of Morgner's texts. Gabriela Scherer published the first book-length study of the development of Morgner's narrative techniques in 1992, and Alison Lewis published her study of Morgner's use of the fantastic in 1995.[4]

The contradictory early reaction to Morgner's novel and the belated new interest in her work can be explained if we understand the significant differences between *Life and Adventures* and the majority of other feminist texts of the early '70s. Today, we can identify many strategies in Morgner's novel as typically postmodern, including the extended use of intertextual connections and the constant attempts to parody and rewrite whole parts of the texts, consciously correcting and reformulating earlier statements, thereby undermining the clear presentation of her message and her authority as author. In the early phases of reception, however, Morgner's aesthetic strategies were perceived as unsystematic, lacking a coherent idea, or as based on a misunderstanding of certain literary rules and genres. Critics have only begun to read her novel differently since the beginning of the '90s. These newer approaches to the novel seem to be better able to deal with the contradictory elements of the text. Critics, more used to the playfulness of other postmodernist texts, do not expect tensions in the

---

4   Marlis Gerhardt (ed.), *Irmtraud Morgner: Texte, Daten, Bilder* (Frankfurt a. M.: Luchterhand, 1990); Agnès Cardinal, "'Be Realistic: Demand the Impossible.' On Irmtraud Morgner's Salman Trilogy," in Martin Kane (ed.), *Socialism and the Literary Imagination: Essays on East German Writers* (New York: Berg, 1991), 147–161; Janhsen and Meyer, "Trobadora Passé? Irmtraud Morgner zum Geburtstag," *Freitag*, 20 August, 1993, and "Spiel-Räume der Phantasie Irmtraud Morgner," in Deiritz and Krauss, op. cit., 209–14; Eva Kaufmann, "Irmtraud Morgner, Christa Wolf und andere: Feminismus in der DDR-Literatur," in Heinz Ludwig Arnold (ed.), *Literatur in der DDR: Rückblicke* (München: text und kritik, Sonderband, 1991) 109–16; Monika Meier, "Konzerte der Redevielfalt: Die Walpurgisnacht-Darstellungen in der 'Amanda' Irmtraud Morgners," *Literatur für Leser*, 4 (1990), 213–27; Dorothee Schmitz, "Wilde Ritte durch die Weltgeschicte oder Schreiben ist Welt machen. Unverdient vergessene Autoren (3): Die Schriftstellerin Irmtraud Morgner (1933–1990)," *Handelsblatt*, 24/25 (February 1995). Scherer, *Zwischen "Bitterfeld" und "Orplid"*; Lewis, *Subverting Patriarchy*.

text to be resolved or for the narrative to move in a teleological fashion to some kind of resolution.

GDR Criticism: Defending the Canon

The unusual form of Morgner's novel was its most irritating aspect for many critics on both sides of the border. This reaction was foreseeable in GDR criticism of the mid-1970s, which had only slowly begun to broaden the scope of its prescribed art theory of socialist realism.

Peter Uwe Hohendahl has shown that official literary scholarship in the GDR did not begin to problematize the question of realism in art until the late '60s. Writers and critics only began to question the traditional conception of the literary heritage, which had been limited to an uncritical appropriation of the classical tradition, in the early '70s.[5] While authors in the GDR had long sought to undermine the official doctrine of socialist realism in their writing, even institutionalized literary scholarship now began to question the narrowly conceived *Widerspiegelungs-* and *Erbetheorie* of the '50s and '60s. Authors and other intellectuals were encouraged by Honecker's assessment at the Eighth Party Congress of the SED in 1971, where he stated: "Since we can attest to the firm position of socialism, there can be no more taboos in the area of art and literature, in my view. That

5   Peter Uwe Hohendahl, "Theorie und Praxis des Erbens: Untersuchung zum Problem der literarischen Tradition in der DDR," in Peter Uwe Hohendahl and Patricia Herminghouse (eds), *Literatur der DDR in den 70er Jahren* (Frankfurt a. M.: Suhrkamp, 1983), 13–52. After the defeat of National Socialism, Soviet occupational forces established antifascist humanism as the basis for the reeducation of the German people in the Soviet occupational zone. Throughout the 1950s and 1960s, cultural officials saw the humanist heritage – as it was embodied in the works of the Weimar classic – as the model for renewal in the GDR. However, Marxism's romantic elements, which had been ignored and repressed in favor of the tradition of Enlightenment, resurfaced in the early '70s, especially in literary works and cultural debates.

concerns the questions of content as well as those of style."[6] Despite the new artistic freedom Honecker's statement seemed to promise, the degree to which the "official" position in art and culture was still imprisoned in bureaucratic crudeness and oversimplifications is obvious in Honecker's naïve distinction of "form" and "content," a distinction that Morgner's writing renders absurd. In addition, the expulsion of Wolf Biermann in November 1976 and the subsequent silencing of a number of avant-garde writers clearly indicated that taboos still existed and would be enforced.

In the *Tauwetterperiode*, which seemed to follow Honecker's speech, official literary scholarship and criticism in the GDR began to carefully promote a basic structural change in the conception of the *Erbetheorie*, broadening the literary canon to include works of the Romantics and the avant-garde, as Hohendahl points out.[7] The concept of a fixed tradition, which could easily be appropriated by the GDR human community (*Menschengemeinschaft*), was replaced in 1977 by a more differentiated and complex theory of literary development. The official literary institutions, however, never questioned the basic conception of an historical model that guarantees the continuity of historical development by dialectical process. The affirmative relationship between the literary tradition and the present-day situation in the GDR was never problematized, and the occurrence of any kind of rupture or contradiction was denied.

Although Morgner's novel directly takes part in the debate over literary tradition, the function of art in a socialist society, and different possibilities for literary forms, this participation is seldom acknowledged in reviews of her novel. It is important to realize, however, that the GDR reviews and criticism not only illustrate the immediate response to her book, but also take part in a larger discourse. By denying the novel's challenges to the official art doctrine, critics attempted to establish their own authoritative position in the debate over art in the

6   Wenn man von der festen Position des Sozialismus ausgeht, kann es meines Erachtens auf dem Gebiet der Kunst und Literatur keine Tabus geben. Das betrifft sowohl die Fragen der inhaltlichen Gestaltung als auch die des Stils. (Honecker, "Bericht des ZK an den VIII. Parteitag vom 15. Juni 1971," reprinted in *Neues Deutschland* 18 December 1971).
7   Hohendahl, "Theorie und Praxis des Erbens."

'70s. A specific kind of language and the recurrence of key terms are discourse markers that designate the critic as a participant in a broader debate. This can most clearly be observed in Werner Neubert's recommendation for the publication of the manuscript in 1974.

In the case of Neubert, one of the more orthodox critics in the GDR and a reviewer for *Neue Deutsche Literatur*, it becomes very clear that the problematic parts of the novel are those that do not easily fit into the official art doctrine. The terms Neubert uses are key words in the broader debate on the function of art in a socialist society. Neubert tries to deemphasize the novel's challenges by fitting them into official norms without investigating them in their own right. As my schematic juxtaposition demonstrates, his essay moves with almost mechanical regularity from one problematic point of the novel to the next, responding to each of the text's challenges with an attempt to negate the critical potential through rebuttal:

Summary of Problematic Points	Rebuttal
1. "Morgner – following her individual talents – has decided to use a fantastic writing style and alienation techniques."	"This does not exclude her use of other, unmediated realistic styles."
2. "She has developed her literary subjectivity to the fullest and takes an original place in contemporary literature."	"This proves to be productive *for her*, while attempts to imitate her style would probably fail."
3. She finds "unusual artistic solutions."	"In view of the dynamic transformations of reality […] it makes sense, in my view, to keep an open mind about such solutions."
4. She uses the "power of fantasy."	"Certainly one has to assume a use of fantasy which remains conscious of its extent and its ideological goal."
5. "Her solutions cannot be dealt with using traditional normative demands for art (e.g. the novel as artistic organism); and Goethe,	"It is important that the author has bestowed on her writing a stable motivation." "In this *individual* attempt one can

	Hegel, and Lukács, and maybe other contemporary theorists might see […] instead of an artistic solution a dissolution of art."	accept her practice; if this technique were to be blown up to the level of a binding aesthetic conception for modern writing, however, it would be questionable. But this is not a real danger."
6.	"Jean Paul's writing style was and is not liked by everyone."	"Nevertheless we admit that he has become a literary enrichment."
7.	Morgner "uses heterogeneous elements."	"The narrative parts, distanced at first view, nevertheless create correspondences with [the points of debate]."
8.	"We have to expect exclamations like: 'That is no novel after all!'"	"If I want to remain credible as a critic, theorist, etc., I have to say: a) you should perhaps be interested in this book, b) do not buy it head over heels […] but ask yourselves if love is possible here."
9.	Morgner's novel as a "lava-like natural phenomenon."	"I will only add what I believe is an important observation: the author views what she writes from a socialist perspective."[8]

Each of the features Neubert mentions is a sensitive topic in the context of GDR literary norms, with each of his arguments related to the broader debate on art in the GDR in the 1970s. His first two points concerning Morgner's individuality and subjectivity directly refer to the debate about individualism in literature. This debate had developed when more and more writers began to question the primacy of an objective neutral style of prose that was part of the official "reflection theory" (*Widerspiegelungstheorie*). Wolfgang Emmerich points out that in the late '60s and early '70s writers began to use fantasy and new narrative methods to express the needs of the individual neglected by the official emphasis on technological progress and rationality as essential for the development of a socialist community.

---

8   Werner Neubert, "Aus einem Gutachten," *Neue Deutsche Literatur*, 22:8 (8 August 1974), 103–5.

Hand in hand with debates about a new subjectivity and individuality, which had started to enter literature, the use of the fantastic is another hotly debated topic in the early '70s. In Rainer Nägele's words:

> The attempt to mediate the concept and experience of subjectivity with societal processes in a new way, or, even more radically, to remove these experiences from forced reconciliation plays a central role in this context. The phenomena of the fantastic in a narrow sense – a "sense" which is far from being fixed but has to be developed – cannot be separated from an analysis of subjectivity.[9]

Because both the fantastic and an emphasis on subjectivity point to a return of suppressed elements in modern industrialized society, the fantastic and subjectivity are closely connected in both Emmerich's and Nägele's analyses. The suppressed other of Enlightenment thought – which Horkheimer and Adorno discuss in their *Dialectic of Enlightenment* – haunts modern humanity. This was also true for the GDR in the '70s, a society almost exclusively concentrated on winning the economic competition with the capitalist West and based on an unshaken belief in technical progress and rationality. Although these problems are not discussed in such terms in the GDR, Neubert recognizes that they are vehemently debated topics in literature. In the texts that appeared in the early '70s in the GDR, the emphasis on the individual, with his or her unfulfilled desires and needs, challenged the fundamental belief in the socialist *Menschengemeinschaft*. In addition, these texts question the theory of an easy appropriation of reality that can be mirrored directly in art. As fantastic elements became more prominent in GDR literature, they endangered the official belief in rational development and progress. That is one reason why Neubert, while acknowledging Morgner's originality, nevertheless feels compelled to warn other writers against imitating her technique.

Neubert's third argument, which emphasizes Morgner's unusual artistic solutions and pleads for openness and flexibility from critics in the face of radical social changes (especially in science and technology), is unusually frank. Neubert acknowledges what writers had

9   Rainer Nägele, "Trauer, Tropen, und Phantasmen: Ver-rückte Geschichten aus der DDR," in Peter Uwe Hohendahl and Patricia Herminghouse (eds), *Literatur der DDR in den 70er Jahren* (Frankfurt a. M.: Suhrkamp, 1983), 194.

been pointing out since the late '60s: the development of the GDR into a highly technological and industrialized society had not been without gaps and contradictions. What had been advertised as a smooth and progressive development, culminating in prosperity and a harmonious community of socialist people, neglected broad areas of human life and needs. By the middle of the '70s even the official managers of cultural life had had to acknowledge that a new model of cultural theory was needed to account for the gray areas of theory of the '50s and '60s. After 1971, when people realized that the traditional art theory no longer corresponded to the realities of modern life, institutionalized GDR culture began to change. Cultural officials started to realize that an exclusive integration of Marxism into the tradition of the Enlightenment was no longer adequate. The new preoccupation with Marx's early works and his previously neglected concept of alienation allowed writers to tackle two burning problems in modern GDR society: the progressive development of increasingly specialized work spheres and the simultaneous formation of groups and classlike structures in the GDR, which contradicted the call for a classless society in the socialist state. The debate over these problems is reflected in Neubert's defense of Morgner's alienation techniques.

Neubert's arguments in points five and six, concerning Morgner's use of fantasy and her refusal to follow the official canon, are closely tied to the debate about the *Erbetheorie*, which was at the center of GDR art theory in the 1970s. Neubert points out that Morgner, in her use of romantic elements and modern montage techniques, breaks with the official theory of literary tradition. Goethe, Hegel, and Lukács – all mentioned by Neubert – had served as guarantors for an unproblematic appropriation of the classical tradition as the natural inheritance of the socialist *Menschengemeinschaft*. Neubert claims that Morgner departs from this tradition without mentioning that Goethe plays an extraordinary role in Morgner's prose – although it seems to be a very different Goethe than the one promoted in official GDR literary theory. The use of romantic poets such as Jean Paul, however, seemed to be threatening to the official literary tradition. Although by the mid-70s the romantic tradition was no longer condemned as reactionary and preparing the way for modern decadent art, Neubert still feels the need to defend the novel from the threat of a too radical departure from traditional aesthetic norms. Neubert is able to admit (in point six) that the literature of the romantics might offer an "enrichment" for literature. He allows Morgner's novel to be an experiment in this direction, but he cannot allow her critique to expand into a new aesthetic theory. While the integration of the romantic period displaced the content of the theory of cultural inheritance significantly, cultural officials were not willing to see this period as an interruption in the smooth and teleological development of art. On the contrary, literary critics took great pains to find a synthesis between classicism and romanticism to save the theory of a teleological development of art and history. The fact that Neubert needs to assure his readers that a "stable [socialist] motivation" is the basis for Morgner's experiments shows that literary scholars had only begun to carefully promote an integration of the suppressed romantic elements into official theory. In order for his recommendation to publish this novel to be accepted, he needs to assure GDR censors that Morgner's ideological position and her political convictions are in accordance with the official party line. Only ideology is able to form a shield against this volcano-like eruption, this "natural catastrophe," as he sees Morgner's novel. Again, Neubert's language is revealing. In the context of GDR ideology, natural catastrophes are precisely those events against which a discourse based on rationality and reason should protect society. The goal of human domination over nature is endangered if nature is allowed to dominate human beings. Although Neubert mentions Morgner's engagement for the "historical, social, sexual, and psychological equality of women" (104), and pretends not to object to her political goals, he treats her text as "other," as a "natural catastrophe" that fundamentally threatens a male discourse of rationality and reason.

Neubert's recommendation – and most of the later review essays in the GDR are essentially of the same nature – indirectly reveals how radical the changes and ruptures in the official theory in the GDR really were. The need to use ideology to disguise the degree of these changes and to cover up the ruptures in theory points to the complexity of the problems endemic to official GDR criticism at the time.

Dissenting Voices in the GDR

Two reviews, one by Annemarie Auer and another one by Gerhard Wolf, differ from the majority of reviews in the GDR. Auer's 1976 review is a long critical essay of forty pages. With its thematization of feminist topics, it is, next to Eva Kaufmann's 1984 essay in *Weimarer Beiträge* on Morgner's development as an artist, the most personal analysis that appeared in the GDR. Auer points out that the word *emancipation* provokes defensive reactions in the GDR:

> And thus back to the literary, before the anger-provoking suffragette word "emancipation" comes into the debate. That one "liberates" oneself with one's writing is accepted much more easily. Liberation through writing is seen as a universal human process among writers, without gender specificity.[10]

Auer herself feels the need to point out that Morgner is not a feminist, but a Marxist – that is, the author does not attack men, but customs (*Sitten*). The fact that this is argued in almost all of the GDR reviews makes clear how threatening the designation "feminist" was in the GDR, a state that supposedly had already succeeded in creating equality among men and women. A single word becomes a discourse marker used to delineate one's political loyalty.

Auer, however, carefully works at undermining her own dictum in the course of her essay. While still trying to rescue Morgner's novel for a GDR theory of art – by a comparison with Schiller, by emphasizing the closure of the novel despite heterogeneous material, and by fitting Morgner's work into a continuous development of GDR literature – Auer emphasizes elements of the novel that openly contradict the official theory of art. She underlines Morgner's critique of (male) instrumental thinking; she criticizes the way official reviews of the novel ignore Morgner's comments as a feminist and trivialize her answers in interviews; and she tries to fit Morgner's novel into the context of women's literature by discussing Anna Segher's reaction to the book. Auer's enthusiastic review of Morgner's text shows clearly that GDR

---

10   Annemarie Auer, "Trobadora unterwegs oder Schulung in Realismus," *Sinn und Form*, 5 (1976), 1068.

critics of the '70s were in conflict with the official theory of art. To get texts published, they had to defend an official conception of art that was directly challenged by the texts they promoted. This conflict became even more marked when both the writer and the critic were women, a fact that unveils the official theory of art as an aesthetic conception that left little space for women's writings.

Gerhard Wolf's review from 1975 goes farthest in accepting the novel's challenges and in attempting to examine the text on its own terms. Even the title of his review, "Abschied von der Harmonie" (Farewell to harmony), points to the fact that Wolf, himself an accepted and prominent author, is not attempting to fit Morgner's text into the official canon, which is supposed to reflect a harmonious, teleological development of art. Wolf finds six *Hauptsätze* (main propositions) in Morgner's novel that point to the singularity of the text's structure by opening up gaps and contradictions, rather than giving answers to preformulated questions. Refusing the kind of authority over the text that was characteristic of most other reviews, Wolf lets the text ask its own questions. His attempt to establish a dialogue, rather than explain away challenges, was thus an exception to the usual practice of GDR criticism, which used texts as instruments to establish and reinforce its own authority.

FRG Criticism (1974–76): Establishing Authority

While the need to establish authority was characteristic of both GDR and FRG critics in the mid-70s, the way to go about it was quite different in the East and West, which points to structural differences in the cultural institutions of the two states. Alice Schwarzer's 1976 review in *konkret* points to a basic difference in the critical discourse of the two German states:

> The *Trobadora* has been received in the GDR in a carefully friendly way. Irmtraud Morgner's exceptional talent is undeniable, even if her contents are discomforting. She was partly praised and partly lectured to, but she was never railed at in the same way as in the FRG (*FAZ*: "debacle," "epic monster," "a lot

of fruitless effort in view of the expensive paper"). That is a little difference even if it is not a fundamental one.[11]

The differences that Schwarzer sees in East and West German critics' treatment of the novel stem from the fundamentally different functions of literature in the socialist GDR on the one hand and the capitalist West on the other. It is surprising how seriously the challenges of GDR writers were taken in this period of the 1970s and how thoroughly they were discussed, even if only to defend the established conventions. Morgner herself pointed to the fact that, in contrast to the capitalist West, those GDR writers who succeeded in getting their texts published had the opportunity to make a difference through their writing. Official cultural functionaries in the GDR were forced to react to radical changes in the literary works of many GDR writers in the early '70s. Wolfgang Emmerich points out that in the late '60s, authors had begun to openly question the *Widerspiegelungstheorie* of art in the GDR, as well as the official literary canon (*Kleine Literaturgeschichte*). In the early '70s, it became impossible even for GDR cultural institutions, which usually react much more slowly, to overlook these basic challenges. Since the procedure leading to the publication of any novel was much more complicated and less dependent on market considerations than in the FRG, it was assumed that a work that reached the point of publication was worth discussing in detail. While literary scholars desperately attempted to fit the challenges of writers into the aesthetic principles of official socialist realism, they were no longer in a position to ignore or suppress new forms of writing. In this sense, GDR writers did have great influence on official art theory in the early '70s. Dependent on celebrated authors for legitimization, cultural officials in the GDR were forced to discuss the questions raised in the texts.

While GDR critics used their authority to defend the aesthetic principles of official socialist realism, in the FRG, where no such theory existed in the form of an official program, critics felt the need to defend their reputation as intellectuals much more strongly. The position in different critical feuds, in different factions, in the formation of "schools" of criticism, and in different literary institutions (certain kinds of news-

11   Alice Schwarzer, "Auch Genossen sind nicht automatisch Brüder," *konkret*, 9 (1976), 57.

papers and feuilletons, for example) is important in establishing the degree of authority with which a critic is able to speak. Catchy review titles, ingenious formulations, and radical judgments are the rule. Whereas GDR critics carefully assessed and asked questions, FRG critics either dismissed works or praised them enthusiastically. The discourse of FRG reviews is marked by critics' need to establish themselves as individual "authorities" through certain catchwords that served as pointers for their position in different debates on literature and art, as well as a thorough vocabulary that marked their own individual voices as critics.

Although the titles of review essays are often chosen by the editor rather than by the critic, they point to the basic market orientation of FRG reviews. Titles of GDR reviews include: "Aus einem Gutachten" (From a recommendation), "Leben und Abenteuer der Beatriz [...]" (Life and adventures of Beatrice), "Irmtraud Morgner: Leben und Abenteuer der Trobadora Beatriz nach Zeugnissen ihrer Spielfrau Laura" (Irmtraud Morgner: Life and adventures of Trobadora Beatrice as chronicled by her minstrel Laura), and "Leben einer Spielfrau" (Life of a minstrel). Most of the GDR critics used the novel's title or careful, moderate metaphors. By comparison, FRG titles are much more provoking and inventive. Some FRG titles read "Marx-Sisters statt Marx" (Marx-sisters instead of Marx), "Trobadora aus der Retorte" (The trobadora from the test tube), "Die Feministin der DDR" (The feminist of the GDR), "Minnesang und Maiunruhen" (Minnesong and Mairevolts), "Sprung in die Gegenwart" (Leap into the present), "Ein Einhorn soll die ganze Welt erlösen" (One unicorn to save the world), "Ein lustiges Klagelied" (A funny mourning song), "Aus dem Dornröschenschlaf erwacht" (Awakened from the sleeping beauty's sleep), and "Unsere 'schöne' Frauenhalter-Kultur" (Our "pretty" culture of kept women). To convince the reader to read the article and to establish their own signature as critics, FRG reviewers and editors were thus forced to be much more original than their GDR colleagues.

Because of the same need, the critics' judgments also tended to be more extreme. The reactions to the work ranged from Gregor-Dellin's "deep disappointment in the novel" ("debacle," "epic monster") and Fritz Raddatz's devaluation ("downpour of horror and wit," "inflation of ideas") to Marggraf's positive review ("Morgner takes the offensive") and Delius's and Schwarzer's enthusiasm ("a book which the left urgently needs," "empowering humor and phantasy").[12] Schwarzer's title, "Auch Genossen sind nicht automatisch Brüder" (Even comrades aren't automatically brothers), for example, emphasizes that Schwarzer, while seeing herself situated on the political Left, defined herself above all as a feminist critic. In addition to showing a political inclination, inventive key words and witty phrases are supposed to help the reader remember the reviewers as individual critics. As critics, FRG reviewers are compelled to advertise themselves and their own political positions as much as to evaluate the text in question.

Just as GDR critics defended their own authority as guardians of the official literary dogma, FRG critics legitimized their authority by mentioning certain art concepts and displaying their knowledge of the "rules" of literature. Morgner's dictum, that none of the critics was ready to examine the novel on its own terms, was valid for both FRG and GDR criticism. Gregor-Dellin complains, for example, that Morgner did not use the opportunity to write a *Bildungsroman* – "and how much the material cried out for it." He never takes the trouble, however, to find out why Morgner chose to quote and at the same time deconstruct traditional genres, such as the educational novel. Although he comes from a different camp of criticism than Gregor-Dellin, Raddatz assumes a similar pose as the protector of conventions of high culture. In "Marx-Sisters statt Marx," he complains that Morgner did not correctly understand the rules of the picaresque novel:

> Irmtaud Morgner's narrative principle of stringing together events without evaluation seems to be based on a misunderstanding of the picaresque novel. *One* great idea formed the basis of the adventures of a Don Quixote de La Mancha, for example; this idea was illustrated and varied through plot and action. Lady Beatrice de Dia, however, walks through reality like Cocteau's figures walked through mirrors – behind them there is nothing.

12   Martin Gregor-Dellin, "Trobadora aus der Retorte: Was die Spielfrau Laura der DDR-Autorin Irmtraud Morgner verriet," *Frankfurter Allgemeine Zeitung*, 10 March 1975; Fritz Raddatz, "Marx-Sisters statt Marx: Neue Bücher von Morgner, Schlesinger, Köhler," *Die Zeit*, 21 Mai 1976; Nikolaus Marggraf, "Die Feministin der DDR: Irmtraud Morgners *Leben und Abenteuer der Trobadora Beatriz*," *Frankfurter Rundschau*, 24 May 1975; F. C. Delius, "Ich habe gelesen," *konkret*, 5 (1975), 43; Schwarzer, "Auch Genossen sind nicht automatisch Brüder."

Aside from the fact that Raddatz is not talking about a picaresque novel to begin with, but rather describes a mock chevalesque novel (the picaresque tradition was created by *Lazarillo de Tormes* and Alemán's *Guzmán de Alfarache*), both Raddatz's and Gregor-Dellin's reviews disregard the possibility that Morgner is purposefully challenging literary traditions, a strategy she even thematizes directly in the novel. The critics' need to fit the novel into fixed categories was overwhelming, and it is telling that, as in GDR criticism, the unconventional form of the text was what bothered FRG critics most. Christa Reinig calls the novel a "family saga"; Ingeborg Drewitz objects that "an ordering hand was missing"; Christa Rotzoll remarks "I do not like it particularly"; and Thomas Zenke complains that Morgner did not fulfill the potential of the medieval hero, using the idea only "to render the fiction absolute."[13] Peter Burri is the only critic who considers the possibility that Morgner is consciously reflecting on literary conventions and traditions:

> Since writing the "untrustworthy narrator" novel (*The Wondrous Voyages of Gustav the World Traveler*), the GDR writer Irmtraud Morgner has been known as an innovator of an old genre: the genre of the picaresque adventure novel, whose fantastic possibilities she uses to mediate current subject matter.[14]

The same need to put labels on Morgner's text can be observed in the political discussion of her work. While GDR critics took great pains to defend Morgner from the accusation of being a feminist, FRG critics almost maliciously underscored the feminist implications of her text. Disregarding Morgner's many statements that she did not consider herself a feminist in the Western style,[15] Western critics – with the

---

13 Christa Reinig, "Ein Einhorn soll die ganze Welt erlösen," *Die Welt am Sonntag*, 8 Aug. 1976; Ingeborg Drewitz, "Sprung in die Gegenwart: Irmtraud Morgners neuer Roman," *Der Tagesspiegel*, 8 August 1976; Christa Rotzoll, "Ein lustiges Klagelied," *Süddeutsche Zeitung*, 13 November 1976; Thomas Zenke, "Aus dem Dornröschenschlaf erwacht," *Frankfurter Allgemeine Zeitung*, 16 November 1976.

14 Peter Burri, "Der zweite Schritt: Ein Roman von Irmtraud Morgner über die Alltagswirklichkeit in der DDR," *Nationalzeitung (Basel)*, 2 October 1976.

15 See, for example, the interview with Oskar Neumann: "I do not see any reason to be a Communist, on the one hand, and a feminist, on the other [...]. I see the only real possibility in the socialist movement; equality is not a woman's problem but rather a human problem. It can only be solved by society as a

exception of Peter Burri, Thomas Zenke, and Alice Schwarzer –
refused to contemplate differences in political labels in East and West.
Marggraf considered Morgner "the feminist of the GDR," while Beatrix Geisel labeled her an "Alice Schwarzer of the GDR."[16]

FRG critics were quick to give a final judgement, but most
neglected the context in which Morgner's novel was written. Using
their own criteria for what art should be, they were just as unwilling to
appreciate or even examine the new and challenging aspects of the
novel as their GDR colleagues, who feared for their official theory of
art. The surprising result was that critics in both East and West Germany complained most about the form of Morgner's novel, suggesting
that critics might establish similar patterns of authority in radically
different discursive settings. While GDR critics feared for their socialist realist theory of art and were most worried by unorthodox political
views, FRG reviewers, threatened by the pluralism of a market-
oriented publishing system, needed to defend themselves as critic
personalities by sticking to traditional concepts of aesthetic theory.
For both groups of critics, the need to position themselves in a certain
discursive setting was thus at least as important as evaluating the text
in question.

FRG Criticism (1985–90): The Critique of Civilization

The reception of Morgner's work in the FRG from approximately 1985
to 1990 is, of course, composed not so much of review essays of Morgner's novel, but mostly of discussions of those parts of Morgner's
oeuvre that had been published by that time.[17] The discussions are
therefore more detailed and profound than in the earlier short critical

whole" ("Weltspitze sein und sich wundern, was noch nicht ist," *Kürbiskern*,
78:1 (1978), 98).

16   Marggraf, "Die Feministin der DDR"; Beatrix Geisel, "Unsere 'schöne'
      Frauenhalter-Kultur," *Mannheimer Morgen*, 25 November 1976.

17   I will not discuss the reviews of Morgner's second novel, *Amanda. Ein
      Hexenroman* from 1983 here.

review articles. Nevertheless, critics still ignored certain postmodernist elements of Morgner's text. In addition, they still did not consider Morgner's feminist discussions in detail and disregarded her attempts to participate in feminist debates on the definition of a female aesthetics.

The second phase of reception in the FDR was strongly influenced by Wolfgang Emmerich's *Kleine Literaturgeschichte der DDR*, which appeared in 1981 and was republished four times, with a new expanded edition being published in 1989.[18] Emmerich, a critic in the Frankfurt School tradition, traced the development of GDR literature in its sociopolitical context. According to him, GDR literature of the '70s and '80s became the medium of a radical critique of civilization and thus participated in the modern critique of reason developed by Adorno and Horkheimer in their *Dialectic of Enlightenment*. His thesis is that GDR literature of the '70s and '80s began to catch up with literary modernism, the reception of which had been interrupted by the socialist realist art doctrine.

> What now takes place [in the GDR] in the course of the 70s and 80s is a historical and philosophical paradigm shift on a large scale. The ideology of progress, mediated through Marxism in its orthodox version, is rejected by critical artists; the belief in the certain arrival of socialism and finally communism is lost [...]. The self-destructive process of Enlightenment, the culmination of rational modernization in "industrial culture" as a process whose limits are not only reached but have long since been surpassed, whose costs cannot be paid anymore, can no longer be ignored [...]. With this GDR literature has approached the "dark" analysis of civilization which has always been a taboo in the official thought of the country: the *Dialectic of Enlightenment* by Max Horkheimer and Theodor Adorno. (271)

According to Emmerich, the literature by women in the '70s played an important role in rethinking the process of Enlightenment, since these texts tried to establish "another reality" as an alternative to the "spell of the outer reality" [Bann der auswendigen Realität].[19]

---

18 In 1996 Emmerich published a new and revised edition of the *Kleine Literatur-geschichte der DDR*. In this discussion of the reception of Morgner's novel in the early '80s, I only refer to the earlier edition from 1989.

19 Emmerich quoting Adorno (Wolfgang Emmerich, *Kleine Literaturgeschichte der DDR: 1945–1988. Erweiterte Ausgabe* (Frankfurt a. M.: Luchterhand, 1989), 285).

Emmerich considers Morgner's works to be important texts that participate in this development:

> Morgner is among those who attempt to reverse the result of the process of repression and who attempt even to recover the "visual thinking," the power of imagination [...]. Her texts practice the transgressing of the borders of empirical reality, which are exposed to the solvent of madness, of the marginal, of the fantastic. (286)

Emmerich's analysis is intriguing, but he places Morgner and most other female authors in the context of a modernity that, according to him, finally found its entrance into GDR literature. Emmerich sees some tendencies in GDR literature that point in the direction of post-modernist aesthetic techniques, but he does not pursue them further, especially not in Morgner's texts.[20] The feminist concerns of women's literature of the '70s are, for him, part of a broader development, a critique of Enlightenment prevalent not only in the GDR, but also in the FRG.[21]

Walter Jens's brilliant laudatio, on occasion of the "Award Ceremony of the Prize for Grotesque Humor" in 1989, displays a similar

---

20   The acknowledgment in Emmerich's analysis of postmodernist tendencies in GDR literature is more pronounced in his 1988 article, "Gleichzeitigkeit: Vormoderne, Moderne und Postmoderne in der Literatur der DDR," in Heinz Ludwig Arnold (ed.), *Bestandsaufnahme Gegenwartsliteratur* (Munich: edition text und kritik, 1988), 193–211.

21   In her important study, *Post-Fascist Fantasies: Psychoanalysis, History, and the Literature of East Germany* (Durham: Duke University Press, 1997), Julia Hell criticizes Emmerich's influential narrative of the development of GDR literature for its adherence to a single, yet twofold teleology: "the move from 'premodernism' to postmodernism was accompanied by an increasing gap between official ideology and literature, a process that would eventually result in the complete separation of the 'best' authors/texts from the GDR's official discourse" (12). Hell wants to intervene in the predominant view of GDR literature as that of the slow emergence of modernism, wedged on one side by a negligible period of 'premodernism' and on the other by a more ambivalently theorized period of postmodernism. While working with a different method-ology than Hell, I am similarly interested in criticizing this type of schematic view of the development of GDR literature from realism to modernism and finally to postmodernism, which seems too simplistic to me. Morgner's oeuvre definitely does not fit into this type of development.

tendency to interpret Morgner's novels as critiques of instrumental reason. Although Jens eloquently points to Morgner's subversive strategies, he places her within the modernist tradition of James Joyce and Thomas Mann and attests to her kinship with Peter Weiss's *Ästhetik des Widerstands*. He emphasizes that Morgner's project is not to *undermine* reason but, on the contrary, to criticize an *instrumental* reason that has reified human existence:

> Nothing more contemptuous exists for Morgner, I think, than the precipitate "Abandonment of Enlightenment, Reason, Law"! She does not promote the revocation of reason – which was a *Gemütsgabe* (gift of the soul) in the eighteenth century – but the fulfillment of reason and its dialectic sublation through the "Romanticism edge." [...] Art forms which prove themselves in the disciplined fantastic of narration, instead of being self-sufficient, always carry the message that it is the task of women [...] – like the Trobadora – to enter history: driven by the current situation of the world, which could culminate in a revocation of creation, and threatened by moments of tension whose destructive power can only be anticipated by fantasy and not by instrumental reason.[22]

Fantasy, disruptive narrative elements, and antirealistic techniques are features highly esteemed in this approach, since they question a reality that has become obsolete and destructive at a time when instrumental reason threatens to erase the emancipatory elements of the Enlightenment movement. On the one hand, Frankfurt School critics are able to appreciate the antitraditionalist gestures of Morgner's text on a much more profound level than orthodox Marxist criticism or the purely aesthetic criticism of early West German reviewers, who for the most part defended traditional genre definitions. Scholars in the tradition of the Frankfurt School thus value the openness of Morgner's text, which refuses any kind of closure in the name of a negation of a bad reality. On the other hand, to save Morgner's text for the "unfinished project of the ('good') enlightenment movement," they cannot allow the novel to reject reason altogether. As I will investigate more closely in chapter 2, however, there seem to be two contradictory moves at work here. On the one hand, openness, fantasy, and a rejection of mimetic techniques are appreciated, but on the other hand, those elements that could threaten a "good" reason and a "good" rationality are disre-

22   Jens, "Die Tausendsassa Irmtraud Morgner," 105.

garded. This tension can be observed in some of the points that both Emmerich's and Jens's analyses share.

First, both Emmerich and Jens are careful to interpret Morgner as a modernist author who stands in the tradition of James Joyce, Thomas Mann, and Peter Weiss. They see Morgner as one of the important young authors who have started to introduce modernist techniques into GDR literature. The literature of women is one element in this modernist movement that strives to question man's reified existence. Because of their insistence on Morgner's participation in the project of modernity, neomarxist scholars fail to examine the specific concerns of Morgner's feminist project in the context of the GDR.

Second, despite the high value put on the negation of closure and mimesis of reality, a certain kind of unifying project creeps back into Frankfurt School criticism. This project is the "unfinished project of Enlightenment," which is supposed to be saved in truly authentic art. That is the reason why Jens has to emphasize that Morgner rightly criticizes instrumental reason, but by no means wants to give up reason altogether.

On the one hand, criticism in the tradition of the Frankfurt School for the first time allows for a profound analysis of Morgner's anti-traditionalist aesthetic techniques, valuing precisely those elements that orthodox Marxism is anxious to interpret away. On the other hand, a specific kind of unifying project, the "project of modernity," is promoted, which is blind to features of Morgner's text that do not fit the project.

US German Studies (1976–83): The Search for a Feminist Utopian Vision

The strongest enthusiasm for Morgner's novel could be observed in the first phase of reception by US scholars of German studies in the late '70s. In her essay "Trobadora in Amerika," Angelika Bammer explains why Morgner's text, together with other feminist texts from the GDR, triggered so much interest in US German studies and women's studies departments. Bammer maintains that it was the specific mixture of Marxism, issues in feminist theory, and a new concern with GDR literature that interested a group of scholars who had just established themselves as a distinct, politically active group in the United States. In this context, Bammer points to the founding of the journal *New German Critique* in 1974, with its special emphasis on Frankfurt School criticism; the journal's second number was a special issue on GDR literature. The Fall 1978 issue included a translation of Irmtraud Morgner's Valeska Kantus story from *Life and Adventures*, followed in winter 1978 by a special feminist issue edited by Helen Fehervary, Renny Harrigan, and Nancy Vedder-Shults, which contained articles on GDR women's writing and a translation of Christa Wolf's "Selbstversuch." Bammer also notes special sessions on GDR literature at MLA conventions since 1975, the organization of the New Hampshire Symposium on GDR Literature, and the establishment of the professional organization Women in German (WIG). These institutions both reflected and propelled a new concern with GDR literature and culture.

The relationship between Marxism and feminism that Morgner's novel investigates was at the center of interest for US scholars, since it seemed to promise an alternative to bourgeois feminism on the one hand and patriarchal socialism on the other. Bammer points out that in the mid-70s, the American women's movement was still largely influenced by a socialist feminist orientation, having had its origin in the protest movements of the '60s. Because Morgner's novel thematized the relationship between a feminist utopian vision and history, and also investigated the preconditions for women's subjecthood, it was greeted with enthusiasm. Bammer writes:

> The debate about the relationship between utopian visions and history in feminist circles attempted to gain a basis on the grounds of historical materialism (the so-called "reality") on the one hand; but, on the other hand, feminists were just as much attracted by the realm of the libido (the fantastic, desire, and the erotic). Morgner's *Trobadora* touched both of these poles; through this, the relationship between utopia and history was grounded as well as recharged with a new, positive tension.[23]

---

23   Bammer, "Trobadora in Amerika," 203.

The first phase of reception in US circles was thus marked by enthusiasm for the new approach that GDR women authors seemed to offer. An example is Biddy Martin's early essay on *Life and Adventures*, in which she comes to the following conclusion:

> Morgner's success in combining political and historical perspectives with a validation of the personal, the subjective, and the imaginative has made *Leben und Abenteuer der Trobadora Beatriz* an extremely important work for women in the East and West. It is an essential affirmation within the GDR of the importance of feminist principles and analyses to the development of socialism. And Morgner's ambitious experiment with form makes the work a very significant contribution to the ongoing exploration and development of aesthetics within and outside of the GDR.[24]

In 1979 Patricia Herminghouse published an important article on Irmtraud Morgner's novel in which she investigated Morgner's use of fantasy as a subversive strategy in the context of other feminist texts from the GDR.[25] Herminghouse analyzed many of the literary allusions in the novel and claimed that Morgner uses fantastic elements to criticize GDR reality and encourage the emancipation of women. Herminghouse saw Morgner's text as the most important example of a unique feminist movement in literature coming out of the GDR.

But as soon as the novel was judged in a second phase of reception in the context of the US and international feminist debates in the early '80s, Bammer explains, the high expectations turned into disappointment and criticism. Sara Lennox and Biddy Martin voiced their reservations and criticism most strongly, postulating that the novel did not accomplish the high goals it had set for itself. Critical voices, disappointed by Morgner's refusal to define the feminist discourse as the most important one in her texts, dismissed her intention as failed and closed the debate for a long time. Martin, after publishing the above-quoted enthusiastic review of the novel in 1979, formu-

---

24   Biddy Martin, "Irmtraud Morgner's *Leben und Abenteuer der Trobadora Beatriz*," in Susan L. Cocalis and Kay Goodman (eds), *Beyond the Eternal Feminine: Critical Essays on Women and German Literature* (Stuttgart: Akademischer Verlag, 1982), 439.
25   Herminghouse, "Die Frau und das Phantastische," 248–66.

lated this new disappointment most eloquently in her article, "Socialist Patriarchy and the Limits of Reform."

> The ruptures introduced into the text and the GDR by other insistent "feminine" desires are foreclosed by the discursive limitations of orthodox Marxist rhetoric and by the supposed historical necessities that govern the development of GDR society. *Life and Adventures* is thematically and structurally marked by the tension between the necessities of the GDR's "really existing socialism" and the unnamed and inassimilable desires, which intervene and which would defy the conceptual and political grasp of conventional wisdom and social structures.[26]

An important factor in the discussions of Morgner's novel in the '80s – a point not mentioned by Bammer – is the debate about the usefulness or dangers of postmodernism for feminist theory. The debate about postmodernism, a term that has had a very different reception in the FRG than in the United States, shows curious patterns of reception in feminist circles.[27] While until the late '80s it played hardly any role in German criticism – and cannot be detected in any of the early FRG reviews of Morgner's novel – it has been at the center of debate in the United States, where books, essays, conferences, and even journals have been devoted to its description, analysis, exploration, and celebration. Though almost all scholars of postmodernism admit the difficulty of defining the concept clearly, postmodernism's concerns are understood to include the new interest in language and form, the transgression of boundaries, and a new self-reflexive stance in literature.

It was striking, however, that this general interest in postmodernism and poststructuralism in the United States, and especially among US feminists, did not influence the feminist criticism practiced in the German departments in the United States. Biddy Martin makes this clear in her essay "Zwischenbilanz der feministischen Debatte":

> But precisely this situation of identity and supposed unity contributes to their [US feminists in the field of Germanistik] isolation, to a certain invisibility

---

26   Martin, "Socialist Patriarchy and the Limits of Reform," 60.

27   See, for example, Habermas's rejection of postmodernism. Ingeborg Hoesterey explains that Habermas sees postmodernism as "dictated by a swing towards irrationality and neo-conservatism, that jeopardize what he considers to be the 'unfinished project' of the enlightenment" ("Postmodernisms," *Yearbook of Comparative and General Literature*, 37 (1988), 161).

within broader feminist debates and discussions among Germanists. Until now female Germanists were represented strikingly seldom in public feminist discussions about the political implications of certain epistemological and critical strategies.[28]

In Germany, feminist critics were among the first scholars to study and apply French poststructuralist theories (after these theories had been neglected in Germany for so long).[29] In the United States, however, Germanists who defined themselves as feminists hardly participated in the debate on postmodernism and poststructuralism at all. Martin points to the tensions that tended to develop in the field of German studies between German feminist critics, who had begun to use poststructuralist theories, and US feminists, who remained committed to empiricist and sociohistorical methods. Morgner's *Life and Adventures of Trobadora Beatrice* is at the center of these discourse displacements and "nonsynchronisms" in the critical debate. To some degree, the mixed response to Morgner's novel – passionate enthusiasm matched by vehement criticism – could be attributed to the unresolved theoretical debates in the field at this time (the late '70s and early '80s).

The critical reviews of the second phase of reception in the United States were written by critics such as Lennox and Martin. Although they were much more open to poststructuralist ideas than the majority of feminists in German studies, they still seemed to have their reservations, for political reasons, about the new French theories, since they feared that an uncritical embrace of them could lead to an abandonment of political activism. Lennox's 1981 article demonstrates this ambivalence toward new French theories:

> It is evident that French feminists, whose thought is rooted in psychoanalysis, structuralism, and linguistics, presuppose a sophisticated understanding of gender and sexuality as socially constituted, particularly through the child's

---

28   Biddy Martin, "Zwischenbillanz der feministischen Debatten," in Frank Trommler (ed.), *Germanistik in den USA* (Opladen: Westdeutscher Verlag, 1989), 171.

29   See Inge Stephan and Sigrid Weigel's influential book *Die verborgene Frau: Sechs Beiträge zu einer feministischen Literaturwissenschaft* (Berlin: Argument Verlag, 1983).

appropriation of language. But as their analysis has been received outside of France, it has intersected with and reinforced certain "essentialist" tendencies in German (and American) feminism which argue that the historical facts of women's difference are ontological qualities instead.[30]

An essentialist view – critics like Lennox were concerned – would paralyse feminists and keep them from taking direct political action.

Martin, on the other hand, demonstrates an explicitly post-structuralist approach:

> Certainly such anti-patriarchal literature in the GDR signals the kind of "insurrection of subjugated knowledges" against a regime of apparently self-evident and absolute certainties which, according to Michel Foucault, character-izes critical epistemological developments in the West during the past ten years. The points of convergence between feminist and post-structuralist thought make Foucault's characterizations of such developments useful in our attempts to elaborate the significance for us of this anti-patriarchal literature in the GDR. What continues to fascinate us about this GDR literature are not only, and indeed, perhaps not primarily, the explicit descriptions, validations and critiques for conditions of women in the GDR; these texts have an immediate informa-tive value, but we read and re-read them not so much for what they say about women, but for what they do discursively, for what they contribute to the theoretical, political and literary projects in which we as Western scholars and feminists are engaged.[31]

Scholars like Martin had begun to recognize the necessity of broadening feminist theory to incorporate poststructuralist thought. In fact, she argues that there are connections and points of intersection between feminist and poststructuralist theory. Her essay nevertheless comes to a negative evaluation concerning Morgner's novel:

> The text removes the difference that Beatriz and her political, cultural and emotional solidarity with Laura have made by subsuming that difference within a conceptual synthesis represented by the heterosexual marriage of Laura to Benno. With the domestication and death of Beatriz, struggle and conflict disappear, unconscious desires are defined as safely conscious attitudes, and the female bonding which has provided the disruptive and critical potential in the text is unconvincingly suppressed in favor of a nervously asserted heterosexuality (72).

30   Sara Lennox, "Trends in Literary Theory: The Female Aesthetic and German Women's Writing," *German Quarterly*, 54 (January 1981), 64.
31   Martin, "Socialist Patriarchy," 60.

64

Martin does not acknowledge the irony in the gestures of closure at the end of Morgner's text. In fact, Benno's nightly masquerade as a Scheherazade figure, telling Laura consoling stories "in Beatrice's style," reveals that the seemingly traditional heterosexual marriage between Laura and Benno is full of disruption and conflict. What Martin overlooks is the possibility that conflict itself acts as a structuring device in Morgner's novel, emerging on a multitude of levels. Whether this conflict, which Martin sees on a thematic level only, gets resolved in favor of any one position, however, is highly questionable. Many elements in the text favor the opposite view, and Morgner never provides unambiguous answers. The Valeska Kantus story as the last will of Beatrice, her ironic way of dying (she loses her balance), the fact that Laura herself is worried about Beatrice's development and in a sense switches positions with the Trobadora, the ironic utopian vision at the end told in a man's voice that masquerades as the Trobadora functioning as a "consolation" for Laura, and the fact that the Trobadora's story has to be told anew (which Morgner later realizes in *Amanda*) – all point to disturbing elements in this supposedly smooth and unambiguous development toward a superficial Marxist and "heterosexual" utopia that silences all disruptive elements. What is disturbing for many feminist critics is the author's clear refusal to privilege any one discourse in her novel. Her refusal especially to imply clearly that feminist questions are the most important issues in her book upset many feminists. In a sense, the radicalism with which Morgner uses poststructuralist techniques – she deconstructs *all* discourses, even the ones that are dear to her heart and certainly important to feminists – is often misapprehended by her feminist critics.

With some justification, one can say that Martin's review closed the debate on Morgner's novel for several years. Lennox, voicing a similarly negative prognosis of the novel, quotes Martin's essay in her article, "'Nun ja! Das nächste Leben geht aber heute an': Prosa von Frauen und Frauenbefreiung in der DDR."[32] Even Rainer Nägele's

---

32   Sara Lennox, "'Nun ja! Das nächste Leben geht aber heute an.' Prosa von Frauen und Frauenbefreiung in der DDR," in Peter Uwe Hohendahl and Patricia Herminghouse (eds), *Literatur der DDR in den 70er Jahren* (Frankfurt a. M.: Suhrkamp, 1983), 224–58.

discussion, "Trauer, Tropen und Phantasmen: Ver-rückte Geschichten aus der DDR," which most consistently uses a poststructuralist approach, concurs with Martin's verdict:

> The gap between narrating and narrated subject, between stories and history seems to have become smaller. But the approach has its costs: where the fabulous story becomes history, difficult compromises are made."[33]

None of these scholars pursues the subversive elements of Morgner's text to the end, too ready to accept Martin's verdict without further investigation.

One West German analysis of Morgner's novel from the early first phase of reception (that is, before the second part of the trilogy appeared) is very different from any of the reviews in the FRG or the United States at that time in its refusal to give definite answers and close off Morgner's multivalent and open structuring. In her 1981 essay, "Die halbierte Geschichtsfähigkeit der Frau," Ingeborg Nordmann emphasizes tensions in the novel as the critical and subversive potential of the text.[34] She views the relationship between Laura and Beatrice quite differently from Martin:

> Morgner is far from constructing a harmonious and completed ("zu sich gekommene") identity Laura/Trobadora. She maintains the tension between the pragmatic adjustment to reality in the GDR and the absolute character of demands of emancipation. This tension aims at the transformation of the traditional antinomies of thinking, acting, and feeling, which include scientific, aesthetic, and emotional spheres [...]. It remains undecided until the end of the novel whether her ability to perceive the distance to utopia as a painful contradiction while nevertheless measuring herself on its claims will succumb to the overpowering force of traditions [...]. The ironic tone of the "positive" outcome leaves unsettled the question of the value of the utopian vision: whether it is distraction from a bad reality or an ever-developing ability to construct oneself in the play of anticipatory forms of existence. (442–3)

33 Nägele, "Trauer, Tropen, and Phantasmen," 214.
34 Ingeborde Nordmann, "Die halbierte Geschichtsfähigkeit der Frau: Zu Irmtraud Morgners Roman *Leben und Abenteuer der Trobadora Beatriz nach Zeugnissen ihrer Spielfrau Laura*," *Amsterdamer Beiträge zur Neueren Germanistik*, 11–12 (1981), 419–62.

66

Nordmann attests to a basic ambiguity in the novel that cannot be reduced to any one of its discourses. The contrasts and tensions established by the connection of disparate parts create a complex and contradictory reality, which provokes a multitude of interpretations.

In feminist analyses, a secret contradiction similar to the one in Frankfurt School criticism seems to be at work. On the one hand, the force of disruption and the techniques to break open the patriarchal discourse are the most valued features of Morgner's work; on the other, the emancipatory project for women is a taboo that cannot be questioned. Again we see patterns of an underlying ideology shaping the reviews of Morgner's novel and patterns of discourse among certain circles of scholars that allow them to ask certain questions, while rendering them blind to other problems that do not fit the project in question.

Morgner's Novel Today: "Kein Ort, Nirgends?"

Angelika Bammer points out that Morgner's novel seems to have been forgotten in critical scholarship in the United States after its enthusiastic reception in the late '70s:

> Nevertheless, in spite of their promising beginning in the 70s, neither Morgner nor her texts have become better known in the U.S. outside of the relatively small circle already mentioned. Except for a short, banal entry in *Who's Who in the Socialist Countries* one looked in vain for directions.[35]

This neglect is not particularly astonishing since, with the exception of a translation of the Valeska Kantus story from Book Twelve and a few other short parts of Morgner's novel, American readers had to wait a long time for a translation of *Life and Adventures*.[36] There are few discussions of the text that refer to or continue earlier debates, or that

---

35 Bammer, "Trobadora in Amerika," 204.
36 A translation by Jeanette Clausen was published by Nebraska University Press in 2000. For a list of shorter excerpts that had been translated before, see the bibliography.

offer new interpretations, and no additional analyses of Morgner's work were written until 1988.[37]

In Germany, critical surveys of GDR literature mention Morgner's *Life and Adventures*, together with the second part of the trilogy, *Amanda. Ein Hexenroman*, as important works in the emergence of a special kind of literature by women. Often these articles are written by US scholars, bearing witness to the influence of American feminists' interest in GDR literature on FRG scholarship. But just as in the US, there are few thorough analyses of Morgner's work. In the context of the topic of gender changes, a theme that has generated much interest among feminist circles, Morgner's Valeska Kantus story has received some attention.[38] None of these analyses offers any new interpretations, however.

At the end of the '80s, there were some hints that this disinterest and silence might be changing. Bammer points to the special 1988 edition of the *American Dictionary of Literary Biography* on "Contemporary German Fiction Writers," which gives Morgner a long entry, praising her as one of the most talented contemporary writers and her novel as the most thorough introduction to life in the GDR. Patricia Herminghouse, in her 1989 survey in *Schreibende Frauen*, judges Morgner's *Life and Adventures* to be one of the most important GDR novels by a woman, introducing a paradigm change in women's writing in the GDR.[39]

---

37 Anneliese Strawström of Sweden wrote a dissertation on Morgner's *Trobadora* in 1987. It traces the "Menschwerdungsthematik" in Morgner's novel on a thematic level.

38 In 1980, Wolfgang Emmerich published three stories of GDR authors from the GDR collection of gender-change stories, *Blitz aus heiterem Himmel*, in a volume called *Geschlechtertausch* (Wolfgang Emmerich (ed.), *Sarah Kirsch/Irmtraud Morgner/Christa Wolf, Geschlechtertausch: Drei Geschichten über die Umwandlung der Verhältnisse* (Frankfurt a. M.: Luchterhand, 1980)). The volume *Die verborgene Frau* by Sigrid Weigel and Inge Stephan also contains an essay by Inge Stephan, "'Daß ich eins und doppelt bin': Geschlechtertausch als literarisches Thema," which discusses Morgner's story (53–175).

39 Patricia Herminghouse, "'Der Autor nämlich ist ein wichtiger Mensch': Zur Prosa [schreibender Frauen in der Deutschen Demokratischen Republik]," in Hiltrud Gnüg and Renate Möhrmann (eds), *Frauen Literatur Geschichte: Schreibende*

An interesting analysis of Morgner's work can be found in an article by Genia Schulz in *Bestandsaufnahme Gegenwartsliteratur*, a special issue of *edition text und kritik*. Her survey of new styles of writing by GDR women discusses Morgner's novel at some length, analyzing the text in explicitly postmodernist terms:

> Today, almost fifteen years after its appearance, one perceives the "post-modern" moment of the text (and its successor *Amanda. A Witch Novel*) more than its pre-bourgeois tradition. Modernism (montage, the collage of different discourses, quotations and self-reflexivity of the writing process) is quoted against itself through the ironic broken interplay of these techniques in the "Novel of Thirteen Books and Seven Intermezzos"; in it not the broken world is expressed, the impossibility of any totality, but an invitation to author and reader for a carefree use of literary set-pieces.[40]

In 1988 Schulz's analysis was the only one that took the aesthetic challenges of Morgner's text seriously, inaugurating the sort of congruous interpretation of the work that this study aims to develop further.

Lately, several other studies of Morgner's work have appeared, indicating that the interest in her texts seems to be growing. In 1992, Gabriela Scherer published the first book-length study of the development of Morgner's narrative techniques in German.[41] Scherer analyzes the development of the narrative structures in Morgner's text and provides a brief overview of Morgner scholarship. The second part of her study analyzes montage techniques, quotations, and laughter in Morgner's texts. Scherer proves that many of the subversive elements that critics have praised in *Life and Adventures* were already prefigured in Morgner's earlier texts. Petra Reuffer's 1988 book, *Die unwahrscheinlichen Gewänder der anderen Wahrheit: Zur Wiederentdeckung des Wunderbaren bei G. Grass und I. Morgner,* is a study on the fantastic in Günter Grass and Morgner's *Life and Adventures*. Reuffer traces the use of fantastic elements and quotations in Morgner's novel, which she sees

Frauen vom Mittelalter bis zur Gegenwart (Frankfurt a. M.: Suhrkamp, 1989), 338–53.

40   Genia Schulz, "Kein Chorgesang: Neue Schreibweisen bei Autorinnen (aus) der DDR," in Heinz Ludwig Arnold (ed.), *Bestandsaufnahme Gegenwartsliteratur* (Munich: edition text und kritik, 1988) 215.

41   Scherer, *Zwischen "Bitterfeld" und "Orplid."*

as a new strategy used by both Grass and Morgner to reinvent the project of Enlightenment against the "technologische Verdummung" (455).[42] In 1995, Alison Lewis published *Subverting Patriarchy: Feminism and Fantasy in the Works of Irmtraud Morgner*, the first book-length study of Morgner's work in English. The study focuses on Morgner's use of fantastic elements in her novels.

Several shorter studies of some important aspects of Morgner's novel have also been published. Michaela Grobbel analyzes Morgner's treatment of the German literary heritage in her works from 1968 to 1972.[43] She treats *Hochzeit in Konstantinopel*, *Gauklerlegende*, and *Die wundersamen Reisen Gustav des Weltfahrers* as postmodern texts, but does not discuss *Life and Adventures*. Synnöve Clason ("Mit dieser Handschrift"), Hanne Castein, and Elke Liebs analyze the use of the literary heritage (including fairy tales, myths, and the reception of romantic texts) in Morgner's novel.[44] Ulrike Sati's study, "Figuren im Gespräch," analyzes the dialogic structures of Morgner's *Life and Adventures*. She argues that Morgner's attempts to find a new female style of writing are marked by dialogic interaction in order to provide openness through a multiplicity of perspectives. Kornelia Hauser and Carlotta von Maltzan trace the motif of gender change in texts by Christa Wolf and Irmtraud Morgner and by Kirsch, Morgner, and Wolf, respectively, and J. H. Reid analyzes the Faust motif in the literature

---

42   Although Reuffer offers some important new insights into Morgner's text and recognizes that Morgner's textual strategies go beyond those of typical modernist works, her study suffers from imprecise quotations and other mistakes.

43   Michaela Grobbel, "Kreativität und Re-Vision in den Werken Irmtraud Morgners von 1968 bis 1972," *New German Review*, 3 (1987), 1–16.

44   Synnöve Clason, "Mit dieser Handschrift wünschte sie in die Historie einzutreten: Aspekte der Erberezeption in Irmtraud Morgners Roman *Leben und Abenteuer der Trobadora Beatriz*," *Weimarer Beiträge*, 36:7 (1990), 1128–45; Hanne Castein, "Wundersame Reisen im gelobten Land: Zur Romantikrezeption im Werk Irmtraud Morgners," in Howard Gaskill, Karen McPerson, and Andrew Barker (eds), *Neue Ansichten: The Reception of Romanticism in the Literature of the GDR* (Amsterdam: Rodopi, 1990), 114–25; Elke Liebs, "Melusine zum Beispiel: Märchen und Mythenrezeption in der Prosa der DDR," ibid., 126–41.

70

from the GDR.[45] Agnès Cardinal sees the investigation of the dividing line between the real and the imaginary and between fact and fiction as the basic concern of the *Salman* trilogy, and Alison Lewis analyzes the concept of subjectivity in novels by Christa Wolf, Irmtraud Morgner, and Christa Moog.[46] In one chapter of her 1991 book, *Partial Visions: Feminism and Utopianism in the 1970s*, Angelika Bammer analyzes Morgner's utopian vision in *Life and Adventures*.[47] While all of these studies offer important details, a longer, more thorough analysis of Morgner's narrative strategies in the context of political and literary debates in the East and West is still missing.

Conclusion

The picture of reception that emerges from these widely contradictory reviews is a complex one. In the first phase of criticism in the mid-70s, the urge to fit the novel into different conceptions of art is over-whelming – in the GDR as well as in the West. Ingeborg Nordmann writes:

> The novel *Life and Adventures of Trobadora Beatriz* by Irmtraud Morgner has provoked a multitude of interpretations and judgments, which agree beyond the recognition or rejection on one point: the ambiguity of the text is supposed to be clarified through the subsequent work of interpretation of the critic.[48]

---

45 Kornelia Hauser, "Weiblicher Teiresias oder trojanisches Pferd im Patriarchat? Geschlechtertausch bei Christa Wolf und Irmtraud Morgner," *Das Argument*, 3 (1991), 373–82; Carlotta von Maltzan, "'Man müßte ein Mann sein': Zur Frage der weiblichen Identität in Erzählungen von Kirsch, Morgner und Wolf," *Acta Germanica* 20 (1990), 141–55; J. H. Reid, "From Adolf Hennecke to Star Wars – the Fortunes of 'Faust' in the GDR," Gaskill *et al.*, op. cit., 142–59.

46 Cardinal, "Be Realistic"; Alison Lewis, "'Foiling the Censor': Reading and Transference as Feminist Strategy in the Works of Christa Wolf, Irmtraud Morgner, and Christa Moog," *German Quarterly*, 66 (summer 1993), 372–86.

47 Angelika Bammer, *Partial Visions: Feminism and Utopianism in the 1970s* (New York: Routledge, 1991).

48 Nordmann, "Die halbierte Geschichtsfähigkeit der Frau," 419.

Nordmann complains that such a firm disposition over the text shuts down those elements the author developed as the productive forces of the technique of the montage novel. These elements, which keep the text open through their opposition to one another are supposed to stimulate the readers' "creative work" in their production of new ways of perception.

Most professional readers were not willing in this early phase of reception to respond to this kind of challenge. Significant passages of the novel were ignored in most reviews, and the new form of the text, which Morgner discusses in depth in the novel itself, is pressed into traditional genres and concepts that bury its critical potential.

The second phase of reception (1985–90), characterized by more theoretical approaches to the novel – Frankfurt School criticism in the FRG and feminist criticism in the United States – is more rewarding than the first and renders a deeper and more interesting picture of the novel's concerns. But even in this phase, the attempt to come to definite answers in regard to the text is obvious. Neomarxist scholars using Frankfurt School criticism, such as Emmerich and Jens, interpret the novel in the context of modernist culture, emphasizing its critique of instrumental reason. Since they postulate a rapid incorporation of modernism into GDR literature as the most important development of the '70s and '80s, they tend to overlook features of Morgner's work that go beyond modernist techniques and thematics. These scholars analyze the emergence of a literature by GDR women in the larger context of modernist development in GDR art, without investigating literature by women from a feminist perspective.

The opposite is true for US feminists in the field of German studies, who look at GDR women's literature with the hope of finding answers to their own theoretical and philosophical questions. The problem of women's subjectivity and the possibility of gaining a specific female voice so long suppressed in patriarchal society are the questions that interest these scholars most. Influenced by a sociopolitical criticism, they tend to neglect the aesthetic innovations in Morgner's novel, analyzing her work mainly on a thematic level. These critics are disappointed that Morgner does not state her feminism more clearly.

From these two earlier phases of reception, we get the contradictory picture of feminist critics complaining about the supposedly overwhelming Marxist discourse in the work, and the GDR Marxists complaining about the feminist concerns of the text, which prevent the reader from seeing the "real" causes for suppression. In a third position, neomarxist critics ignore feminist concerns entirely, subsuming the text under the general development of modern literature.

Only in the 1990s, some studies are beginning to discuss Morgner's text in the context of postmodernism. None of these analyses has evaluated the special combination of feminist and postmodernist textual strategies in Morgner's novel. In discussing the political usefulness of incorporating postmodernist elements into feminist theory, Morgner's novel was far ahead of other feminist texts in the GDR and in the FRG. The special concerns displayed in *Life and Adventures*, which I will discuss in the following chapters, are proof of Morgner's internationalism and political engagement. Coming from a feminist writer in the GDR, these ideas demonstrate Morgner's ability to think beyond the borders, not only between East and West, but also between different political and theoretical positions.

Chapter II
The Critique of Instrumental Thinking

Kleine Literaturgeschichte der DDR: 1945–1988, Wolfgang Emmerich's highly influential account of the development of GDR literature, notes a strange *Ungleichzeitigkeit* (nonsynchronism) in the literary development of East and West Germany. While the literary techniques of modernism had long since triumphed in Western literature, GDR literature, according to Emmerich, continued to be absorbed in a premodernist narrative technique – namely socialist realism – until the late 1960s.[1] Following Georg Lukács's theories, GDR authors clung to the Hegelian idea that art should mirror social totality directly, guided by a rational concept of social change. Not until

1   Emmerich designates socialist realism as a "pre-modernist literary technique" (cf. *Kleine Literaturgeschichte*, 280) although it was developed in the 1930s, well after the advent of modernism. Emmerich's definition has its justification in the genesis of socialist realism. Socialist realist techniques were developed by Soviet writers and theoreticians as a politically motivated alternative to modernist techniques and formal experiments of modern writers, which were considered formalistic and decadent. Although even before the revolution, writers like Maxim Gorki wrote realist novels with revolutionary themes (e.g. *The Mother*, 1906), socialist realism only became the official doctrine in the USSR after 1934, when A. Zadanov, secretary of the Central Committee, proclaimed it as the only literary technique able to further and express the revolutionary goals of the Communist party. Socialist realist techniques were supposed to combine a political and ideological position of socialism with the artistic means of realism. Georg Lukács, the theoretician responsible for introducing and developing the concept of socialist realism in Germany who then became the main theoretician for the young GDR, demanded that writers go back to premodernist techniques of realism to mirror societal reality directly and to "objectively" analyze the historical situation that would automatically show the future victory of socialism. In this sense, and from the self-understanding of its practitioners, socialist realism can be called a premodernist literary movement. It is important to note, however, that this definition does not designate a temporal sequence but is a definition based on the proclamations of the theoreticians of socialist realism, which in turn resulted from political considerations more than from artistic reflections.

the second half of the 1960s did GDR artists carefully begin to experiment with such modernist narrative techniques as flashbacks, discontinuous narrative time, interior monologue, stream of consciousness, ironic breaks, and changes in narrative perspective (281). In discussing GDR literature of the 1980s, Emmerich states:

> Within about fifteen years GDR narrative literature repeated in modified form a process which (West) European prose literature had already gone through between 1910 and 1930. GDR prose, in other words, has become modernist, that is, "contemporaneous" with the Western world. (284)

The reason for this development, which Emmerich calls a change of paradigm, could be found in the changed economic situation of the GDR in the late 1960s. The GDR had successfully completed its economic reconstruction after the war and had become one of the leading industrial countries. The phase of the antifascist socialist revolution in the GDR had passed and with it the need for the unquestioned identification of intellectuals with the young GDR state. Artists and intellectuals began to ask if the historical development had really culminated in the promised arrival in the socialist society of free, emancipated individuals. Had the constant struggle moved society toward a "rational community of human beings," a society free of repression and inequality? The Marxist utopian vision of the future had become questionable in a society that still carried the "birthmarks" of the past and whose "new" values almost exclusively focused on economic growth and technological progress. Emmerich writes,

> A chain of traumatic experiences, long the sole property of Western intellectuals, has entered the consciousness of GDR artists and intellectuals, for whom the unwavering belief in socialism had served to repress it. Now, however, the self-destructive process of enlightenment cannot be ignored any longer; the culmination of rational modernization in industrial culture is a process whose limits have not only been reached but surpassed, and whose costs cannot be paid any longer. (271)

Emmerich gives a short list of examples of disappointments experienced by GDR intellectuals, including the failure of revolutionary liberation movements in the third world, the stagnation of the democratization process in their own country, ecological disasters, and the threat of atomic destruction. The impact of these experiences on GDR intellectuals, Emmerich argues, can be compared to the experiences of the Frankfurt School critics more than forty years earlier: the failure of revolutionary movements in the 1930s (especially in the USSR) and the experience of the emergence of fascism. According to Emmerich, GDR intellectuals had therefore begun to repeat the "dark critique of civilization" epitomized by Theodor W. Adorno and Max Horkheimer's *Dialectic of Enlightenment*.

This chapter analyzes Irmtraud Morgner's *Life and Adventures of Trobadora Beatrice as Chronicled by Her Minstrel Laura* against the foil of Frankfurt School aesthetic theory, examining both the text and the limitations of such a theory in its analysis. Theodor W. Adorno is the Frankfurt School critic who most decisively developed a theory of aesthetics, so I will be using Adorno's writings on art and aesthetics – his last work, *Aesthetic Theory*, and especially his writings on the novel and the task of the cultural critic.[2] Since many critics have pointed out that Adorno's aesthetic theory is based on a specific historical model – that is, his interpretation of the history of Western rationality – I will be looking at *Dialectic of Enlightenment*, which remains the fundamental text of Adorno's social theory, in order to point to the connection between Adorno's historical pessimism and his aesthetic theory.[3] Although Morgner's *Life and Adventures* follows Adorno's historical criticism in its basic gesture of criticizing instrumental reason, applying Adorno's theories to the novel reveals important differences. Contrary to Emmerich's claims, these differences result from a changed cultural situation in the GDR in the 1970s. Certain features of Morgner's text go beyond Adorno's theoretical claims for modern art, showing that Morgner responds not

2   Theodor W. Adorno, *Aesthetic Theory*, published after the author's death in 1970 by Gretel Adorno and Rolf Tiedemann; I will be quoting from the 1984 translation by C. Lenhardt. *Notes to Literature* was first published by Adorno in three volumes in 1958, 1961, and 1965; I will be quoting from the 1991 translation by Shierry Weber Nicholsen. *Prisms* was first published in 1955; I will be quoting from the 1981 translation by Samuel Weber and Shierry Weber.

3   *Dialectic of Enlightenment* was written in collaboration with Max Horkheimer and first published in 1944. I will be quoting from the 1972 translation by John Cumming.

only to the concept of an organic work of art in GDR aesthetic theory, but also to a modernist aesthetics that Adorno advocated.[4]

Emmerich's analysis has almost become a "classic" in criticism of GDR literature. Most critics, even if they do not agree with his Frankfurt School perspective, agree with him that GDR literature has started to make up for a literary modernism that had earlier been suppressed. Although I, too, agree with Emmerich's basic argument, the close analysis of one single GDR author shows that the development Emmerich describes is less mechanical and unambiguous than one might think. Morgner's novels prove that GDR authors are not necessarily lagging behind aesthetic developments in Western literature but have – almost unnoticed by Western critics – participated in an aesthetic discussion that involves questioning modernist techniques in literature and art, as well as the ideological consequences that arise from such a criticism.[5]

Emmerich sees the foremost symptom of a paradigm shift in GDR art in the preoccupation in GDR literature with a new concept of the subject. He points out that from the late 1960s on, authors began to display a radical subjectivity in their work that went far beyond the harmonious concept of subjectivity in the official art doctrine of socialist realism. The conflict between the individual and society, which the official GDR ideology never acknowledged in the socialist state, became the prime focus of many GDR authors.

---

4   Georg Lukács's concept of the organic work of art had important connections to a classical concept of art, which Adorno criticized. Both Lukács and Adorno interpreted aesthetic concepts from an historical point of view, but while Lukács went back to the concept of the organic work of art of the nineteenth century and accused modernist art works of decadence, Adorno criticized the classical ideal of the organic work of art and promoted a modernist aesthetic.

5   In her book *Postfascist Fantasies*, Julia Hell similarly criticizes this schematic narrative about GDR literature. See note 21, chapter 1.

The Status of the Subject in Frankfurt School Criticism

A similar reevaluation of the status of the subject in history could be observed in the writings of the Frankfurt School. While orthodox Marxism postulated the proletariat as the revolutionary subject of history, Frankfurt School critics saw the status of the subject as fragile. Disappointment over the course of the revolutionary movements in Europe in the 1920s and 1930s (a failed revolution in Germany and a problematic development of the revolution in the USSR) and the emergence of fascism forced a fundamental reevaluation of orthodox Marxist theories, which had promised the automatic self-destruction of capitalism and the arrival of socialism with the proletariat as the driving force and the true subject of history.[6] The *Bund proletarisch-revolutionärer Schriftsteller* (Union of Proletarian-Revolutionary Writers), with Georg Lukács as their most prominent theoretician, tried to apply Marx's dialectical materialistic method designed for political economy to the superstructure of literature and art. They arrived at *Widerspiegelungstheorie* (reflection theory), which, together with a general concept of realism, was supposed to favor the organic work of art as an expression of the interests and concerns of the proletariat. The work of art was supposed to mirror all the factors that objectively determine our life in a way that turns the artwork itself into an "organic totality" showing the "typical" and the "objective laws of reality." Lukács's concept of realism, which became very important for the official GDR literature in the 1950s, goes back to the aesthetic norms of nineteenth-century realism and classicism in its demands for "closed" and "organic" forms.[7]

---

6   For a discussion of the split among Marxist critics in the Weimar Republic, see Helga Gallas, *Marxistische Literaturtheorie: Kontroversen im Bund proletarisch-revolutionärer Schriftsteller* (Neuwied: Luchterhand, 1971).

7   Lukács's theory caused heated discussions and was rejected by many leftist writers already in the 1930s. The "Realismus-Debatte" (debate over literary realism), which took place in exile between Lukács and writers who also considered themselves to be communists (e.g. Bertolt Brecht and Anna Seghers) attests to this controversy. Lukács was sharply criticized for using concepts that had originated in a nineteenth-century bourgeois ideal of artistic production, instead of developing new forms of proletarian art, a task that

Even after falling out of favor in 1956, Lukács's general concepts continued to influence literary theory in the GDR until the late 1980s.[8]

Frankfurt School critics like Adorno and Horkheimer, on the other hand, began to modify Marx's approach significantly. In view of the failure of the European revolutionary movements, these theoreticians saw that the objective conditions for the overthrow of the old society were present, but the subjective conditions for a successful revolution were lacking. For Frankfurt School critics, the logical consequence of this situation was the need to reflect upon consciousness and subjectivity in their analysis of culture and ideology. The incorporation of psychoanalysis into Marxist analyses of society, studies of the authoritarian personality, the application of Weberian ideas about rationality, studies of mass culture and the culture industry, and finally Adorno's increasing interest in art and aesthetics all attest to this fundamental reevaluation of the status of the subject.[9] The high point in this new shift from critical theory to a "critique of instrumental reason" is *Dialectic of Enlightenment*.[10]

In the foreword to *Dialectic of Enlightenment*, Horkheimer and Adorno state the fundamental question that had led to the project:

> It turned out, in fact, that we had set ourselves nothing less than the discovery of why mankind, instead of entering into a truly human condition, is sinking into a new kind of barbarism. (xi)

writers like Brecht believed to be important. Lukács, however, rejected all attempts to reach new aesthetic forms and accused authors who used formal experiments in their works of being "decadent" and "formalistic."

8   On the development of GDR literary theory, see Hohendahl, "Ästhetik und Sozialismus," 100–62.

9   For a full account of the genesis of Frankfurt School criticism, see Rolf Wiggershaus, *Die Frankfurter Schule: Geschichte, Theoretische Entwicklung, Politische Bedeutung* (Munich: Hanser, 1986); Martin Jay, *The Dialectical Imagination: A History of the Frankfurt School and the Institute of Social Research, 1923–1950* (Boston: Little, Brown, 1973); and David Held, *Introduction to Critical Theory: Horkheimer to Habermas* (Berkeley and Los Angeles: University of California Press, 1986).

10   Cf. Seyla Benhabib, *Critique, Norm, and Utopia: A Study of the Foundations of Critical Theory* (New York: Columbia University Press, 1986).

They reject the Marxian thesis of the humanization of the species through social labor. History, they claim, does not display an emancipatory dynamic, as Marx had postulated, but is instead a history of domination, determined by humanity's relation to nature. Horkheimer and Adorno replace Marx's notion of the class struggle with the conflict between man and nature, begun in precapitalistic society and likely to go on after the end of capitalism.

Enlightenment, in Horkheimer's and Adorno's analysis, is not only a correlate to the struggle for emancipation by the bourgeoisie, but engages the whole spectrum of Western thought. The emancipation of humanity from nature through reason means not only an objectification of nature, but also a suppression of the inner nature in human beings. Myth, with which Horkheimer and Adorno claim the process begins, is already marked by Enlightenment reason, and Enlightenment regresses into myth.[11] Reason, the instrument that helps human beings escape the fear and domination of nature, itself becomes an instrument of domination: a domination over nature as well as a domination over inner nature.

Reason, as Horkheimer and Adorno see it, radically separates subject and object. Nature becomes the object or the Other that man, as subject, can utilize for his own ends. Reason is governed by an identity logic that seeks to make unlikes alike in order to turn things into concepts. All phenomena are subsumed under the totalizing process of reason, with everything, which does not fit, into the category of rational thinking – all otherness – being repressed. In order to dominate nature, however, man's inner nature needs to be dominated as well. The process of objectification is not a process of self-actualization but one of self-denial disguised as self-affirmation.

One of the key passages in Horkheimer's and Adorno's account of Western rationality is the analysis of Homer's *Odyssey* showing that since the beginning of Western thought, the struggle for self-

11 Myth for Horkheimer and Adorno is already part of the dialectic of Enlightenment thinking. It already contains the destructive potentials of an instrumental thinking that later becomes overwhelming. Horkheimer's and Adorno's interpretation and use of the concept of myth is significantly different from the structuralist and poststructuralist view of myth, as it can be seen, for example, in Lévi-Strauss.

preservation and autonomy has been linked to sacrifice, renunciation, and repression. Odysseus, the prototype of the rational bourgeois individual, escapes myth and masters nature by rational calculation. Nature constantly threatens his status as an autonomous individual, and it can be overcome by a pragmatic policy of self-interest. Odysseus's reason is an "instrumental reason" that must carefully calculate the price of survival. Only through a repression of his instincts and through continual self-sacrifice can he survive the temptation of nature that would otherwise destroy his individuality.

The Subordination of Woman as Part of Nature

While Morgner takes up many of the themes contained in *Dialectic of Enlightenment* in *Life and Adventures,* Adorno and Horkheimer's discussion of the status of women in modern society seems to be especially interesting for a writer whose main theme is the position of women in the modern GDR. For Horkheimer and Adorno, the subordination of women as part of nature is only one of the manifestations of the effects of "instrumental thinking" in modern society, but their analysis of man's need to define woman as other in order to dominate her is compelling and has many parallels in modern feminist thought.

One of the key passages in *Dialectic of Enlightenment* that discusses the status of women in modern society is an analysis of Odysseus's encounter with Circe, which for Horkheimer and Adorno shows not only the Enlightenment's repression of sexuality, but also the subordination of women as representatives of nature. Circe represents the double status of women: she embodies that which is both attractive and threatening to men. Her magical powers seduce men to give themselves up to instinct. She promises them happiness and fulfillment, but threatens their autonomy by turning them into swine, i.e. into unreasoning beasts. Although she does not actually hurt the men, the liberation of their own instincts, which turns them back into nature (animals), means a loss of their identity. For Horkheimer and Adorno, it is "the repression of instinct that makes them individuals" (70).

82

Odysseus resists Circe's magic. He sleeps with her, but not until he has forced her to swear an oath that secures his position. Through an exchange protected by a contract, her power is broken. The relationship between man and woman takes on the character of an exchange, with marriage representing a later stage in this development. The repression enacted in this exchange is twofold. First, woman is repressed as nature and otherness: "As representative of nature woman in bourgeois society has become the enigmatic image of irresistibility and powerlessness" (71–2). Second, the exchange features the repression of man's desire for woman, which equals self-denial: "In this way she reflects for domination the pure lie that posits the subjection instead of a redemption of nature" (72). Since man perceives his sexual instincts as threatening, he has to project his sexuality onto women and repress them as the other, the opposite of reason.

The question of how we can escape an Enlightenment logic that is repressive and leads to self-destruction touches upon Adorno and Horkheimer's pessimistic prognoses for a political praxis – or any kind of praxis – that would be able to reverse this development. Their analysis of Western thought is all encompassing, describing basic mechanisms of our consciousness and our ability to think and reason. In fact, according to Horkheimer and Adorno, even language itself is part of Enlightenment's domination of otherness. They argue that in the emancipation from the mythic past, the unity between name and object, which rested on the congruence of name and thing, is replaced by the concept, which is based on a logic of substitution. In the separation between living things and dead matter and the conception that certain sites are the places of demons and gods, the separation between subject and object has already begun:

> When the tree is no longer approached merely as a tree but as evidence for an Other, as the location of *mana*, language expresses the contradiction that something is itself and at one and the same time something other than itself, identical and not identical. Through the deity, language is transformed from tautology to language. The concept, which some would see as the sign-unit for whatever is comprised under it, has from the beginning been instead the product of dialectical thinking, in which everything is always that which it is, only because that which it is not. (15)

The distance between subject and object is the precondition for any abstraction. Since language begins to separate the object from its concept, language is already domination.

Here the aporetic structure of Horkheimer's and Adorno's critical theory becomes apparent. If rational thinking is always already caught up in an identity logic that represses any kind of particularity, the same necessarily must be true for critical theory itself, which uses the same tools, the very same reason, to carry out its critique. Horkheimer and Adorno acknowledge this dilemma in their introduction to *Dialectic of Enlightenment*, emphasizing that it cannot be resolved, but only redeemed through the hope that the critique of Enlightenment can nonetheless evoke the utopian principle of nonidentity logic. We can evoke the other but we cannot name it, just as the Jewish God must not be named but may only be evoked.[12]

The search for a nonidentity, a nondiscursive moment of truth, must therefore be the task of the critic. The goal of the critic (Adorno speaks mainly about the cultural critic here, but the same would be true for the writer and artist) is to illuminate those cracks in the totality, those fissures in the social net (and the discourse), those moments of disharmony and discrepancy through which the untruth of the whole is revealed and the glimmers of another life become visible.

12   Adorno's concept of a utopian other that cannot be named but only evoked is very close to the interest of poststructuralist thinkers in "difference," "the repressed," or the "unnamable," as Derrida calls it. Adorno's goal of showing how an instrumental reason suppresses all otherness in Western culture comes close to the effort of poststructuralists to deconstruct a "logocentrism" that has ruled our Western civilization. Common to both Adorno and poststructuralist critics is the close attention that both pay to language and writing. Especially in Adorno's later writings – above all in his late aphorisms – his complex style (which many have criticized as convoluted and difficult) is a conscious choice, used not only to draw attention to the fact of *how* something is said, but also to show that language can never express the "real" thing.

The New Claim to Fantasy as the Other of
Instrumental Thinking

Emmerich posits that this is exactly the gesture of GDR artists in the late 1970s. With the recognition that their own system, the socialist society, was not excluded from the process of domination and self-domination and that even in socialism instrumental reason had become the driving force of modernization, artists could not continue "to mirror the bad reality":

> The utopian vision has become smaller if it has not been destroyed. In this situation the writer cannot speak the official language any longer if he does not want to risk his credibility. Literature finally becomes counter-language, "poetic protest against the harmlessness of scientific and journalistic mastering of reality" (Werner Mittenzwei). The topics of literature become larger and go beyond the problems of their own small country, and literature now aims at the fundamental problems of humanity and at the question of its survival. Literature becomes a critique of civilization, which cannot ignore the realistic threat of the apocalypse any longer.[13]

Against the claim of a socialist realist theory that art should mirror the totality of social forces directly (Lukács), artists now refuse the mimesis of the bad reality ("Mimesis ans Verhärtete und Entfremdete," as Adorno called it), positing an alternative "reality" determined by fantasy, imagination, and fiction.[14] For Emmerich then, Irmtraud Morgner's novel *Life and Adventures of Trobadora Beatrice* is a prime example of this new claim to fantasy as the other of instrumental thinking. "Against a terrible coalition of male domination, violence, war, and pure technological rationality," he says, "she posits a recovery of the living imagination and of *concrete thinking* [plastisches Denken]" (285).

Morgner's playful experimentation with myth, fairy tales, legends, and other cultural texts, together with her realistic descriptions of life in the GDR, renders our everyday reality strange and lets the reader experience new possibilities of thinking. She enchants reality to encour-

13   Emmerich, *Kleine Literaturgeschichte*, 273.
14   Cf. ibid., 285.

age the reader to imagine new alternatives to it. She destroys our day-to-day experiences, oversteps borders, and challenges a thinking that is determined by rationality, objectivity, and order. According to Emmerich, she does what Heiner Müller argues should be the main function of art today: "the mobilization of fantasy."[15]

A reading of Morgner's novel against the foil of Adorno's theories reveals an essential correspondence between Morgner's analysis of modern society and that of Adorno. Both writers agree in their most fundamental evaluation of the history of rationality and Western civilization. A closer look at Morgner's clever use of historical facts and her reinterpretation of cultural texts reveals a fascinating affinity with theories of the Frankfurt School surprising in a novel written in the GDR, a country where these theories were never officially received or appreciated. A reading of *Life and Adventures* from the perspective of a Frankfurt School critic also points to the changed status of these theories at the time that Morgner was writing, however. In the transformed historical situation of the 1970s and early 1980s, the use of Frankfurt School theories by a contemporary writer must necessarily reflect the events that occurred since the creation of this body of criticism, especially the (post)modernism debates in architecture and art. An analysis of Morgner's use of Frankfurt School theories sheds light not only on the aesthetics of her own novel, but also on the status of critical theory today and the current debate on modernism and postmodernism.

Recovering the Nonrational Forces of Fantasy and Imagination

Morgner's novel opens with the words, "Of course this country is a place of wonders" [Natürlich ist das Land ein Ort des Wunderbaren], setting up from the very beginning the thematic ambiguity between

15   "[D]ie politische Hauptfunktion ist jetzt, Phantasie zu mobilisieren." Quoted in ibid., 286.

reality and fiction. The reader is tempted to read this sentence as part of the official GDR doctrine positing that the socialist state is the only alternative to the inhuman capitalist system of the West, and therefore contains "wonderful" possibilities for a free and emancipated community. In fact, later in the novel Beatrice ironically calls the GDR "the promised land" [das gelobte Land].[16] The reader soon learns, however, that the "wonderful" does not refer to the wonderful possibilities of socialism in the GDR, but to the literal meaning of the word – "full of wonders," in the sense of the improbable or magical, only accessible through imagination and fantasy. The "miracle" that happens to the fictional character – Irmtraud Morgner in the streets of the GDR – consists of a woman approaching her with the story of the adventures of an eight-hundred-year-old trobadora, Beatrice de Dia, who supposedly lived and died in the GDR.

The assumed "wonders" of socialist society are ironically contrasted to the "miracles" of Beatrice's life, a very different level of wonders, which nevertheless, much like the belief in the "socialist miracles," are also immediately accepted by the characters in the book: "I tolerated, who knows why, the unsolicited weight of the package" [Duldete, wer weiß warum, das unverlangte Gewicht] (3). From the very beginning, however, this second level of wonders turns out to be a burden for the author Irmtraud Morgner, since the acceptance of Beatrice's adventures as true causes a questioning of the relationship between fiction and reality, a taboo in the existing socialist state. "When I became aware of the burden, I tried to get rid of it" [Als sie mir bewußt wurde, versuchte ich die Last loszuwerden (7)]. The "burden" is the developing conflict between a rational, objective description of reality and an imagination that oversteps our conventions of reality from the very first sentence of the novel.

Not only does the sentence, "But of course this country is a place of wonders," ironically refer to the official GDR doctrine as ideology,

16   The title of chapter 12 in the second book, for example, reads, "Parnitzke finds the optimal woman of his life; Beatrice buys a train ticket to the promised Land" [Parnitzke findet die optimale Frau seines Lebens, Beatriz kauft sich eine Fahrkarte ins gelobte Land]. The first chapter of book four has the title, "The trobadora's arrival in the promised land" [Ankunft der Trobadora im gelobten Land].

it also unveils the socialist system as based on the same kind of rationality as the West, a reason that suppresses any nonrational experience. Imagination is a "burden" in a system based exclusively on rationality and reason. The political system of the "promised land" – much like the Middle Ages, which Beatrice had to escape, and the capitalist West – also seems to suppress imagination and fantasy as nonrational and other. It turns out that the GDR is based – just as the capitalist states of the West are – on Horkheimer and Adorno's "instrumental reason," which has to repress the Other to turn the world into concepts. The text artfully exposes the gaps between the norms of the ideal and the reality of existing conditions as contradictions, a procedure that Adorno had claimed to be the task of authentic art.

The urgency of the task of recovering the nonrational forces of fantasy and imagination is motivated by the destructiveness of instrumental thinking, fully apparent at a time when the threat of nuclear war was immediate.[17] The importance of recognizing the dynamics of this kind of rational thinking is emphasized throughout the Valeska Kantus story, Beatrice's "revelation" made public by Laura after Beatrice's death. It is the story of a female scientist who, through a sudden sex change, gets the chance to understand male thinking from the inside. Valeska concludes her story with the following statement:

> My teaching, which urges women to believe in themselves and in the transformation just described, is pragmatic. Shenya advised me to work miracles in order to spread word about the teaching. [...] Because people believe great truths more readily in unlikely clothing. If I had the prospect of winning over a majority of women to a temporary transformation by having myself nailed to the cross, I might accept even this means. The danger of humanity's self-destruction through war causes me to see as right every means that can extort peace.[18]

The emancipation of women, the main concern in Morgner's novel, figures both thematically and structurally as the emancipation of desire and imagination from the bonds of pragmatism and rationality.

17   This threat is already thematized in *Rumba auf einen Herbst* (originally written during the early 1960s), which is set at the time of the Cuba missile crisis in 1962. The threat of nuclear war is present in the image of the second sun in *Rumba*.
18   Morgner, *Life and Adventures*, 465.

As in Horkheimer's and Adorno's account of Western thinking, femininity is identified with historically repressed forms of knowing, desiring, and relating that threaten a male order of reason and are unthinkable within the boundaries of a hierarchical social order.

The tensions between male instrumental thinking and the unnamed and inassimilable desires of women repressed throughout history develop around the fantastic legend of Beatrice de Dia, the medieval trobadora who enters the GDR in the late 1960s after having awakened from an 810-year-long sleep. Beatrice, who had been charmed out of history with the help of a magic potion because the conditions for women in the Middle Ages had become unbearable for her, lets the reader experience the GDR from her "strange" perspective, one that renders the everyday conditions of our world unfamiliar and "unnatural." Beatrice brings the fantastic, the extravagant, the impossible, and the erotic to bear on the apparently "natural" order and exposes the political nature of conventional distinctions between rationality and imagination. Beatrice's bonds with mythical and "real" female characters represent the structural and thematic intervention of unconscious and "irrational" desires into the repressive stability of GDR socialism and expose male rational thinking as domination and repression of the other.

The threat that Beatrice and female bonding pose to social hierarchy and ideological certainties is shown throughout the text by the fears and rationalized denials of most male characters, who feel threatened by a world without absolutes, hierarchies, and surrogate gods of any kind – the sort of world that Beatrice and other women in the book seem to represent. The character of Uwe Parnitzke is an example of one of these men. In spite of his willingness to work for a better future, he is shaken to the roots by the world without fathers and authorities that Valeska and Beatrice open up for him.[19] Parnitzke

19   Julia Hell analyzes the literature of this generation of writers in her book, *Postfascist Fantasies,* as the product of the confrontation with the SED's ideological discourse on the Communist family lineage and its unconscious fantasies. She claims that these texts by writers like Christa Wolf rethematize the issue of father–son (or father–daughter) relations and the trope of the substitute fathers, narrating the break with the "real" father/parents. Hell maintains that the identification with the paternal image of Stalinism, which stands at the

shows most clearly how the Marxian potential for utopian thinking has regressed into an instrumental thinking determined by hierarchies and domination.

Morgner's Use of History and Myth

But *Life and Adventures of Trobadora Beatrice* is above all a phantasmatic novel. Morgner mixes myth, legends, and fairy tales with contemporary reality. Beatrice is a legendary trobadora from the Middle Ages whose life story consists of a fantastic mixture of legends and tales, though the character is based on the life of the Comptessa de Dia, who actually lived in Provence in the twelfth century.[20] Virtually nothing is known about the historical Trobairitz de Dia, not even a death date or whether her name was really Beatrice. The few facts known about the life of the actual Comptessa have triggered heated debates among medievalists. Preserved are a two-sentence *Vida* (Life), which Morgner adapts as the opening lines of book 1, and four *cansos* (love songs) attributed to a Comptessa de Dia, as well as a *tenso* (a dispute between two poets) attributed to the troubadour Raimbaut d'Aurenga (d. 1173) that some scholars have seen as evidence of the love relationship between Raimbaut and the Comptessa de Dia. The four *cansos* (two of which Morgner includes in *Life and Adventures*, book 1, chapter 9, and book 4, chapter 5) can be found in Meg Bogin's

core of the 1950s dominant ideology, and its sudden loss, is nowhere more convincingly articulated than in Irmtraud Morgner's *Life and Adventures*. Uwe's identity, which is defined in terms of a lack – "I am a man who has lost a father" – is organized around this traumatic experience. His story of "looking for a new father" – which is really taken from the censored novel *Rumba* – is typical of a whole generation.

20   For an analysis of Morgner's use of the historic figure Comptessa de Dia, see Peter Hölzle, "Der abenteuerliche Umgang der Irmtraud Morgner mit der Trobairitz Beatriz de Dia," in Jürgen Kühnel, Hans-Dieter Muck and Ulrich Müller (eds), *Mittelalter-Rezeption* (Göppingen: Kümmerle, 1979), 430–45.

The Women Troubadours.[21] Peter Hölzle points out that Morgner is not affected by the uncertainties about the exact facts of the life of the historical Comptessa. She uses the four songs (plus three additional ones that might have been written by the Comptessa) as well as the information of the *Vida* and mixes this material with fictional information. What is interesting for Morgner are not so much the exact historical facts about this trobadora, but the special character of the songs that bear her name. Peter Hölzle maintains:

> Scientists have called these songs "an unusual artistic manifestation of the most passionate and sensuous poetic temperament of female poetry of all ages and countries" (Hans Gerd Tuchel). Some researchers were shocked by the songs, and as a result they did not talk about them all, or the songs' artistic merit was measured up until the 1940s according to a puritan moral. The supposed impudence of the "Comtessa de Dia" was a comfortable excuse for quite a few researchers of troubadour-lyric – all of them men – to suppress the irritating role change between longing troubadour and distanced lady (because it does not fit into the conventions of troubadour lyrics).[22]

On the one hand, Morgner uses these unique historical documents because they challenge the supposedly secure conventions of art and cultural history. On the other hand, she does not hesitate to add fictional information to these materials. In retelling the Comptessa de Dia's life, Morgner rewrites the Tristan motif of the magic love potion; Beatrice's eight-hundred-year-long sleep is a rewriting of the fairy tale "The Sleeping Beauty"; her sister-in-law is the legendary mermaid Melusine, half dragon, half woman; Beatrice's companions in the fight for a better world are the Greek goddesses Demeter and Persephone and the Amazon queen Penthesilea; in Hades Beatrice meets Pluto and various kinds of devils; there are rewritings of typical episodes from Arthurian tales (for example, Beatrice goes on an *aventuire* to find the legendary unicorn whose name is Anaximander); and finally, the author rewrites the biblical legend of Jonah and the whale.

Morgner's novel disregards the laws of time, place, and probability, but her fantastical use of existing mythological texts and legends

---

21   See Meg Bogin, *The Women Troubadours* (New York: Paddington Press, 1976), 82–91.
22   Hölzle, "Der abenteuerliche Umgang," 439–40.

is hardly arbitrary. Rather, it functions to unveil certain patterns of thinking that have been prevalent throughout Western history. Morgner's rewriting of patriarchal myths exposes the roots of instrumental thinking in a mythology that has already become rational. Like Horkheimer's and Adorno's account of the emergence and dialectic of Enlightenment thinking, Morgner's rewriting of patriarchal myths highlights the ideological roots of mythology.

Her retelling of myths unveils a power struggle between male and female forms of knowledge. Persephone and Demeter, for example, reappear throughout the novel, locked up in a bunker, stripped of their magical power by God, who only allows them a small contingent of miracles per year:

> "There's still an arbitrary quota on the deeds allocated to us," Persephone lamented. "Sometimes we get three or four entitlement vouchers a year, sometimes only one. But there have also been years when Mr. Lord God didn't grant us a single miracle. He can't kill us because we're immortal; that angers him. But he can keep us idle – that's worse than dead." (16)

As in Horkheimer and Adorno's account, Morgner's text makes clear that male rationality has replaced and suppressed the older matriarchal order and female forms of knowledge. Zeus has been dethroned by the Christian god, and Pluto, the ruler of the underworld, by the Christian devil, but both religions are based on a male reason, since – as Penthesilea tells Laura – Zeus and God, as well as Pluto and the devil, have signed a contract that allows them to share power and dominate the female magical forces of Demeter and Persephone. Female power needs to be suppressed because it disrupts the male rational order:

> "Did you meet Beatrice in Genoa?" asked Laura, after bringing the schnapps. Penthesilea fished out her gum, stuck it under the tabletop, downed the schnapps, and replied, "In Hades. I'm in a hurry. [...] With so many new arrivals, it's no wonder that the organization leaves something to be desired. During the three months that Pluto has Persephone with him as his wife, the situation is even more chaotic. Because the deposed queen of the underworld cripples the service workers' discipline with her songs of revenge, which decry wars as the worst perversion of the patriarchy. About half the work force is devils. The other half was taken over by Pluto. To be sure, he has been stripped of power too, but he's made a deal with the devil, which is why he isn't sitting in a holding cell like Persephone but can move about, under guard." (220–1)

92

The mythical underworld has been turned into a modern industrial company run by modern management techniques based on male instrumental reason. "Bunkers," "contingents," "dispatch personnel," "entries (arrivals)," and "wars" describe the modernized version of the Greek underworld based on the same male principles that, as Horkheimer and Adorno maintain, were already operative in Greek mythology itself.

This fact becomes apparent in the second book of the novel with the abduction of Persephone from her mother, Demeter. Morgner stays fairly close to the story line of the original version in her retelling of the myth and only changes the emphasis of certain facts. In Persephone's recounting of her past, Zeus's behavior is characterized as diplomatic, witty, and motivated by his attempt to preserve power. The text points out that already in the original Greek myth, woman is the representative of nature; she is the goddess of nature. Her powers over nature need to be controlled by the male gods, since Demeter's wrath – she commands the fields to stop bearing fruits and threatens to wipe out humanity – undermines the power of the male gods, who are dependent on man's devotion. In Morgner's version of the story, Zeus displays the same behavior that Horkheimer and Adorno point out in Odysseus.[23] He uses his wits and his cunning to overcome Demeter's (read: nature's) wrath and to escape powerlessness: "Zeus, who feared he would lose his worshipers and thus his divine existence, tried conciliatory gifts" (59). Like Odysseus, Zeus tries to preserve his power through exchange maneuvers and manipulating his environment. His tactics are based on rationality motivated by his need to control the world around him.

While Zeus and Pluto's behavior aims at controlling the Other, love and pain motivate Demeter's wrath. Through their use of violence, cunning (Pluto), and pragmatism (Zeus) – both forerunners of an instrumental reason in Horkheimer and Adorno's understanding of the word – the female magical power is broken. Already in mythology the result is domination over nature and over female mythical forces, culminating in the destructiveness of modern rationality as seen in the modern version of Hades. As Penthesilea tells Laura in book 9, the

---

23   Throughout the *Odyssey* and even more in the *Iliad*, Zeus favors Odysseus regularly, although Odysseus's tutelary goddess is Athena.

millions of arrivals in Hades of dead and mutilated bodies from modern wars can only be managed by the male gods with the same kind of effectiveness and "rationality" that has caused the wars in the first place.[24] Modern rationality has turned back into myth, and Western Enlightenment thinking has regressed to a new kind of barbarism unsurpassed in history.

If it is the task of the critic to rediscover the contradictions and discrepancies in the identity logic of reason and rationality, as Horkheimer and Adorno claim, women should be the prime sites where this discrepancy can be detected. The position of woman, who stands for otherness and nature in the logic of Enlightenment thought – for that, which has to be repressed in order for the male individual to gain subject status – must necessarily be an ambiguous one. Adorno and Horkheimer write:

> Woman is not a being in her own right, a subject. […] She became the embodiment of the biological function, the image of nature, the subjugation of which constituted that civilization's title to fame. For millennia men dreamed of acquiring absolute mastery over nature, of converting the cosmos into one immense hunting ground. It was to this that the idea of man was geared in a male-dominated society. This was the significance of reason, his proudest boast. Woman was weaker and smaller. Between her and man there was a difference she could not bridge – a difference imposed by nature, the most humiliating that can exist in a male-dominated society. Where the mastery of nature is the true goal, biological inferiority remains a glaring stigma, the weakness imprinted by nature as a key stimulus to aggression.[25]

Women do not participate in the male logic of instrumental reason. They are not allowed to gain subject status but remain objects for male domination. Since woman is not nature, however, but is turned into an *image of nature* by a male logic of domination, she displays, as Horkheimer and Adorno point out, the domination of male reasoning on her own body. This becomes apparent in Morgner's retelling of Penthesilea's past:

24 Penthesilea's description of Hades reminds the reader of the male master efficiency of Auschwitz. The experience of this unspeakable kind of barbarism was the impulse for Horkheimer and Adorno to develop their theories about Western rationality in *Dialectic of Enlightenment*.

25 Adorno and Horkheimer, *Dialectic of Enlightenment*, 247–8.

94

The woman called herself Penthesilea. Laura recalled having read the name in books. "Didn't a certain Achilles once fall in love with you?" asked Laura facetiously. "After he chopped me up in a duel," answered Penthesilea, also facetiously, putting her right thumb and index finger to her teeth and pulling a string of chewing gum to arm's length. "After all, Achilles wasn't so strong that he could fall in love with a woman like me. Only in death did I seem desirable to him. Even heroes need a downhill slope in order to function." Penthesilea tipped back her curly Afro, threaded the string of gum back into her mouth, and laughed so immoderately that Wesselin started whimpering. (220)

In Morgner's interpretation of the myth, Achilles has to kill Penthesilea in order to love her. The motivation for Achilles' behavior is fear. Achilles can only become a hero when he destroys any object that would challenge his status as subject. Morgner's interpretation is surprisingly close to Adorno and Horkheimer's analysis:

The bourgeoisie profited from female chastity and propriety – the defense mechanisms left by matriarchal revolt. Woman herself, on behalf of all exploited nature, gained admission to a male-dominated world, but only in a broken form. In her spontaneous submission she reflects for her vanquisher the glory of his victory, substituting devotion for defeat, nobility of soul for despair, and a loving breast for a ravished heart. At the price of radical disengagement from action and of withdrawal into the charmed circle, nature receives homage from the lord of creation. Art, custom, and sublime love are masks in which nature reappears transformed into her own antithesis. Through these masks she acquires the gift of speech; out of her distortion emerges her essence. Beauty is the serpent that exhibits a wound in which a thorn was once embedded. Behind male admiration of beauty, however, lurks always the ribald laughter, the withering scorn, the barbaric obscenity with which strength greets weakness in an attempt to deaden the fear that it has itself fallen prey to impotence, death, and nature.[26]

Woman becomes the scar, the stigma that bears witness for male domination. In becoming the mask of dominated nature, she uncovers the male lie of reconciliation with nature. Penthesilea's "maßloses Gelächter," the uncanny laughter of the dead woman, is witness to men's weakness and fear. Morgner's version of patriarchal mythology uncovers the psychological bases for a male instrumental reason.

Morgner's satiric retelling of patriarchal myths does not represent an attempt to reconstruct a "real" but neglected women's history

26   Ibid., 249.

or to mythologize biological difference. The possibility of going back to a concept of the biological essence of women in order to reverse power structures is ruled out in the text's critique of a radical separatist wing of feminism represented by Persephone and Demeter and their followers.[27] The attempts of Persephone and Demeter to regain power, together with their group of radical feminists, are wearisome for Beatrice, since they want to use the same means that men have used for their goals to reinstate matriarchy. For Morgner, reinstating female forms of knowledge does not mean returning to a female biological essence. Women's forms of knowledge represent a utopian hope since women have been socialized differently, not necessarily because they are biologically different. Their status outside of male power represents a glimmer of resistance and the hope for a utopian other.[28] Beatrice balances Persephone and the radical wing of the feminist opposition in the novel. Because she has been asleep for eight hundred years, she has not been corrupted by the power struggle, which has worn down the other mythological characters in the novel. Thus Beatrice offers truly new and utopian possibilities based on creativity and eroticism. The irony of this situation is that only

27   Of course, Morgner's description of the different feminist fractions is a parody of different feminist groups in the West, especially in the FRG. I identify these groups and Morgner's use of parody in chapter 3.

28   Compare Adorno's discussion of the utopian possibilities of women in his essay on Veblen: "As a late apologist of the feminist movement he [Veblen] has absorbed the experiences of Strindberg. For Veblen woman becomes as a social phenomenon what she is for herself psychologically – a wound. He perceives her patriarchal humiliation. He compares her position, which he includes among the relics from the periods of the hunter and warrior, to that of the servant. Free time and luxury are allotted her only to strengthen the status of the master […] on the one hand, precisely by virtue of her debased situation as 'slave' and object of ostentation, the woman is in a certain sense exempted from 'practical life.' […] By virtue of her distance from the process of production she retains certain traits which characterize the human being who is not yet entirely in the grasp of society. […] Hope cannot aim at making the mutilated social character of women identical to the mutilated social character of men; rather, its goal must be a state in which the face of the grieving woman disappears simultaneously with that of the bustling, capable man, a state in which all that survives the disgrace of the difference between the sexes is the happiness that difference makes possible" ("Veblen's Attack on Culture," in Adorno, *Prisms*, 81–2).

through an escape from a bad, male-dominated history is Beatrice able to enter history truly as other.

Morgner's use of mythology highlights the ideological and psychological bases of mythology itself. As in Horkheimer and Adorno, mythology is already based on rationality, and rationality regresses into myth, into a new barbarism, as described by Penthesilea in her report on Hades. Morgner's strategy, to unveil mythology as rational and to show at the same time how rationality regresses into myth and barbarism, can be observed throughout the *Life and Adventures* and becomes even more pronounced in the second novel of Morgner's trilogy, *Amanda*.[29] Beatrice is reborn in *Amanda* as a siren after her death at the end of the first novel – a siren, however, who has lost her voice. The novel describes Beatrice's attempt to recover her voice in order to prevent the self-destruction of humanity. The snake Arke, Beatrice's helper and coach, says of her project:

> Not the development of abstract thinking, but its claim of exclusiveness, which not only prevented the development of plastic thinking but also destroyed its achievements, made my life difficult. I was depressed that the history of thinking kept progressing like the other one: in a warlike fashion. [...] Thus the remnant that was destroyed was the plastic appropriation of the world. In myth and religions we can still see these images. But for us atheists they just are museum pieces. Some results of this appropriation have been preserved; but the use of this kind of appropriation here and in other industrial countries was lost in thinkers' wars. Only a few poets dare to preserve this facility, which is innate in all people and therefore necessary.[30]

29 In *Amanda,* Morgner retells Beatrice's story with Beatrice herself as the narrator. The witch Amanda, Laura's alter ego, struggles to reunite with her human half, Laura. The reader learns that all women are split like Laura into a human half that functions in our everyday society and a witch half that is held captive by the devils in "Hörselberg." The novel tells of the witches' attempt to overthrow the oppressive regime of the devils by joining forces with their human halves.

30 My translation. "Nicht die Entwicklung des abstrakten Denkens, sondern dessen Ausschließlichkeitsanspruch, der eine Weiterentwicklung des bildhaften Denkens nicht nur verhinderte, sondern seine Errungenschaften zerstörte, machte mir das Leben schwer. Mich deprimierte, daß die Historie des Denkens nach wie vor ebenso ihren Fortgang nimmt, wie die andere: kriegerisch. [...] So ein Rest, der zerstört wurde, ist die bildliche Aneignung der Welt. In Mythen und Religionen

The exclusive domination of abstract thinking in our society, according to Morgner, has led to aggression and wars while other forms of thinking, such as imagination and a mimetic relationship to nature, have been lost.

Like Horkheimer and Adorno, Morgner sees her task as the recovery of those few traces in history that point to other forms of relating to the world. Mythology is one area that still bears traces of images that originated from different ways of relating to nature. The critique of an abstract instrumental reason is the motivation for Morgner's attempt to go back to mythology and history. As in Horkheimer and Adorno, the suppression of women associated with nature since the beginning of history shows the destructiveness of a monolithic regime of abstract thinking that suppresses any other forms of knowledge. The goddesses Demeter and Persephone, the Amazon queen Penthesilea, legendary figures like the mermaid and witch Melusine, and the medieval trobadora Beatrice, whom Morgner herself calls a heretic and witch (see *Die Hexe im Landhaus*), are all fantastic representatives of a female potential that has been suppressed in a male-dominated history.

Morgner also rereads history to specify the points that culminate in the victory of instrumental reason. After Greek mythology, a second important stage in male-dominated history is the late Middle Ages, with the persecution of witches. Morgner uses the image of the witch throughout both of her novels. In *Amanda*, she claims that all women are split into two halves, one functioning in everyday reality and the other representing the witch in all women. But even in *Life and Adventures* all female characters have witchlike qualities.

In her analysis of the use of the witch image in contemporary feminism, Silvia Bovenschen uses *Dialectic of Enlightenment* to explain the phenomenon of witch persecution in the Middle Ages. Bovenschen points out that in the persecution of the witches, the

könnten die Bilder zwar noch besichtigt werden. Von uns Atheisten jedoch nur museal. Etliche Resultate dieser Aneignung blieben erhalten; die Fähigkeit der Aneignung ging hier und in ähnlichen Industrieländern verloren in den Denkerkriegen. Nur einige Dichter wagen die in allen Menschen angelegte und demnach nötige Fähigkeit zu bewahren" (*Amanda*, 375).

attempt to dominate women as representatives of nature took a new radical form. This wave of hatred against sensuous women was based, according to Bovenschen, on the charge of their complicity with the secret powers of nature:

> The sympathetic relationship of women to nature, the magic-mimetic forms of appropriating nature, its successes (using herbal drinks), its failure (the laying on of hands), being as they were secular attempts of controlling life, threatened the Church; but they simultaneously stood in the way of the triumph of instrumental reason.[31]

Not only her supposed closeness to nature, but also the sexuality of the woman as witch has threatened men. Bovenschen gives many examples throughout history of the erotic woman who is cast in the role of the witch by a male-dominated society. The need to suppress nature as the other of reason is the basis for the persecution of witches.

Morgner's female characters can be called witches because they are all sexual figures whose demand to live their own eroticism greatly upsets men. Beatrice sees women's ability to express themselves as sexual beings without suppression as the principal mark of a changed society. Since she expects to have awakened at a time when the old *Frauenhalterordnung* (society in which women have the status of slaves) has been abolished, she naturally assumes that she is now able to show her sexual desires as a free individual without being punished. She excuses the rude behavior of the engineer and the demolition master who awakened her as an exception: "Two brutes did a patriarchy make. It wasn't so bad" (10). She openly flirts with the driver who picks her up on the highway:

> Beatrice delighted him with admiring glances. They were meant not for external assets, since beauty was conspicuously absent, but internal ones. Ethical. No hollow cavalier badge – helpfulness. Self-evident brotherliness. Sisterliness. Beautiful human community. Beatrice admired its representative. (14)

She finds out that her assumptions are wrong when she is brutally raped by the driver. Not only are women still punished for expressing

---

31   Silvia Bovenschen, "The Contemporary Witch, the Historical Witch and the Witch Myth: The Witch, Subject of the Appropriation of Nature and Object of the Domination of Nature," *New German Critique* 15 (Fall 1978), 98.

their sexuality openly, but we repeatedly see that Beatrice's open display of her own desires shakes the male order to its roots:

> Beatrice thanked the police officer and praised the gleam of his even white teeth, which set off his brownish skin tone beautifully. The smile disappeared. Throat-clearing. Embarrassed coughing. Return of the passport through the slot with a wish for a speedy recovery. (91)

Men repeatedly classify Beatrice as either a prostitute or insane, modern equivalents of witches, since her confident exercise of her own sexuality places her outside of the male order.

Not until Laura tells her "a story that Laura Characterized as too true" (book four, chapter 19), describing the unequal and hierarchical relationship between men and women, does Beatrice understand that the times have not changed. Laura explains to her "in this country, eroticism is the last domain that belongs to men. In all other areas the laws of our land grant women equal rights" (114). If women are not able to express their own desires and are still persecuted as sexual beings, Beatrice realizes, all attempts to reach emancipation will have failed:

> "What?" shrieked Beatrice, as if a nerve had been struck by the dentist's drill, "I've slept 808 years for nothing. All of a sudden, I understand that I'll still have to deny my vocation: deny myself. No wonder I can't find proper employment. Customs don't allow it. One can't find what doesn't exist. A passive troubadour, an object that sings of a subject, is logically unthinkable. A paradox." (114)

The continuity of women's suppression becomes apparent in Beatrice's words. The suppression of women's sexuality forces them into passivity; it turns women into objects for male desire and prevents women from assuming the status of the subject. The obvious paradox is that it is the *male* sexuality that constitutes and legitimizes their subjectivity. This was precisely Beatrice's problem as a female troubadour in the Middle Ages.

By making a female troubadour the heroine of her novel, Morgner points to the institutionalization of the concept of *minne* in the Middle Ages as another point in history that establishes women's suppression in order for men to win subject status. Her emphasis on a male rationality as the basis of the institution of *minne* in the Middle Ages is apparent in her use of Erich Köhler's theories of the courtly love service, quoting directly page-long excerpts from his ground-breaking interpretation. Köhler was one of the first to understand the concept of courtly love in the Middle Ages in sociohistorical terms. He interpreted the institutionalization of the courtly love service as an attempt by the high aristocracy to secure their power in binding the lower nobility to the courts. According to Köhler, rational considerations shaped the institutionalization of courtly love in the Middle Ages. In fact, this concept continues to influence our concept of romantic love until today. The concept of *minne* inscribed the woman's position as that of an object that channels men's desires in order for men to gain subject status. Köhler's interpretation of the courtly love tradition interests Morgner because his research proves that the concept is based on rationality and is aimed at controlling the inner nature of man.

By inserting Köhler's sociological interpretation of medieval courtly love into her novel, Morgner makes clear that her fantastic use of the female troubadour as heroine is not an attempt to rewrite history or to set her fictions in opposition to historical facts; on the contrary, the fictional story makes historical contradictions visible. Morgner says in an interview with Eva Kaufmann: "I write historical novels of the present. And the fantastic element has, aside from its utopian component, another function: to make the historical visible."[32] In the novel, Laura uses Köhler's theories to prove to the fictional character Irmtraud Morgner (whom she wants to convince to buy Beatrice's manuscript) the possibility of a female troubadour in the Middle Ages. Laura explains:

> So the courtly lady was responsible for enabling the man to fulfill his class obligations at the highest level, whereby the nature of high, that is, courtly love was to be sought in the tension between hope and expectation, the only thing which could guarantee that the lover's efforts would not flag. [...] The meaning

---

32 Eva Kaufmann, "Interview mit Irmtraud Morgner," *Weimarer Beiträge* 9 (1984), 1494–514. Reprinted as "Der weilbliche Ketzer heißt Hexe. Gespräch mit Eva Kaufmann", in Marlis Gerhardt (ed.), *Irmtraud Morgner: Texte, Daten, Bilder*, 42–69 (Frankfurt a. M.: Luchterhand, 1990), 64.

of the adoration of the lady, the meaning of courtly love itself, consisted in perfecting and increasing the merit of the male wooer. Thus as long as Beatrice de Dia did not block her source of virtue, that is, did not disturb the tension between hope and expectation in her cansos to Raimbaut d'Aurenga but if possible increased it further, her extraordinary activities were completely accepted. A medieval minnesinger of the female sex is historically conceivable. A medieval love poet of the female sex is not. (30)[33]

History and fiction are artfully intertwined. The fictional story of Beatrice de Dia renders visible the specific contradictions in the history of the position of women in society.

Rationality is paid for by a suppression of external and internal nature, but the suppressed nature leaves its marks. The hegemony of instrumental thinking destroys man himself. On her journey to Paris, Beatrice finds out that Raimbaut d'Aurenga's name (the Provençal d'Aurenga is d'Orange in modern French) has become the name for the exfoliant Agent Orange, designed to kill the vegetation of large areas of jungle that – as an unintended side effect – injured and caused genetic defects in thousands of people in the Vietnam War (book 1, chapter 21: "Wherein Beatrice learns, among other things, about the biocide preparation bearing Raimbaut's name.")[34] Modern science turns against humanity itself and leads to a new kind of barbarism. In the figure of the medieval troubadour Raimbaut d'Aurenga the text establishes a connection between the institution of chivalry and the

---

33   Cf. Erich Köhler, *Ideal und Wirklichkeit in der höfischen Epik* (Tübingen: Niemeyer, 1970).

34   Raimbaut d'Aurenga is the troubadour in the service of Beatrice's husband; he is Beatrice's first lover. In accordance with Morgner's interpretation of the Middle Ages as a point in history in which rationality gains another important victory, she emphasizes Raimbaut's cunning and pragmatic realism. Laura explains to Irmtraud Morgner: "Beatrice de Dia had brought Sir Raimbaut d'Aurenga to the court of Almaciz and inspired him to sing, as custom and husband demanded. The art of this troubadour sounded exceedingly pleasant to the ears of Guilhem de Poitiers, for Raimbaut extolled wealth and virtue as compatible, something his rivals more or less questioned. They made a virtue out of their material need while Raimbaut who was no less poor, would cast a sprat to catch a mackerel. Beatrice thought he was a bad poet" (30). Raimbaut's art is influenced by his pragmatic desire for success and thus the use of his name, Agent Orange, for a chemical weapon did not happen by chance.

destructiveness of modern technology, making visible the dialectic of Enlightenment. Again, it is the suppression of women that makes the contradiction visible.

As long as the Trobadora stayed within the limits of the accepted conventions, she was allowed to speak. Beatrice could write poems in which she criticized Raimbaut d'Aurenga, as long as she succeeded in hiding her irony behind the conventions of the medieval canto:

> And the very same day she composed a canso to the arrogant troubadour. In which she fed and praised him with words that disqualified his pretentious art. Sir de Poitiers was surprised by his wife's skills. But not unpleasantly so. The court society, jaded by boredom, received the lady's cansos with applause and were lavish in their praise for the trobadora's beauty, character, and kindness. Since he believed the high nobility was exemplary and, for that reason, chosen and appointed by God to rule, Raimbaut, of course, failed to notice he was disqualified. And he wasn't the only one. (31)

However, as soon as Beatrice takes up her own voice, "shameless, conscious of her worth" [schamlos, wertbewußt (35)], and as soon as she talks about real love between two subjects, the court reacts with consternation and her husband burns her poems.

Because she has now become a "Liebessängerin" instead of staying within the limits of courtly love, in which she should be the object instead of in the subject position, she is persecuted by her environment and has to "leave history." Morgner writes about her:

> The Trobadora Beatrice de Dia is a historical figure, a provençal troubadour of the 12th century, but a female one. To be a troubadour does not only mean to address a single person, but to address or sing to the whole world. For this you need to be convinced that the world will hear you, which requires positioning oneself as a subject in the 12th century. Beatrice de Dia was a person who overstepped borders, a heretic. The name for the female heretic is witch.[35]

Beatrice de Dia was a witch because she expressed her own desires in her poem. Because woman is supposed to function as the object for men's domination, Beatrice decides to leave history and wait for a time when the instrumental thinking that suppresses women as objects and nature will be abolished.

35 Irmtraud Morgner, *Die Hexe im Landhaus: Ein Gespräch in Solothurn. Mit einem Beitrag von Erika Pedretti* (Zürich: Rauhreif Verlag, 1984), 16.

The fact that this kind of thinking still predominates, that instrumental reason is still the basis of Western societies, in capitalist as well as socialist states, is the painful realization that Beatrice has to accept when she comes to the GDR. She is still not allowed to be a trobadora because to discover her own subjectivity, to speak in her own voice, to accept women's desires as real, threatens men's position. Although the laws in the GDR grant women formal equality, Beatrice has to find out that "eroticism is still the last domain of the men." Equality in the workplace has not resulted in the true emancipation of women promised by orthodox Marxism. The suppression of emotional desires and the continuing pervasiveness of rigid psychological structures remain the true causes of domination.

As with Horkheimer and Adorno in their *Dialectic of Enlightenment*, Morgner's project is to establish an archaeology of the self.[36] She uses images of women in history to unveil the ideological basis for their suppression, important for an understanding not only of history, but also of the present. Morgner appropriates the image of the witch to take over the myth and use it against the enemy who introduced it. On the one hand, this use of mythology and history contains an ironic critique of the male mystification of the female. On the other hand, it makes possible a resistance that was denied to the historical witches and to other suppressed women in history. In an active understanding of their own history, women can reappropriate those behavioral possibilities, which they possess because of their widespread exclusion from the sphere of production and other important areas of life. Because of their exclusion from a subject position in a male system of rationality, they have preserved utopian possibilities that might challenge the course of history. The potential for resistance is rooted in the anachronistic female role: the dysfunctionality of woman's role in history allows for utopian thinking.

But here we encounter a point of difference between Adorno and Morgner in their treatment of history. Although Adorno's analysis of an all-dominating male reason that suppresses all otherness is compelling

36   Cf. Benhabib's Foucauldian interpretation of *Dialectic of Enlightenment* as an investigation of "the psychic archaeology of the self" (*Critique, Norm, and Utopia,* 165).

and offers convincing explanations for the continuous suppression of woman in history as either temptress (witch) or desexualized being (Mary), he does not examine how the suppression of women has worked at specific periods in history. His analysis is all encompassing and neglects particular historical forms of oppression, as well as historical forms of resistance. This, however, is Morgner's project in her novel. Although she agrees with Adorno's overall explanation, she insists on historical specificity to find points of resistance that can be utilized to change the position of women in society. She rejects Adorno's totalizing analysis of history and instead turns to different moments of historical experience, which she constantly compares and contrasts with one another. This type of historical specificity under-mines the tendency to offer the totalizing perspectives characteristic of Adorno. Her concept of history is closer to Lyotard's concept of "petits récits," which replace the "grand narratives" of history. In *The Postmodern Condition*, Lyotard explains:

> We no longer have recourse to the grand narratives – we can resort neither to the dialectic of Spirit nor even to the emancipation of humanity as a validation for postmodern scientific discourse. But as we have just seen, the little narrative [petit récit] remains the quintessential form of imaginative invention, most particularly in science.[37]

Morgner's montage of "petits récits" enables her to put Lyotard's "imaginative invention" into practice.

The Problem of Political Praxis

Morgner's rejection of Adorno's totalizing historical analysis points to problematic aspects in Adorno's aesthetic theory. These problems, which have been discussed intensively in the secondary literature on

---

37. Jean-François Lyotard, *The Postmodern Condition: A Report on Knowledge*, Geoff Bennington and Brian Massumi (trans.) (Minneapolis: University of Minnesota Press, 1984), 60.

Adorno, concern the possibility of a political praxis. Adorno's turn to the autonomous work of art seeks to preserve a utopian moment of resistance and serves to realize the emancipatory aspects of a good Enlightenment. Although Adorno's point is to show that the plight of Enlightenment and cultural rationalization only reveals an identity logic that is constitutive of reason, he still insists on the emancipatory potentials of a critique of Enlightenment and reason. This critique, however, necessarily has to use the same rationality, and the same tools of this reason that it condemns. Since political praxis has become impossible, Adorno insists on a philosophy of art as the only possible answer to the dilemma of social praxis.[38]

Although Morgner clearly emphasizes the utopian possibilities of reappropriating repressed female forms of knowledge, the question of how this potential can be applied in a society based on an all-dominating instrumental reason is a difficult one. Morgner's experiments in the text with different models and strategies for emancipating women create a tension that never gets resolved. Morgner explores this tension to show that there cannot be an easy answer to the problem of how women can enter history as subjects. An exploration of these tensions in *Life and Adventures* points to a similar problem with the possibility of political praxis in Adorno. Both Morgner and Adorno are pessimistic about reversing the logic of the Enlightenment movement. But while Adorno harbors hope and sticks to his theory of art as the last bastion for a utopian preservation of alternatives,

38   "The only possible ingress into art is the idea that something on the other side of reality's veil – a veil woven by the interaction of institutions and false needs – objectively demands art. It demands a kind of art that can speak for what is hidden by the veil. Unlike discursive knowledge, art does not rationally understand reality, including its irrational qualities, which stem in turn from reality's law of motion. However, rational cognition has one critical limit, which is its inability to cope with suffering. Reason can subsume suffering under concepts; it can furnish means to alleviate suffering; but it can never express suffering in the medium of experience, for to do so would be irrational by reason's own standards. Therefore, even when it is understood, suffering remains mute and inconsequential – a truth, incidentally, that everybody can verify for himself by taking a look at Germany after Hitler. What recommends itself, then, is the idea that art may be the only remaining medium of truth in an age of incomprehensible terror and suffering" (Adorno, *Aesthetic Theory*, 27).

106

Morgner has given up this utopian vision and deconstructs *all* ideas of change, insisting rather on the process of renegotiation and dialogue.

The difficulty for women's attempts to assume the status of subjects becomes apparent in the relationship between Beatrice and Laura. With these two women, Morgner demonstrates two ways that women could change the course of history and take political action. Because Beatrice had literally stepped out of history for a while, she represents women's utopian possibilities in terms of fantastic impulses and extravagant, absolute desires that disrupt the conformism and pragmatism of male-controlled GDR society. Beatrice is the (ironic) personification of Adorno's thesis of the utopian potential of the woman who has not taken part in the movement of the dialectic of Enlightenment because she has been excluded from the sphere of production.[39] Laura's pragmatic realism, on the other hand, seems to represent the "new" generation of socialists who, although critical of flaws in GDR society, are willing to work within the system to change society and improve the conditions for women. Laura's strategy is to support small changes through a constant courageous struggle. She pursues a politics of small steps. When Beatrice reacts with despera- tion and wants to try to convince Persephone that she needs to go back to sleep, Laura is irritated:

> She condemned conclusions like these as weak. Actually, she shared her father's view of people who don't face the realities of life. Accepting the realities wouldn't have to mean wholesale affirmation, she continued. In any case, the process of life demanded pride, realpolitik, a talent for improvisation. And consisted of the ability to struggle through. Miracles, okay, but no private ones for slackers. (114)

Laura's view is clearly influenced by her father (whose philosophy of "Realpolitik" is representative of a patriarchal rationality that again boils down to an instrumental reason). Laura alone cannot be a true alternative. She behaves like a man with different goals. Beatrice, in contrast, claims that more radical measures are necessary:

---

39   Cf. Adorno: "By virtue of her distance from the process of production she retains certain traits which characterize the human being who is not yet entirely in the grasp of society" (*Prisms*, 82).

Beatrice called Laura squeamish. Facing realities could only be judged a sign of strength if you had good luck. "A person who is condemned to life imprisonment and doesn't make plans to escape is not proud but cowardly. Didn't you also bewail the lack of solidarity among women? That's natural among those who have been humiliated for millennia. Their hopes of escaping from a hopeless situation could only be based on miracles, that is, on individual actions. I have exited history because I wanted to enter history. To appropriate nature. First of all, my own. Tackle the making of humanity head-on. This end justifies all magical means." (114–15)

For women to become subjects, the traditional order of rationality needs to be disrupted. But the only way for Beatrice to appropriate her own nature is to break radically with a reality that does not allow her to become a subject. She literally steps out of a bad history to offer a true alternative. Although Beatrice's role is clearly to challenge the conventions and pragmatism in the GDR, the success of such disruptions of the logic of instrumental thinking is doubtful, because as soon as Beatrice reenters history, she begins to change. She becomes more and more realistic and domestic and loses her radical possibilities. Eventually she "loses her balance" in the confrontation with the everyday reality of women in the GDR (she falls out of a window while cleaning) and dies. Her utopian possibilities do not seem to have a chance once she tries to introduce them into reality as an active force.

Laura, on the other hand, undergoes a reverse development. Her views become more radical; she becomes like Beatrice and eventually takes her place. (At the end of the novel, she is co-opted in Beatrice's stead to the round table at King Arthur's castle, which is now headed by the Queen of Sheba and consists of men and women in equal numbers.) In letting Laura survive, it seems as if the text supports a strategy of synthesis (Beatrice's utopian abilities and Laura's pragmatism are synthesized in the end), but even Laura's position at the end of the novel is not realistic and secure.[40] She now lives in a fantastic world, outside of reality, and her husband, Benno – himself an ironically utopian man – has to tell her fairy tales to console her. The irony of

40   In her excellent discussion of the novel, Biddy Martin criticizes what she interprets as the closing gesture of the novel. I will come back to this final gesture (which I see differently) in chapter 3.

108

Benno's story does not allow the reader to see the utopian reconstruction of GDR society as a realistic possibility. Neither strategy, Beatrice's or Laura's, succeeds fully in the end. Instead of reaching closure at the end of the novel, the relationship between Beatrice and Laura can merely explore different possibilities for women. The text examines and contrasts political and aesthetic strategies, but there does not seem to be a clear choice of the best means for women to enter history. Morgner both employs and subverts the concept of pleasure as a radical break with our everyday reality (personified through Beatrice) and the politics of small changes within the system (personified through Laura). It appears that the process of renegotiating our reality as well as some form of dialogic exchange (in the fantastic vision of the round table) is more important than any final result.

In fact, the only way for women to gain freedom in the text is to use magic. Beatrice uses a magic potion to step out of history, Valeska experiences a magical sex change, Vera Hill acquires the magical ability to walk on a rope to be able to combine her roles as scientist and mother, and Laura only finds a truly utopian male partner through the magic workings of Melusine, who sends Benno "down from heaven." On the one hand, these examples again point to the importance of fantasy and imagination as counterforces to an ordered world; on the other hand, the metaphors Morgner uses to describe the fates of these women ironically show how difficult it is for women to gain subject status. Although magic, fantasy, and imagination can save the world, their success is highly questionable and utopian in the literal sense of the world: they do not have a place in our world today. This can be seen in the highly symbolic deaths that all these "magical" women suffer: Beatrice loses her balance and falls out of the window while cleaning, Valeska dies in an accident, and Vera falls to her death in response to the doubts and persecution of her magic by her neighbors.

Morgner's pessimism about true change is similar to Adorno's. Although he had pointed out that the utopian possibilities of women offer some hope, Adorno writes:

Opposed to this [the utopian possibilities of women], however, is a counter-tendency the most prominent symptom of which Veblen designates as the conservatism of woman. She rarely takes part as subject in historical development. The state of dependence to which she is confined mutilates her. This counterbalances the opportunity offered her by her exclusion from economic competition. Measured against the man's sphere of intellectual interests, even that of those men absorbed in the barbarism of business, most women find themselves in a mental state that Veblen does not hesitate to term imbecilic. Following this line of thought, one might reach the conclusion that women have escaped the sphere of production only to be absorbed all the more entirely by the sphere of consumption, to be captivated by the immediacy of the commodity world no less than men are transfixed by the immediacy of profit. Women mirror the injustice masculine society has inflicted on them – they become increasingly like commodities.[41]

Although this analysis does not fit the conditions in the GDR, where women do take part in the sphere of production, even in the socialist state women do not actively shape the society they live in.

Unlike the women that Adorno talks about (women who are excluded from economic competition and from the sphere of production), Morgner's characters are all working-class women. But the text makes clear that even working-class women in the GDR suffer the "mutilations" that Adorno talks about. They have uninteresting jobs with few responsibilities, and they have to work a second shift at home because men refuse to share the housework. This situation literally keeps women in a constant position of suppression. Laura recalls the subservience of her grandmother:

The entire time I knew my grandmother, her most favored position was stooped over. Standing, her calves, hollows of knees, and thighs in a straight line. To her last days she could maintain this position any length of time without feeling rush of blood to her head or other ailments. In this position she washed the floors, waxed, weeded, planted, cut mushrooms, and gathered twigs. [...] She had acquired the ability to work in a stooped-over position in her younger days. As a servant girl. The entire time I knew her, she hated birds. (413)

The bent position, which had become the second nature of Laura's grandmother, represents and mirrors the mutilations in her mental state. She suffered from the same loss of creativity that Adorno

41   Adorno, *Prisms*, 82.

ascribes to the woman who is in an object position, with no chance to develop her intellectual and creative abilities. She has even lost the ability to appreciate beautiful birds.

Morgner makes clear that this situation has not improved in the socialist state. Olga Salman, Laura's mother, suffers from the same kind of mutilations (which Morgner calls "posture faults" [*Haltungs-schäden*]) as her grandmother. Although married to the model of a working hero of the GDR, her life at his side, without creative work or responsibility, leaves her without energy to improve her condition. In fact, Persephone grants her wish to leave history, like Beatrice, through hypnosis, since she cannot bear her situation any longer:

> She had lost the strength to hold onto cheerful hopes. All she could hold onto were dark hopes. Not because her life had been especially hard. Its emptiness had embittered her. And marked her: the corners of her mouth had turned down. She had lost all curiosity. All that interested her on television was the weather report. A remnant of pleasure in shopping still remained, it stirred at the sight of fabrics. But the thought that Olga Salman wouldn't get out of the house anyway banished her pleasure in sewing, making purchasing fabrics seem useless. Olga Salman, the tailor, had uncut the fabrics lying in cupboards! Even her daughter wouldn't have believed it before seeing it with her own eyes. (415–16)

Olga Salman is marked by a society that does not allow her to become a subject. Morgner calls this kind of society – which exists in the socialist countries as well as in the capitalist West – a *Frauenhalter-gesellschaft*. Women have the status of slaves and are treated like objects. Even Beatrice is in danger of submitting to the existing conditions and losing her creative ability. In fact, Laura tells Beatrice about her grandmother's "posture faults" [*Haltungsschäden*] because Beatrice is on her way to submitting to the role of a house slave, as her mother and grandmother had.

> Beatrice took over the kitchen work from Laura during the holidays. Also systematically. This made Laura uneasy. Indeed, she even started to resist. And it seemed to her high time to talk with Beatrice with her preventative intentions about her grandmother's bad posture. (413)

Although Laura had tried to convince Beatrice to become more realistic, she learns by watching Beatrice adapt to the everyday conditions in the GDR that compliance with the real situation of women in society destroys her critical and creative potential. Although a realistic view of society seems necessary, the dangers of becoming too much of a realist are apparent. Beatrice, by becoming more and more like Laura, loses her revolutionary potential:

> On 28 January, when the cease-fire arranged as part of the Vietnam agreement had been in force for one day, Laura noticed that Beatrice had even begun to look like her. "Why are you training yourself so hard?" she asked, shocked. "Do you want to double me? Do you want to render yourself superfluous?" (415)

As soon as Beatrice's utopian possibilities come in close contact with reality, they are in danger of being lost.

Morgner's analysis of the possibilities that women have to enter history features an important difference from Adorno's theories. Adorno's pessimism about the possibilities of political praxis leads him to aesthetics as the last possibility for preserving some utopian vision of an alternative truth.[42] As a result of his totalizing critique in *Dialectic of Enlightenment*, Adorno reached a position where the logic of history could be analyzed, but organizing direct political opposition was impossible. Adorno turned to aesthetics to find a way out of this dilemma. He offered the authentic work of art as that emphatic opposition that could no longer materialize in political organization.[43] The authentic work of art, however, had to insist on the autonomy of art, according to Adorno, since domination and repression character-

---

42   "Art is able to utter the unutterable, which is Utopia, through the medium of the absolute negativity of the world, whose image is composite of all that is stigmatized as ugly and repulsive in modern art. While firmly rejecting the appearance of reconciliation, art none the less holds fast to the idea of reconciliation in an antagonistic world" (Adorno, *Aesthetic Theory*, 48).

43   Compare Peter Uwe Hohendahl's analysis in "Autonomy of Art: Looking Back at Adorno's 'Ästhetische Theorie,'" in Judith Marcus and Zoltan Tar (eds), *Foundations of the Frankfurt School of Social Research* (New Brunswick, NJ: Transaction Books, 1984), 210.

ized reality.[44] Only in the authentic work of art could a moment of objective truth be preserved:

> Truth content in art works is the materialization of the most advanced consciousness, including the productive critique of the status quo both in art and outside of it. It is a kind of unconscious historiography, one that sides with what has been vanquished. (274)

Although Morgner's text does not offer any kind of positive concept of political opposition, political engagement is not excluded from her novel. Political reality and political discussions enter the text from all sides and are woven into the network of different narrative perspectives with the help of irony. Morgner's strategy is to thematize the problem of political action without rejecting it in favor of aesthetics. She plays through and experiments with different political strategies without claiming that any strategy can give a final answer or offer "objective truth." Although Morgner's basic stance as an author is very close to Adorno's most decisive demands for modern art, there are important differences between Adorno's hope that the authentic artwork contain traces of an objective truth pointing to an end of suppression and Morgner's more radical abolition of any concept of truth or authentic experience.

---

44 "Aesthetic identity is different, however, in one important respect: it is meant to assist the non-identical in its struggle against the repressive identification compulsion that rules the outside world. It is by virtue of its separation from empirical reality that the work of art can become a being of a higher order, fashioning the relation between the whole and its parts in accordance with its own needs. [...] The manner in which art communicates with the outside world is in fact also a lack of communication, because art seeks, blissfully or unhappily, to seclude itself from the world. This non-communication points to the fractured nature of art. [...] Thus in all dimensions of its productive process art has a twofold essence, being both an autonomous entity and a social fact in the Durkheimian sense of the term. [...] The unresolved antagonisms of reality reappear in art in the guise of immanent problems of artistic form. This, and not the deliberate injection of objective moments or social content, defines art's relation to society" (Adorno, *Aesthetic Theory*, 6–8).

The Concept of Art and "Objective Truth"

Like Morgner, Adorno emphasizes the need for any authentic work of art to assume a self-reflexive stance in an age of alienation and the impossibility of any authentic experience. For him, irony and negativity are the most important narrative modes for modern literature to assume in order to resist the domination of a bad reality. In his famous essay, "The Position of the Narrator in the Contemporary Novel," Adorno identifies a strange paradox as characteristic of the contemporary novel: although the novel depends on narration, the task of narrating has become impossible in view of the disenchanted world.[45] The novel, the literary genre of the bourgeoisie, relies on realistic description of the world. But to narrate something as it is has become impossible in a world that no longer allows for authentic experience:

> For telling a story means having something *special* to say, and that is precisely what is prevented by the administered world, by standardization and eternal sameness. Apart from any message with ideological content, the narrator's implicit claim that the course of the world is still essentially one of individuation, that the individual with his impulses and his feelings is still the equal of fate, that the inner person is still directly capable of something, is ideological in itself, the cheap biographical literature one finds everywhere is a byproduct of the disintegration of the novel from itself. (31)

If the narrator tries to retell the world, she or he merely perpetuates a bad reality. To avoid a mimesis of the alienation and self-alienation that determines our world, the novelist has to renounce simple realism:

> If the novel wants to remain true to its realistic heritage and tell how things really are, it must abandon a realism that only aids the facade in its work of camouflage by reproducing it. (32)

The most important consequence of this, according to Adorno, is the disappearance of the aesthetic distance between narrator and subject,

---

45   Adorno, "The Position of the Narrator in the Contemporary Novel," in Shierry Weber Nicholsen (trans.) *Notes to Literature* (New York: Columbia University Press, 1991), 30–36.

and between narrator and reader. It is impossible for narrators to stand above the things they talk about; there is no place for contemplative distance. The narrator has to abolish the aesthetic distance between author and reader and instead reveal the process of narration itself:

> When in Proust, commentary is so thoroughly interwoven with action that the distinction between the two disappears, the narrator is attacking a fundamental component of his relationship to the reader: aesthetic distance. In the traditional novel, this distance was fixed. Now it varies, like the angle of the camera in film: sometimes the reader is left outside, and sometimes he is led by the commentary onto stage, backstage, into the prop room. (34)

This description seems to fit Morgner's narrative techniques perfectly. The radical variations in narrative modes in the novel (stories, diary entries, letters, newspaper reports, discussions, interviews, theoretical treatises, scientific theories, speeches, law texts, business contracts, poems, songs, parts of other novels, fairy tales, mythical stories, legends, and dreams) destroy the distance between narrator and reader, as Adorno had demanded. But although montage and the use of citations are nothing new in literature and have been designated as defining characteristics of modern literature, Morgner's radical approach has stunned readers and critics.

In its radicalness Morgner's approach is much closer to certain forms of surrealist and dada art than those modernist texts that Adorno promoted. In fact, Adorno had little patience with the disjunctive and montage-like techniques of surrealism, in large part because of his (highly problematic) indebtedness to a notion of the avant-garde as cohesive and organic (though he does not acknowledge as much).[46] Morgner's plea in *Life and Adventures* for the "operative montage novel" that lives from its interruptions and the joining of radically different texts shows this difference. The heterogeneous fragments of the novel open the text up for the intervention of the reader, who actively has to assign those fragments meaning and order, which the text refuses to offer. Through this technique, a multiplicity of readings

---

46 Compare, for example, Adorno's critique of surrealism in his essay "Rückblickend auf den Surrealismus," in Shierry Weber Nicholsen (trans.) *Notes to Literature* (New York: Columbia University Press, 1991).

becomes possible and is even encouraged. In an interview that Laura, as Beatrice's minstrel, grants to the *Aufbau Verlag*, the emancipatory and subversive potential of such a montage novel is elaborated:

> The orthodox novel form requires sustaining a concept over several years. In view of violent political movements throughout the world and an appalling information explosion, that is possible nowadays only for lethargic or stubborn characters. What I'm offering is the novel form of the future. Which is part of the operative genre. [...] An absolutely ideal genre for interventions. [...] Apart from temperament, short prose is in keeping with a normal woman's life rhythm, which is socially and not biologically conditioned and constantly diverted by the interruptions of household responsibilities. [...] An ensemble of short prose brings the life movements of the epic "I" clearly into the book with no need to frame it with respect to content. Truth about life in books cannot exist without the author's belief in himself. A mosaic is more than the sum of its stones. In the composition they have a strange effect with and against each other under the eye of the viewer. Reading should be creative work: pleasure. [...] Our society has a tendency to totalize: all revolutions have such a predilection. You can only write short stories with the consent of the readers. They have the job of completing the total. The genre is based on the reader's productivity. Short prose gives an extract, the detail. Precisely. Precision of detail carries more weight than the heaviness of wishy-washy epic literature. And it has to be wishy-washy, because epic literature can't be forced. (176)

Morgner not only leads the reader into the "prop room" of writing, as Adorno demanded, but also consciously undermines the distance between narrator and reader until a distinction between them becomes impossible. Like Adorno, Morgner rejects the totalizing perspective of the epic genre, since modern society's flood of information and its tendency to subsume everything under a totality leave no room for specificity and difference. Morgner instead pleads for an ensemble of short prose that renders the reader active and democratizes the relationship between author and reader. In this way, her novels are "negative epics" in Adorno's sense of the word.[47]

47   Cf. Adorno: "Forty years ago, in his *Theory of the Novel*, Lukács posed the question of whether Dostoevsky's novels were the foundation for future epics, or perhaps even themselves those epics. In fact, the contemporary novels that count, those in which an unleashed subjectivity turns into its opposite through its own momentum, are negative epics. They are testimonials to a state of affairs in which the individual liquidates himself, a state of affairs that

This kind of writing challenges traditional realist conventions and displaces – much as Adorno had demanded – the transcendent and omniscient narrator. The juxtaposition of genres and the disrespectful irony subvert textual and extratextual limitations on meaning and possibility. There is an apparent refusal in Morgner's text to privilege one form of knowing over another, to distinguish the important from the unimportant or the global from the small and close-at-hand. The combination of the most disparate texts exposes the process of writing as a political exercise of choice, exclusion, and control.

Morgner's deconstruction of the process of writing as a political choice, which in turn abolishes any kind of normative dimension, reveals an important difference from Adorno. Although Adorno had demanded that the work of art must uncover the "lie of representation," he nevertheless introduced a normative aspect into his theory of art.[48] A concept of "objective truth," a notion that seemed to have become impossible for Adorno in his analysis of Western thinking, creeps back into his aesthetic theory. Art is for Adorno the only area of life that can resist the domination of the identity logic that suppresses authentic experience. Thus, the authentic work of art preserves an "objective truth value" because it is separated from the world of reification and domina-

converges with the pre-individual situation that once seemed to guarantee a world replete with meaning. These epics, along with all contemporary art, are ambiguous: it is not up to them to determine whether the goal of the historical tendency they register is a regression to barbarism or the realization of humanity, and many are all too comfortable with the barbaric" ("The Position of the Narrator in the Contemporary Novel," 35).

48 "Today art is most valid when it proves itself intransigent to the deception of realism, refusing to put up with all that is innocent and harmless. If it is to live on, it must elevate social criticism to the level of form, de-emphasizing manifestly social content accordingly" (Adorno, *Aesthetic Theory*, 354). Compare the German here: "Ihr (der Kunst) verbindlichstes Kriterium heute ist, daß sie, allem realistischen Trug unversöhnt, ihrer eigenen Komplexion nach kein Harmloses mehr in sich duldet. In jeder noch möglichen muß soziale Kritik zur Form erhoben werden, zur Abblendung jeglichen manifesten sozialen Inhalts" (*Ästhetische Theorie*, 371).

tion.[49] Adorno explores this thesis again and again in his writing on art. Already in *Dialectic of Enlightenment*, he explains that although art always has to work with general concepts (language, style, tradition) to be understood, it can show through its failure to represent something in these general terms that there is something that exists beyond these general concepts. Through its negativity, through the conscious exposure of its failure to reach identity, art is able to transcend a bad reality and retain the utopian hope for a true generality. Art therefore preserves in its form the hopes and sufferings, the expectations and contradictions of the human race.[50]

Adorno concentrates only on the artistic production of the work of art, rejecting the analysis of the reception of artworks as positivistic and irrelevant.[51] His aesthetic theory is ultimately a theory of modern-

49   Adorno talks repeatedly about the "objective moment of truth" preserved in the authentic work of art in his *Aesthetic Theory*. See, for example: "To experience the truth or untruth of art is more than a subjective 'lived experience': it signals the breaking-through of objectivity into subjective consciousness. Objectivity mediates aesthetic experience even when the subjective response is at its most intense" (347).

50   "Style represents a promise in every work of art. That which is expressed is subsumed through style into the dominant forms of generality, into the language of music, painting, or words, in the hope that it will be reconciled thus with the idea of true generality. This promise held out by the work of art that it will create truth by lending new shape to the conventional social forms is as necessary as it is hypocritical. It unconditionally posits the real forms of life as it is by suggesting that fulfillment lies in their aesthetic derivatives. To this extent the claim of art is always ideology too. However, only in this confrontation with tradition of which style is the record can art express suffering. That factor in a work of art which enables it to transcend reality certainly cannot be detached from style; but it does not consist of the harmony actually realized, of any doubtful unity of form and content, within and without, of individual and society; it is to be found in those features in which discrepancy appears: in the necessary failure of the passionate striving for identity" (Adorno and Horkheimer, *Dialectic of Enlightenment*, 130–1).

51   Compare Adorno's criticism of reception analysis in *Aesthetic Theory*: "That is why, if we want to determine the nature of the relation between art and society, we must look not at the sphere of reception, but at the more basic sphere of production. Concern with the social explication of art has to address the production of art rather than study its impact (which in many cases diverges completely from art works and their social content, a divergence that can in turn be explained sociologically). Since time immemorial human responses to art works have been

ism and the avant-garde. While he criticizes the concept of the organic work of art as it was developed in European classicism, he insists on the autonomy of art as the precondition for its historic truth-value. Adorno's own historical analysis prevents him from supporting anything but the modernist work of art, understood as autonomous, as Russell Berman points out.[52] The concept of objective truth in the autonomous work of art proves to be another attempt at totalization that Adorno had criticized in Enlightenment thinking. Despite his rejection of any kind of "objectivist" theory (for example in his criticism of positivism), Adorno's aesthetic theory becomes problematic precisely in its utopian moments, which – against Adorno's will – display an objectivist teleology that Morgner is not willing to follow.

In one of her letters, Beatrice warns Laura of the dangers inherent in "great conceptions," which reduce reality and meaning to the fictional coherence of global theories:

> Beatrice said novelists were people who hid their ideas in the heads of other people, from cowardice. And Beatrice warned her friend absolutely to avoid a great work. She wrote: "That's exactly what our best people suffer from, precisely those in whom the most talent and the most tireless striving resides. [...] For the present day wants its rights; the thoughts and feelings that come unbidden to the poet every day, these will and must be expressed. But if one has a greater work in mind, nothing can compete with it." (185)

exceedingly mediate; they are not directly related to the specificity of a work but are determined by society as a whole. In short, the study of effects fails to show what is social about art" (324).

52   Cf. Russell Berman's analysis: "The defense of the monadic work of art, furthermore, was based on a particular historical model. Increasing autonomy corresponded to a rising curve of commodification over four or five millennia of market exchange. Modern formalism thus was a continuation and refinement of the traditional response to conceptual terror. This historical scheme, an attempt to retain the universal history of Hegel and Marx, evidently precludes the possibility of perceiving the qualitatively new, for the new is only more of the old. Neither the orthodox procrustean efforts to grasp all art in terms of reflection theory nor Adorno's similarly universal explanation of formal resistance to the domination of the enlightenment is able to postulate fundamentally new or different aesthetic functions" ("Adorno, Marxism, and Art," *Telos* 34 (Winter 1977–78), 165).

The insistence on openness functions as a form of opposition to artistic conventions and an artistic praxis that is exclusive and repressive. The question of "truth" in art gets a new twist and the process of writing can neither be objective nor contain any kind of objective truth; instead, writing is always a political decision. The text's insistence on openness and process is most apparent in Morgner's use of the concept of the author.

Morgner's Concept of Author, Subjectivity, and Representation

The text's epistemological, thematic, and structural tensions are developed around Beatrice's relationship to GDR men and women, especially to her minstrel Laura Salman, who in turn discusses the implications of writing with Irmtraud Morgner, who appears as a character in the text. In a preface to the text, Laura sells the chronicles of Beatrice's life to the GDR author Irmtraud Morgner, who reluctantly accepts the task of publishing Beatrice's life story, though she knows that getting involved in Beatrice's experiences will mean overstepping the borders of our conventions: "Oh, this irresistible pull of curiosity, I'd known all along that I wouldn't escape responsibility" (4). *Verschuldung* (responsibility) is used in an ambiguous way here, since it not only refers to a monetary debt (Morgner has to give Laura one month's pay for the manuscript), but also to her becoming guilty for challenging the conventions of realism and traditional art, especially those of the official art doctrine in the GDR. From the beginning, not only the distinction between fiction and reality, but also that between experience and its representation is destroyed. The novel becomes a work about representation.

Through a complex network of mediation, the process of representation becomes more and more artificial. The experiences of Beatrice are several times removed from the reader: Laura, as Beatrice's minstrel, rewrites and edits Beatrice's stories (some of which were already written by someone else and then copied by Beatrice); the fictional

120

character Irmtraud Morgner then receives the stories from Laura and supposedly functions as editor of the book, which lists Morgner as the author above its title. The transaction between Laura and Morgner establishes a network of female narrative voices whose distinct identities become more and more blurred. The novel consists of a multiplicity of authors. In addition to the "real" author Irmtraud Morgner, the text contains several other authors: Morgner's fictional counterpart; Laura, who writes Beatrice's biography; and Beatrice, in whose name Laura and Morgner write. Moreover the chronicle contains stories by the mermaid Melusine. Melusine, the reader is told, copied some of her stories from the book *Rumba auf einen Herbst,* the author of which is Irmtraud Morgner. The circle is closed and yet wide open, since it is impossible for the reader to figure out which narrative voice is responsible for which story. Any kind of controlling authorial voice is deconstructed and distinctions between experiencing, documenting, and "fictionalizing" become problematic.

Although Adorno had also demanded that the authentic work of art display a radical self-reflexivity and unveil "the lie of representation," Morgner seems to question the possibility of representation itself.[53] Morgner's mixing of different narrative perspectives, the montage of radically diverse genres, her intertextual references and citations, and the many discussions about writing and reading in the novel all emphasize the self-reflexivity of the text, deconstructing the concept of a controlling authorial voice and even the idea of representation itself. The truth value that Adorno sees in the concept of negativity, in the representation of the "lie of representation" through which alternative notions of emancipation can become apparent without the author having to name them, is itself problematized in Morgner's text. Morgner reduces to absurdity the idea that

---

53   "It has often been noted that in the modern novel [...] reflection breaks through the pure immanence of form. But this kind of reflection has scarcely anything but the name in common with pre-Flaubertian reflection. The latter was moral: taking a stand for or against characters in the novel. The new reflection takes a stand against the lie of representation, actually against the narrator himself, who tries, as an extra-alert commentator on events, to correct his unavoidable way of proceeding. This destruction of form is inherent in the very meaning of form" (Adorno, "The Position of the Narrator," 34).

any kind of representation can show how an object is, in itself, showing its "truth." Everything is already representation; experience is only possible through entering the dialogue between different narrative voices without any claim for rational control or authentic subjectivity. Any kind of so-called authentic truth is already always subject to a certain historical and political reading. The reader is just as much an author as the author is a reader. The distinction between reading and writing is systematically undermined.

Another example of Morgner's technique of deconstructing the idea of representation itself is the "Valeska Kantus Story." Beatrice's last will, read by Laura at her funeral, is the "Gospel of Valeska," a report of the female scientist Valeska Kantus, who through sudden, unprecedented metamorphosis is changed into a man. The report consists of Valeska's experiences as a man and discussions between her and her female friends about the possibilities and the meaning of the incident. Not only does Beatrice's last will not contain her own voice, but it is Laura who interprets the manuscript written by someone else as Beatrice's last will and revelation:

> Three days before her death, Beatrice had told her friend Laura about a strange encounter. Which Laura interpreted after the fact as a premonition of death. The trobadora claimed to have recognized, on the train to the potash mine in Zielitz, a man she had once met in Hades. [...] But in Hades the man had still been a woman. Valeska Kantus by name. [...] Beatrice had turned over to Laura a manuscript written by the man who, while still a woman, had allegedly been snatched from the jaws of clinical death following a traffic accident. Laura read it on the day of the trobadora's burial. As a revelation. (442)

The mixing of voices contains multiple readings of events all highly ambiguous in themselves. Laura reads the manuscript that Beatrice gave her as Beatrice's revelation, as the sum of her experiences and her authentic voice, while Beatrice had interpreted the voice of the man as the voice of someone else she met in Hades, a place that is really a nonplace.

The manuscript itself contains a "gospel" that is actually a specific reading of the position of women in society. The discussions between Valeska and her female friends center on the question of the possibility for women to become subjects and to enter history. Through her sex change, Valeska learns that the suppression of women throughout history is not the result of biological differences, but of a certain reading of these differences. After she discovers the metamorphosis in the mirror,

> Valeska burst into immoderate laughter. In view of the growth, on which legions of myths and power theories were based. Proof of having been chosen. Key to a privileged life, scepter of domination: a little flesh with wrinkly, at best blood-engorged skin. Valeska lacked the appropriate role training for a serious, self-admiring glance to her midsection: the prejudice. (450)

The "real" oppression of women is the result of a reading of seemingly banal and unimportant differences between men and women.

Because Beatrice's revelation consists of a chain of readings and rereadings, the notion of any kind of authentic experience becomes impossible. The subject position becomes extremely fragile, constantly undermined by other voices that precede the subject. Readings and interpretations are the basis for any kind of experience. Any kind of "truth" is always already lost. Morgner's subject in *Life and Adventures of Trobadora Beatrice* seems to be a radicalization of Adorno's pre-individual subject as it reveals itself in what he calls the "negative epics" of modernism.[54] Morgner's subject is a nonsubject, an indistinguishable multiplicity of voices, and a subject that becomes more and more dependent on fantasy and magic for its existence, only revealing itself in dialogic form. But her subject seems to be more of a "post-individual" than Adorno's "pre-individual" subject is. The process described in her novel is not so much a "falling back into mythical times," as Adorno had claimed, but rather the overcoming of our traditional notions of subjectivity with the help of magic and fantasy.[55] The subjectivity of Morgner's author is dependent on a network of voices without clear boundaries between the different subjects. The concept of the author is dissolved into a chain of masks behind which stands another mask.[56] There does not seem to be much room in

---

54 Cf. Adorno, "The Position of the Narrator in the Contemporary Novel," 35; see especially n. 49.

55 For a more detailed discussion of Morgner's use of fantasy and utopia, compare my essay "Places of Wonder: Fantasy and Utopia in Irmtraud Morgner's *Salman Trilogy*," *New German Critique*, 82 (Winter 2001), 167–92.

56 Morgner is closer to Michel Foucault and Roland Barthes in her notion of subjectivity than to Adorno. I will come back to this point in chapter 4.

Morgner's text for Adorno's claim that the authentic work of art contains "objective truth." On the contrary, everything is the result of readings that always already precede the subject. Morgner pushes Adorno's concept one step further in emphasizing the same impossibility of originality and universality in art itself. Her strategy results, I would argue, in part from Morgner's special position as a female author and from her choice of subject: women.

Woman as Author

Morgner insists that her deconstructive form of writing is based on specifically female modes of experience. "Feminine" forms of writing and knowing are explicitly associated with the unconcluded and the erotic. In a conversation with Laura about the planned project of publishing Beatrice's story, the character Irmtraud Morgner says:

> What? Now I've gotten myself into something! Which nobody wants. The impression it makes! "Have you joined the women's libbers?" my publisher asked me recently. "Do you need that?" Working with these testimonies is systematically destroying my reputation. People have already started looking for blue stockings under my trousers. Men search my face for ugly traces. And grandiose style doesn't sell anyway. I should have gotten a hardship bonus under these conditions. I must insist on clarity. I demand a logical presentation of evidence or my money back, thank you. (25)

It turns out that aesthetic conventions are male conventions. A "dark style" (a form of writing that refuses great concepts and logical explanations) is suspicious precisely because it is associated with a threatening femininity. Morgner unveils our traditional aesthetic concepts as ideological.

But the ideological basis of aesthetics is not only the fault of a "bad" male aesthetics; it is true for all writing, even the "good" female forms of writing. This becomes apparent as soon as we find out what "proofs" Laura and Morgner use to justify their own choice of subject and style. Laura tries to convince Irmtraud Morgner that there are objective historical proofs for the possibility of a female troubadour.

124

But this conviction is deconstructed in the text, not only because the character convinces the author, but also because Laura's proofs turn out to be a specific reading of history (a feminist version of Erich Köhler's interpretations) rather than objective fact. With tongue in cheek, Morgner repeatedly undermines her own aesthetics. The form of the work of art contains no "promise" anymore. Rather, it is a subversive strategy whose function is to question aesthetics, not to set normative demands.

The need for Morgner's strategy becomes apparent when Adorno's theories are considered in relation to Morgner's own position as a female author and gendered subject. While for Adorno authentic art has to be an expression of the alienation of the subject in modern society, Morgner's subjects are not only modern subjects, alienated because they live in an age of late capitalism; they are also women who never had the chance to become subjects in the first place. They are different from Adorno's male subjects, whose own project of an escape from nature through domination has turned against them and threatens to destroy their subject position.

Morgner's gendered author position constitutes an additional difficulty. Adorno's examination of the subject proceeds from a male perspective. When he claims that any authentic art shows how subjectivity turns against itself and regresses back into myth, he speaks of a male subject, one that has performed the task of escaping from nature to gain autonomy. Woman for him is the mask of nature that did not take part in Enlightenment's project of individuation, because men did not allow women to become subjects and suppressed them as part of nature. In Adorno's system, Morgner's characters would never be able to speak. Any attempt to make the other speak would be suspect as nothing but ideology, since it would have to support the illusion of a world in which the other can express itself. Adorno's analysis of the position of women in modern society tends toward essentialism, a view that does not allow for any kind of female resistance.

In Adorno's analysis, woman as the mask of nature becomes something that the male critic can *read*. In fact, Adorno emphasizes that it is the task of the critic to decipher the traces of suppression that become apparent in the contradictions of the logic of reason. Woman herself, according to Adorno, is such a trace, a "Wundmal." The difficulty for the female author and critic is that she is herself the mask that has to be read. To decipher the "wounds" and "stigmas" that a repressive system leaves, the critic must assume a standpoint outside the object examined. Woman needs to be read and the traces of suppression she displays offer hope, but how can the mask read itself? How can a woman step out of history? Ultimately, and against Adorno's own intentions, the critic is always a male critic in Adorno's text who, by reading woman, turns her into an object again. Adorno does not ask how it would be possible for women to gain subject status or how women could possibly recover their own voices. Morgner's own technique, then, is an ironic play with the perspective of the critic, who is supposed to be outside of the time and object she examines. By letting the critic Beatrice literally step out of history and time, Morgner ironically demonstrates the impossibility of an "objective" standpoint.

While Morgner does not share Adorno's insistence on rationality and reason, subverting not only the notion of the "objective" critic who could use such rationality but also more radically deconstructing the notion of the author and subject, she also rejects the normative demands for art that can be found in Adorno's theories. One important reason for this is the time difference that separates Adorno and Morgner.

The Historicity of Adorno's Aesthetic Theory

Peter Uwe Hohendahl has examined Adorno's aesthetic theory in connection with the cool reception it received from the West German Left in the early 1970s, and has pointed out that "Adorno evidently had not changed his position. In his last work [*Ästhetische Theorie*] he reiterated his critique of unmediated engagement and once more presented modernism and the avant-garde as the only viable responses to the increasing brutality of advanced capitalism."[57] The rejection of Adorno's aesthetic theory by the Left resulted, in Hohendahl's view, from the changed status of the avant-garde, a shift Adorno neglected. Between 1967 and 1970 West Germany witnessed an almost unparal-

57   Hohendahl, "Autonomy of Art," 207.

leled breakdown of the literary system. Radicals called for the end of literature and criticism, since the capitalist system had appropriated them and turned them into meaningless toys of the culture industry. Unlike Adorno, the New Left did not believe in the possibility of aesthetic opposition any longer, since it had become clear that the attempts of the avant-garde movements to overcome the gap between aesthetic and practical spheres and regain political impact had failed. Peter Bürger's study of the failure of the "historical" avant-garde and the changed function of art as a result of this failure offers the import- ance of the institution of art as an additional aspect for the evaluation of Adorno's aesthetic theory.[58]

Because Adorno failed to criticize the concept of autonomy and despite his radical historicization of art, he again introduced a nor- mative aspect into theory, according to Bürger. Bürger claims that although the "historical" avant-garde did not succeed in destroying the institution of art based on a radical separation between aesthetic and practical spheres, its failure shows that art institutions are decisive for the function and effectiveness of art in society. After the failure of the avant-garde, Bürger maintains, no single aesthetic movement or theory could claim to be the most progressive form of art. After 1945, realistic and avant-garde art legitimately existed side by side. In this sense, Adorno's aesthetic theory has become historical since it applies to the period of modernist art, a period that had come to an end after the failed attack of the "historical" avant-garde on the complacency of modern aestheticism.

The criticisms raised by Bürger and Hohendahl seem important in the application of Adorno's aesthetic theory to a contemporary novel, one produced much later than the historical avant-garde that Adorno analyzes. Because of the chronological difference, the question of political praxis poses itself in a different way for the author. Morgner's text reveals repeatedly that art can no longer be "unconscious historical analysis" [*bewußtlose* Geschichtsschreibung],[59] but on the contrary,

---

58   Peter Bürger, *Theorie der Avantgarde* (Frankfurt a. M.: Suhrkamp, 1974).

59   Cf. *Aesthetic Theory*: "In aesthetics it is legitimate to speak of the primacy of the object only in relation to the idea that art is an unconscious form of historio- graphy, the memory of what has been vanquished or repressed, perhaps an

aesthetic choices are always motivated by political strategy reflecting how a work of art functions in society. Adorno, as well as Lukács, rejected Brecht's practice of political engagement in literature for different reasons: Lukács could not tolerate a nonorganic work of art, while Adorno rejected the conscious political engagement of Brecht's works as tendentious, since for him works of art had to be "unconscious historical analysis."[60] Yet Morgner's work seems significantly influenced by Brecht's theory of alienation. Like Brecht, Morgner is very conscious of the institution of art and examines how art functions in society at specific times in history. Like Brecht, Morgner knows that it is impossible to destroy the institution of art, as the failure of the historical avant-garde movements has shown. She insists instead on the examination and renegotiation of the function of art in society.

The evaluation of the development of art after the historical avant-garde and after 1945 explains Morgner's rejection of Adorno's normative demands on the authentic work of art, even though she agrees with Adorno's basic analysis. She follows Adorno's criticism of instrumental reason because it offers her valuable explanations for the suppression of women in history, but she does not accept Adorno's description of what an authentic work of art has to look like. Although her text uncovers the "lie of representation," her novel is not the "dark epic" that Adorno had demanded. On the contrary, her playful experimentation with a variety of genres and narrative perspectives emphasizes enjoyment and almost an indulgence in the pleasure of narration.[61] Moreover, her strategies are consciously chosen for the active engagement of the reader and are ultimately politically motivated. Political analysis, theoretical discussions, highly modernist pieces of art, and different forms of realistic narration stand side by side in the text without discrimination. These features of Morgner's text point beyond a mere reactivation of fantasy and imagination as counterforces to an instrumental reason, as Emme-

anticipation of what is possible" (366). Adorno repeatedly calls works of art "windowless monads" (7).

60   Compare Adorno's criticism of Brecht's political engagement in his essay "Engagement," in Shierry Weber Nicholsen (trans.), *Notes to Literature* (New York: Columbia University Press, 1991).

61   The concept of "jouissance" comes to mind here. I will come back to this important point in chapter 3.

rich had claimed. In fact, Morgner, unlike the avant-garde art that Adorno promotes, not only reacts to the concept of the organic work of art that had been the official doctrine in the aesthetic theory of the GDR, but insists that the text also has to take the development of art after the historical avant-garde into account.

The belatedness of literary theory in the GDR, what Emmerich describes as the GDR artist's only now repeating the "dark critique of civilization" of the Frankfurt School, is more complex than apparent at first sight. The text situates itself in a field of tensions between the realistic organic work of art of GDR literary theory, the *nonorganic* art forms of high modernism that Adorno promoted, and those art forms that point beyond modernism. Although Frankfurt School criticism provides an important basis for recognizing these tensions, analyzing those features of Morgner's text that do not fit into Adorno's aesthetic theory moves toward a discussion of the problematic concept of postmodernism.

In going beyond normative aspects in Adorno's theory, it appears that Morgner consciously uses the tensions and problems in Adorno's theory in a very productive way. The normative aspect of Adorno's theories has been very much emphasized in recent discussion of postmodernism in order to save Adorno for a project of Enlightenment and against a political relativism perceived as dangerous.[62] This aspect might be present in Adorno's aesthetic theory, but it is also constantly undermined by his own self-reflexive gestures. Adorno's style of writing, for example, seems to point away from the belief in closed systems and totalizing forms of analysis.[63] This becomes most apparent in his aphorisms and in collections such as *Minima Moralia*.

62 Cf. Jürgen Habermas's famous "Adorno-Preisrede" (translated as "Modernity vs. Postmodernity" and reprinted in *New German Critique* 22 (1981), 3–14). He speaks of the "unfinished project of modernity" that is in danger of being threatened by new forms of theory.

63 In fact many scholars have pointed out that there are definite links between Adorno and deconstruction in Adorno's insistence on those heterogeneous fragments that cannot be grasped through conceptual thought, his rejection of any kind of identity logic, and his denial of the intentionality of signification. Indeed both Derrida and Foucault have acknowledged their indebtedness to Frankfurt School thought. Compare Martin Jay's discussion of parallels between Adorno

For Morgner, the tensions in Adorno's writings seem to be the most productive aspects of his theory. They point to unresolved problems between a utopian vision of true emancipation and a totalizing critique of an all-encompassing logic of rationality. Adorno's notorious pessimism, his criticism of metaphysical closures, and his insistence on negativity, in fact, are very close to Derrida's practice of deconstruction. They lead to a questioning of conventional forms of rational argumentation that have been taken up by many critics and authors of contemporary fiction. Morgner's insistence on the "small narratives" that might offer points of resistance, her strategy of questioning the concept of the subject and of representation, her constant gesture of subverting her own aesthetic strategies, offering instead a process of rereading, renegotiation, and dialogue in her text as the only way to discover one's own "voice-range," shows that she emphasizes those elements in Adorno's theories that point to open ends, disclosure, and other forms of rationality.

If Morgner's novel can be interpreted as displaying certain postmodern qualities, then her postmodernism is certainly not a rejection of and total departure from modernism, but is rather involved in a renegotiation of constitutive terms of the modern. In playing through different textual possibilities, oscillating between different voices and different readings, the text becomes a field of experimentation and a testing ground for different theoretical approaches. It is in feminist criticism that the possibility of political action takes on a new urgency.

and poststructuralism in *Adorno* (Cambridge: Harvard University Press, 1984); Terry Eagleton's *Walter Benjamin or Towards a Revolutionary Criticism* (London: Verso and NLB, 1981) and *Marxism and Deconstruction: A Critical Articulation* (London: Methuen); and Jürgen Schulte-Sasse's "Theory of Modernism versus Theory of the Avant-Garde," the foreword to *Theory of the Avant-Garde* by Peter Bürger.

CHAPTER III

"Excavating the Voice Range of Woman": The Intersection of Feminist and Postmodern Theory in *Life and Adventure*

Morgner's stated intention in *Life and Adventures* was to create a space from which women could enter history and make their voices heard. She described Beatrice's journey as a quest to "free her own voice range" (58) [die eigene Stimmlage freilegen] and to define herself as a subject in order "to enter history" (113). Although Morgner sharply criticized modern society as a "Frauenhaltergesellschaft," a society in which women have the status of slaves,[1] she refused to define herself as a feminist or even admit that what she was writing about were exclusively "women's concerns":

> I do not like the word feminist, because it has a fashionable, apolitical ring for me, because it provokes the assumption that women's process of becoming human could only be a concern of women. But this is a problem for humanity. Emancipation of women is impossible without the emancipation of men and the other way around. *Life and Adventures* was written by a communist.[2]

While Morgner's reservations with the term "feminist" arose in part because of the different understanding of the term in the East and the West, Morgner remained a convinced Marxist throughout her

---

1   In one of the information visits of Benno Pakulat, Morgner lets her character state: "There aren't any great women writers. Can't be. Greek culture was based on slaveholding, modern culture on holding women as slaves" (284). Morgner herself made the same argument in a study group at the VIIth Schriftstellerkongreß in 1974 (Irmtraud Morgner, "Rede auf dem VII. Schriftstellerkongreß der DDR." *Neue deutsche Literatur* 8 (1978). Reprinted in Marlis Gerhardt (ed.), *Irmtraud Morgner: Texte, Daten, Bilder* (Frankfurt a. M.: Luchterhand, 1990)).

2   Karin Huffzky, "Produktivkraft Sexualität souverän nutzen: Ein Gespräch mit der DDR-Schriftstellerin Irmtraud Morgner." *Frankfurter Rundschau*, 16 August 1975, 111.

life.[3] In *Life and Adventures,* for example, she lets Beatrice say "a woman of character can only be a Socialist today" (105, 402). As a consequence, many feminists were disturbed at what they perceived to be a privileging of a critique of Western capitalism over feminist considerations.

These differences in perception, I will argue, arose in part from the complex structure of *Life and Adventures.* The contradictory early reaction to Morgner's novel and the belated new interest in her work can be explained if we understand the significant differences between *Life and Adventures* and most other feminist texts of the time. Unlike other feminists in the early 1970s, Morgner used postmodern strategies to promote feminist goals. On the one hand, *Life and Adventures* takes part in a debate over how to define "woman," a debate that has been going on since the emergence of the women's movement. On the other, the text discusses questions of representation and the status of the subject, topics that have become key issues in postmodernist texts. In combining feminist and postmodernist strategies, Morgner's novel anticipates the current debate about the differences between and intersections of poststructuralist and feminist theories. As a text concerned with the possibility and usefulness of a definition of woman and the consequences of such a definition for political practice, *Life and Ad-*

---

3   In several interviews, Morgner repeated her conviction that the "abolishment of the exploitation of human beings by human beings" [Abschaffung der Ausbeutung des Menschen durch den Menschen] through a socialist revolution was the precondition for the "abolishment of the exploitation of women by human beings" [die Ausbeutung der Frau durch den Menschen]. Compare, for example, her statements in an interview with Richard Zipser in "Stellungnahmen" (Irmtraud Morgner, "Stellungnahmen," (Interviews with 39 GDR Writers), in Richard A. Zipser (ed.), *DDR Literatur im Tauwetter: Wandel – Wunsch – Wirklichkeit,* Vol. 3 (New York: Peter Lang, 1985), 23). It is important to add, however, that Morgner did not see the exploitation of women as a "secondary contradiction," as in orthodox Marxist ideology. Ingeborg Nordmann points out that Morgner criticized orthodox socialist ideology by emphasizing Marx's early emancipatory statements, as well as other utopian socialist thinkers like Fourier, over the more economically oriented later Marx (Ingeborg Nordmann, "Die halbierte Geschichtsfähigkeit der Frau: Zu Irmtraud Morgners Roman *Leben und Abenteuer der Trobadora Beatriz nach Zeugnissen ihrer Spielfrau Laura." Amsterdamer Beiträge zur Neueren Germanistik,* 11–12 (1981), 426).

ventures makes important contributions to the debate on the political nature of postmodernism.

In this chapter, I will read Morgner's *Life and Adventures* as a "feminist" and a "postmodernist" as well as a "political" text, with each of these terms in quotation marks to indicate that the combination of these elements in the novel encourages a reexamination of certain narrow definitions of feminism, postmodernism, and politics. The result will force us to abandon the simple, polarized pigeonholing of texts and theories as either historical or ahistorical, essentialist or anti-essentialist, political or nonpolitical, emancipatory or reactionary. A discussion of Morgner's novel in the context of the debate on postmodernism is useful because it can point to certain elements in the text that were overlooked in early critical responses. It can also explain in part why this text has been discussed in such contradictory terms.[4]

Like many critics, I distinguish between postmodernism as a cultural designation and postmodernity as the designation of a social and historical period or "condition."[5] In this sense, postmodernism can be understood as a response to postmodernity, a historical condition with economic, political, and social determinations.[6] Postmodernity corres-

---

4   It is interesting that critics in the 1990s who begin to read Morgner's narrative techniques as postmodern textual strategies seem to have different expectations than earlier critics. It seems that these critics are better able to recognize the conflicting movements and contradictory elements in the novel as productive energy, rather than claiming that Morgner's novel lacks a coherent concept or is based on a misunderstanding of certain literary rules. Several critics, however, still feel compelled to distinguish Morgner's textual strategies from those in other postmodern works they suspect of being merely "playful" and lacking "seriousness" and political relevance. Scherer, for example, agrees with Grobbel's final evaluation, which is that "Morgner's strategy to go beyond merely playful elements by inserting a clearly visible socio-political criticism, lifts her texts above the framework of the postmodern literary analysis" (quoted in Gabriela Scherer, *Zwischen "Bitterfeld" und "Orplid."*)

5   Compare, for example, Linda Hutcheon, *Poetics of Postmodernism: History, Theory, Fiction* (New York: Routledge, 1988), 23.

6   Compare Jochen Schulte-Sasse, "Modernity and Modernism, Postmodernity and Postmodernism: Framing the Issue," *Cultural Critique*, 5 (1986–87), 6. Unlike Schulte-Sasse, Fredric Jameson does not make a distinction between postmodernism and postmodernity, but uses the term *postmodernism* for both, a socioeconomic periodization and the designation for a cultural and aesthetic

ponds in the most general terms to a situation that can be characterized by the West's loss of unqualified faith in the "project of modernity," a modernity that starts at the latest with the Enlightenment and the Industrial Revolution in the eighteenth century.[7] Linda Hutcheon points out that such diverse theoretical positions as Derrida's challenge to the Western metaphysics of presence; Foucault's investigation of the complicities of discourse, knowledge, and power; Vattimo's paradoxically potent "weak thought"; and Lyotard's questioning of the validity of the metanarratives of legitimation and emancipation have all been used to define the term *postmodernity* in philosophical circles.[8] While there can be, as Andreas Huyssen asserts, as many postmodernisms as there are "modernisms," each of which must be understood in terms of historical developments,[9] there does seem to be some agreement concerning some specific characteristics of postmodernism. Many scholars point to post-

phenomenon. He asserts that postmodernity has its cause in a fundamental change in the conception of the self in recent economic developments in capitalist society. He speaks of a shift to a late multinational capitalism, and, as a critic in the Marxist tradition, defines postmodernity in terms of the socioeconomic development. For him, postmodernism is not only a style but a "cultural dominant." Postmodernism *is* the "cultural logic of late capitalism," since, in Jameson's eyes, it not only replicates the socioeconomic effects of postmodernity, but reinforces and intensifies them. The problem with this equation of postmodernism and postmodernity is—as Hutcheon also points out—that there seems to be only one kind of response possible to late capitalism. Jameson sees postmodernism as complicitous with late capitalism without allowing for the possibility of a relation of subversion or criticism. (Cf. Fredric Jameson, "Postmodernism, or the Cultural Logic of Late Capitalism," *New Left Review*, 146 (1984), 53–92.)

7   Rick McCormick points out that some critics set the beginning of modernity with Descartes in the seventeenth century, and others with the rise of capitalism in Italy and France after 1450. Modernism, on the other hand, is usually said to begin with impressionism in the 1860s (Richard W. McCormick, *Politics of the Self: Feminism and the Postmodern in West German Literature and Film* (Princeton: Princeton University Press, 1991), 10).

8   Linda Hutcheon, *The Politics of Postmodernism* (London: Routledge, 1991), 24.

9   Andreas Huyssen, for example, points to "Ungleichzeitigkeiten" ("nonsynchronisms," a term he borrows from Ernst Bloch) in the development of different modernisms and postmodernisms in Europe and the United States ("Mapping the Postmodern," *New German Critique*, 33 (Fall 1984), 5–52).

modernism's self-reflexivity, its emphasis on the investigation of the social and ideological production of meaning and the effects of representation, its attempt to move beyond a certain binary "either/or" logic in favor of a logic of the "both/and" (Rick McCormick's phrasing), its use of parody and what some critics (Charles Jencks and Linda Hutcheon, for example) have called "double-coding" in postmodernist texts. More specifically, postmodernist fiction has come to contest the modernist ideology of artistic autonomy and individual expression, as well as the deliberate separation of high art from mass culture and everyday life.[10] Many of these characteristics are present in *Life and Adventures,* such as the extended use of intertextual connections, and recurring attempts to parody and rewrite whole parts of the text, thereby consciously correcting and reformulating earlier statements, which undermine the clear presentation of her message and her authority as author.[11] These features were very different from other feminist projects of the early 1970s.

Feminisms in the Early Seventies

It is difficult to read feminist texts from the former GDR in conjunction with those from the West, since in the early 1970s a feminist movement did not exist in East Germany in the same way it did in the West. Institutionally there was no women's movement, as Bathrick points out, "simply because the official public sphere prohibited any collective public presence that was not organized as an ideologically proper representation of the female experience."[12] Yet, there were a growing

---

10   Compare Huyssen, "Mapping the Postmodern," 53–4.
11   Ingeborg Nordmann, in her early article from 1981, had already analyzed Morgner's montage technique as a montage of text parts that criticize one another and undercut each other's authority. Nordmann maintained that the function of this technique was twofold: it served to produce a socialist teleology, but it also destroyed any kind of teleological sense through its technique of decomposing all perceptions of reality ("Die halbierte Geschichtsfähigkeit der Frau," 461).
12   Bathrick, *The Powers of Speech,* 54.

number of outstanding women writers in the GDR who began to discuss women's issues in their fictions.[13] As Angelika Bammer argues, public political engagement of women writers "did not take the form of political activism on behalf of women's liberation," but rather tended to be played out in the cultural sphere through protest, which "was registered in the form of fictions."[14] A comparison of Morgner's novels to feminist texts in the West is fruitful, not only because Morgner's texts articulate a consciousness that is unmistakably feminist, but also because her novels, together with those by Christa Wolf and other women writing in the GDR, were widely read and influenced the development of feminist literature in West Germany.[15] In the case of Morgner's *Life and Adventures*, a comparison with other feminist texts of the time helps to contextualize the early feminist critique of the novel.

In the early 1970s, the time Morgner's novel was published, the agitative beginnings of the contemporary feminist movement in West Germany, which had grown out of the activism of the 1960s (partly influenced by the American civil rights movement, the antiwar movement in the Vietnam era, and the student movement), could still be felt. The first unmistakable sign of organization came in the spring of 1968, when the Action Council for Women's Liberation [Aktionsrat für die Befreiung der Frauen] was formed in West Berlin. Female students began to criticize the Socialist German Student Federation [Sozialistischer Deutscher Studentenbund] for its failure to take the oppression of women seriously. As in most leftist organizations, the student movement saw the oppression of women as a secondary contradiction [Nebenwiderspruch] that would vanish automatically

13 For the development of the feminist movement in the GDR, see Patricia Herminghouse's essay, "Legal Equality and Women's Reality in the German Democratic Republic," in Edith Hoshino Altbach *et al.* (eds), *German Feminism: Readings in Politics and Literature* (Albany: State University of New York Press, 1984), 41–6.

14 Bammer, "The American Feminist," 18–19.

15 Angelika Bammer shows in her study on utopianism in feminist texts from the 1970s that "the case of East and West Germany is only one example of the remarkable degree to which feminism (in its first decade at least) was simultaneously national and transnational. As texts and theories crossed borders they not only carried their original feminist formations with them, but were instrumental in the shaping of different feminisms elsewhere" (*Partial Visions*, 65).

with the advent of the socialist society. Female students were forced to subordinate their own demands to the general, "more important" concerns of the student movement, a movement dominated by men. Helke Sanders's speech at the national convention of the German SDS in September 1968 attests to the discontent of its female members.[16]

Despite these difficulties, women formed autonomous women's groups with storefront day-care centers [Kinderläden] and fought for an anti-authoritarian education. Women's centers were opened in 1972, followed by houses for battered women. The concern of these women's groups included the fight for women's sexual autonomy and the organization of protest actions against the §218, the law prohibiting abortion.[17] In the GDR, women had to remain silent on these issues in public, although family violence, rape, and homophobia existed there as well. Abortion was not legalized until 1972. In fact, the GDR, with its difficulty in maintaining its population, was the last of the socialist states to grant this right. As Patricia Herminghouse maintains, the ideology of "family" remained a bastion of conservatism in the GDR.[18] The large number of feminist publications that appeared during the early 70s and female authors' preference for documentary literature demonstrate the need feminists felt to make their voices heard in order to change history.[19] To counter male stereotypes about women, feminists tried to

16   Helke Sanders, "Rede des Aktionsrates zur Befreiung der Frauen bei der 23. Delegiertenkonferenz des SDS im September 1968 in Frankfurt." *Frauenjahrbuch* 1, (1975). Reprinted as "Speech by the Action Council for Women's Liberation," in Edith Hoshino Altbach *et al.* (eds), *German Feminism: Readings in Politics and Literature*, Edith Hoshino Altbach (trans.) (Albany: State University of New York Press, 1984), 307–10.

17   One example is the campaign in the magazine *Stern*, "Ich habe abgetrieben" [I had an abortion], organized by Alice Schwarzer in 1971.

18   Herminghouse, "Legal Equality," 43.

19   Sigrid Weigel, in her book *Die Stimme der Medusa: Schreibweisen in der Gegenwartsliteratur von Frauen* (Dülmen-Hiddingsel: tende, 1987), points to Erika Runge's *Frauen: Versuche zur Emanzipation* (Frankfurt a. M.: Suhrkamp, 1969), Alice Schwarzer's *Frauen gegen den $ 218* (Frankfurt a. M.: Suhrkamp, 1971), Ulrike Meinhof's *Bambule* (Berlin: Wagenbach, 1971), Britta Noeske's *Liebe Kollegin: Texte zur Emanzipation der Frau in der Bundesrepublik* (Frankfurt a. M.: Fischer Taschenbuch, 1973), and Alice Schwarzer's *Der kleine Unterschied und seine großen Folgen* (Frankfurt a. M.: Fischer, 1975). Patricia

"set the record straight" by publishing "realistic" accounts of women's experiences. While the realist bias of the early phase of feminist writing shows up most clearly in the great amount of documentary literature at this time, it can also be observed in a different manner, in the so-called "new subjectivism" that emerged in literature in the mid-70s. Women authors played a major role in this trend, since they were eager to represent women's authentic feelings, wishes, and experiences. Diaries and so-called "I"-texts or identification literature [Identifikationslitera-tur] appeared in great numbers. Two books especially, Verena Stefan's *Häutungen* (1975) and Karin Struck's *Klassenliebe* (1973), have been regarded as the beginning of feminist literature in West Germany. Although Stefan's text includes a critique of a traditional language that perpetuates male dominance, both Stefan and Struck seek to record what they thought of as authentic experiences of women uncontami-nated by male ideology. Written in a confessional or thinly disguised autobiographical mode, texts such as these tended to emphasize the supposed sameness of women's experience and had variants of the dominant motif of "woman-as-victim" as their theme.[20] The tendency to develop the notion of sexual difference and the attempt to define a "feminine essence" is not unique to West German feminist literature of the early 1970s, however; it can also be observed in the literature of US feminists at that time.[21]

Herminghouse analyzes a similar trend in documentary literature in the GDR, such as Sarah Kirsch, *Die Pantherfrau* (Berlin, Weimar: Aufbau Verlag, 1973), and Maxie Wander's *Guten Morgen du Schöne: Protokolle von Frauen* (Frankfurt a. M.: Luchterhand, 1977) ("Legal Equality," 46).

20   Bammer, *Partial Visions*, 68. Compare also her more detailed analysis of Stefan's text on pp. 67–79.

21   Angelika Bammer states that a great number of these texts "were predicated upon two basic cultural feminist assumptions: (1) that gender difference was given, and (2) that women's 'difference' should be seen as positive. [...] This affirmation of femaleness as a positive identity was not limited to cultural feminism, however; it was a vital dimension of 1970s feminisms in general" (*Partial Visions*, 93).

Morgner's Postmodern Feminism

Morgner's different agenda, which I define as a feminist agenda that employs postmodernist strategies, can already be detected in the postscript to her novel *Die wundersamen Reisen Gustavs des Weltfahrers. Lügenhafter Roman mit Kommentaren,* published in 1972, where she quotes from the letter of the novel's fictional author Bele H.:

> In a different letter, the author claimed that women had an underdeveloped historical consciousness, since they had not entered history as subjects. In order to live as human beings, in order to enter history, they would have to exit history: to appropriate nature. First their own. [22]

This passage has been read as Morgner's commitment to the feminist movement, her goal supposedly being the discovery of a female essence [die eigene Natur] repressed by a male-dominated history. Looking at the quotation more closely, we find a strange wording that seems to be typical for Morgner's texts. Bele H. talks about "entering history" [in die Geschichte eintreten] like entering into a building, i.e. something artificially constructed rather than given and unchangeable. Her paradoxical wording of "having to exit history in order to be able to enter it" presupposes an understanding of history as something contrived. Morgner emphasizes the constructedness of history in which women have not been present as subjects. The ability to produce history, she goes on to say, defines human beings as gendered and determines their status. As Morgner lets her character claim, "[W]omen have an underdeveloped historical consciousness, since they have not entered history as subjects." But to enter history means for women to appropriate their own nature [sich Natur aneignen. Zuerst ihre eigne]. Again Morgner uses an unusual verb when she talks about women's "nature." For Bele H., "sich Natur aneignen" does not seem to involve the simple task of

---

22   My translation. "In einem anderen Brief behauptete die Verfasserin, Frauen hätten ein schwach entwickeltes Geschichtsbewußtsein, weil sie wesentlich noch nicht in die Geschichte eingetreten wären. Um als Menschen zu leben, das heißt in die Historie einzutreten, müßten sie aus der Historie austreten: sich Natur aneignen. Zuerst ihre eigne" (155).

rediscovering a natural femaleness that is given and easily available, but women instead have to "appropriate" nature. "Aneignen" means to make something one's own as well as to assert power over something or someone. The statement that it is women's task to "appropriate" their own nature points out that women's nature has not been their own so far. Morgner's strange wording unmasks the concept of "nature" in patriarchal societies as something artificial, constructed by human beings, or, more specifically in the context of the quote, constructed by men to define women and thereby to prevent them from assuming the status of subjects. Again, Morgner points to the constructedness of concepts that have long been seen as "natural" and "given."

In fact, the "author" Bele H. creates a highly ironic game with the conception of nature versus civilization/history in this passage. In the tradition of the Enlightenment and German idealism, "Menschsein," being human, means to assume one's historicity, a process that implies change and progress. Paradoxically, to be a female "Mensch," Bele H. claims, means to become "nature" first, to assume one's "natural" identity. At first sight it seems that Bele H. assumes a Rousseauist position of going back to nature. Her unusual wording, however, throws this position into question since it is not clear what women's "natural" identity is. The irony in Bele H.'s words distances the reader from familiar conceptions and models of "nature" and "history," and we are forced to reconsider core ideas of Western culture.[23] In fact, unlike most West German feminists of the time, Morgner deconstructs many such core ideas of Western culture in her texts: through a simple, but highly artistic play with words and linguistic structures, she probes the ground of certain concepts and ideas. She questions the mechanisms operative in the construction of such concepts, thereby rendering them insecure and open for renegotiation.

In addition to deconstructing familiar concepts of "nature" and "history," Morgner plays with the concept of the author. *Die wunder-samen Reisen* has at least four "authors": Irmtraud Morgner, whose name is on the cover of the book; Bele H., who is the fictional "author" [Verfasserin] and the author of the letter quoted at the end of the book;

---

23   In addition, Bele H.'s statement plays with the Marxist concept of "Mensch-werdung," of course, interpreting it from a feminist perspective.

Dr. phil. Beate Heidenreich, the fictional editor of the text and a friend of Bele H.; and Gustav, Bele H.'s grandfather, who actually tells the "mendacious stories" of the novel. This strategy of creating a chain of voices instead of speaking as an individual autonomous author is continued in *Life and Adventures*. Not only does Beatrice meet Bele H. on her journey to Split, where they debate key notions of "women's nature" (bk. 8, ch. 22), but Irmtraud Morgner, the intrusive and manipulative author, appears in the novel as a fictional character, who discusses writing strategies and the conditions for production of a text with her own character, Laura Salman. Morgner creates a multiplication of the author in the text, for Laura, as the chronicler of Beatrice's life, is also an "author." In fact, the chain of voices includes not only Laura, Beatrice, and Irmtraud Morgner, but all the female characters of the novel. They are connected through texts that they write and read *with each other, for each other*, and *in each other's names*. The intermezzos in *Life and Adventures*, for example, are parts of *Rumba auf einen Herbst*, that the beautiful Melusine copies into her own Melusinean notebooks.[24] Laura writes stories using Beatrice's name, and Beatrice writes stories in "Laura's style" (for example the story "Berta vom blühenden Bett," bk. 8, ch. 10). In book 8, we find a letter from Beatrice asking Laura to find an author who can write a poem for Wenzel Morolf in Beatrice's name (205). At Beatrice's funeral, Laura reads as Beatrice's last will Valeska's "Gospel" [Gute Botschaft], which Beatrice had received from a man she

---

24 These parts of *Rumba auf einen Herbst* are not the only texts that Melusine quotes in her "Melusinische Bücher" [Melusinian Books], however. Chapter 19 of her fourth Melusinian Book contains the transcripts of an interview with the master chess player Dr. Solowjow (bk 8, ch. 2), Melusine's seventy-third book contains an article she has copied from a magazine (bk 10, ch. 4), her ninety-fourth book contains excerpts from the memoirs of Krupskaja (bk 10, ch. 13), her 189th book consists of quotations from Laura's notebook (bk 10, ch. 18), her 311th book is a summary of the results of the Vietnam War produced by the Stockholm Institute for International Affairs (bk 11, ch. 25), her 396th book is a copy of Olga Salman's petition (bk 11, ch. 28), her 103rd book contains excerpts from the GDR health book "Mann und Frau Intim" (bk 11, ch. 32), and her 161st book is the copy of a newspaper report in *Neues Deutschland* (bk 11, ch. 34). The Melusinian Books thus form a third text (together with Laura's chronicle of Beatrice's life and *Rumba auf einen Herbst*) inside of *Life and Adventures*, which itself also consists of a multiplicity of voices.

had met in Hades "when he was still a woman" (442). Valeska's "Gospel," however, contains among other citations Bele H.'s words from *Die wundersamen Reisen* spoken by Shenya, Valeska's friend and lover. Moreover, Beatrice had also repeated Bele H.'s words of the quoted passage from *Die wundersamen Reisen* almost verbatim as her own when she first met Laura. Many passages consist of quotations from different characters in the novel. Sometimes the quotations are slightly changed, sometimes they are repeated verbatim.[25] All of these postmodernist devices, which include a multiplication of beginnings, endings, and narrated actions, the parodic thematization of the author, a complex play with multiple coding through allusion and allusive commentary, citation, playfully distorted or invented reference, recasting, transposition, deliberate anachronism, and the mixing of two or more historical and stylistic modes, help to undermine the notion of a stable female identity.[26] The texts in the novel do not have one single author, but contain a multiplicity of voices. Thus, the individual autonomous author who has control over her own text does not exist in Morgner's novel. Speaking, writing, and even experiencing are not forms of individual expression, but always occur in dialogue with other voices (other people's as well as other texts'). The subject is not simply split into more than one voice as in other modernist texts, but it constitutes itself only in exchange with other subjects and texts.[27]

25 In the chapter "Benno Pakulat höchstpersönlich," for example, Benno repeats Laura's story "Café au contraire" with yet another role change (315). On his third "Information Visit," he repeats words that Beatrice before had put into the mouth of her ideal image of her lover Raimbaut d'Aurenga in a chapter called "Laura's Protocol of the Trobadora's Memories of the Real Raimbaut d'Aurenga Who Does Not Comply with Reality" (bk 1, ch. 18). And in the last chapter, Benno begins to tell Laura 1,001 nightly stories in "Beatrice's style" to console his mourning wife. In the first of these stories, he not only retells the story of Beatrice's life in the Middle Ages as Laura had told it to Irmtraud Morgner in the first chapter of book 1, but he closes his story with the exact same words that Irmtraud Morgner had spoken at the very beginning of the novel in "Vorsätze."

26 Matei Calinescu lists many of these textual strategies as typical postmodernist devices; cf. his *Five Faces of Modernity: Modernism, Avant-Garde, Decadence, Kitsch, Postmodernism* (Durham: Duke University Press, 1987), 303–4.

27 Alison Lewis analyzes the notion of subjectivity in texts by Wolf, Morgner, and Moog. She interprets the use of doubles in many texts by East German woman

Morgner plays with the concept of authenticity in the very first paragraphs of the novel. In "Vorsätze" [*foreword* as well as *resolutions*], she lets the editor of *Life and Adventures*, Irmtraud Morgner, pledge that her chronicle of Beatrice de Dia's life uses nothing but authentic documents and sources: "I immediately started reordering and editing these sensational testimonies for publication. The book you are reading follows the sources rigorously in describing all essential events. Sections of text are reproduced unchanged in a new sequence that is accommodating to the reader" (5). Since the reader already knows that the documents themselves are very strange and full of miracles and magic events, this pledge by the novel's fictional editor is an ironic commentary on the so-called authentic texts so popular among feminists at the time. Morgner's goal of undermining the authority of our traditional concept of the author who speaks as a single individual can be observed in her use of self-parody as well. In *Life and Adventures* Morgner uses almost all of her earlier texts, parodying them by adding corrected versions of her own earlier statements. Most striking are the commentaries of the resurrected Beatrice in the second part of the trilogy, *Amanda*, in which Beatrice tells the reader how *Life and Adventures* came to be written:

> Laura changed from the department of history to the department of German literature and married – as the book *Life and Adventures of Trobadora Beatrice* fairly correctly describes – Uwe Parnitzke in her third semester after a few romantic relationships [...]. She took up work as my minstrel and produced texts with my name on them, which were really written by Amanda [we find out in the second part of the trilogy that Amanda is Laura's second half]. Because only she could write like this. I had no idea and remained ignorant for a long time. But I am not angry at Laura and Amanda for deceiving me. Amanda used my name for a good purpose [...]. And I still claim that the

writers as "acts of transference," acts in which the writer authorizes another female subject to speak. Although the notion of the double seems to me too narrow for Morgner's technique of creating a multiplicity of voices in *Life and Adventures*, I agree with Lewis's thesis that Morgner creates an alternative model of female subjectivity that stresses the intersubjective aspect in the formation of female identity ("Foiling the Censor").

author of the novel had no idea either. That is how this book [*Life and Adventures*] willingly or unwillingly turned out to be an irresponsible novel.[28]

For Morgner texts are not stable and closed entities, but are constantly rewritten and added to. *Life and Adventures* makes clear that even the rewritten text is open for a new rewriting by the reader. There is no final author-ity and no final text. All the author can do is enter into the dialogue of texts and encourage the reader to do the same. In contrast to other feminist projects of the 1970s, Morgner's goal was not to find a "female essence" through women's authentic experiences, but rather to focus on the debate among feminists itself. Her technique of constantly rewriting different stories and events from many different perspectives, consciously giving up her own authority as author, draws attention to discourse formation and the power of language.

Intertextual Games

Another strategy used by Morgner to deconstruct the notion of the autonomous stable subject is her highly artistic play with a variety of different intertexts. Morgner's technique of using her characters' names to create allusions to different texts is a good example. The two main characters, Laura Salman and Beatrice de Dia, have highly symbolic names and are connected in the novel through the allusion to Dante, Petrarch, and the Middle Ages. In Dante, Beatrice is the one who guides the author on his path through paradise and the circles of heaven. She is

28 My translation. "Laura wechselte vom historischen zum germanistischen Institut und heiratete, wie im Buch 'Leben und Abenteuer der Trobadora Beatriz' einigermaßen richtig beschrieben ist, im dritten Semester nach wenigen Romanzen den Assistenten Uwe Parnitzke [...]. Sie nahm also bei mir Arbeit als Spielfrau und lieferte mir Texte mit meinem Namen, die tatsächlich Amanda schrieb. Weil nur sie so schreiben konnte. Ich war ahnungslos und blieb es lange. Aber ich verarge Laura und Amanda nicht, daß sie mich hintergingen. Amanda nutzte meinen Namen für einen guten Zweck [...]. Und daß die Romanautorin ebenfalls ahnungslos war, unterstelle ich nach wie vor. So ist aus dem Buch gewollt oder ungewollt ein unverantwortlicher Roman geworden" (*Amanda*, 120–1).

the essence of virtue, beauty, and wisdom and becomes the symbol of philosophy in *The Divine Comedy*. Through Beatrice, whom Dante has come to love with idealistic admiration, he points out how love becomes the guiding principle of his poetry. Beatrice in *Life and Adventures* constantly moves between death and resurrection, frequently visiting Hades or awakening from a deathlike sleep of eight hundred years. Like Beatrice in *The Divine Comedy*, she is a figure who moves between different worlds and oversteps boundaries. In *Life and Adventures* it is the physicist Wenzel Morolf who compares himself to Dante to prove that scientific and poetic creativity are not so different from one another (seventh intermezzo). Morolf starts to talk about Dante because he witnessed a woman's death that day (Beatrice losing her balance while cleaning windows and falling to her death). He feels depressed and compares his state of mind to that of Orpheus, who looked back too early and thereby lost his lover Eurydice whom he had tried to guide out of Hades. Morolf claims that both the scientist and the poet need a certain kind of faith and spiritual fervor [geistiger Fanatismus] to have the courage to ask questions that nobody has asked before.

Laura Salman's first name reminds the reader of Petrarch's poems to Laura, which had set new standards for the lyric production of the fifteenth and sixteenth centuries. Petrarch's sonnets did not show the loved woman as the "donna angelica," but instead emphasized her worldly beauty and showed her as she interacted with nature. These poems break with the conventions of the troubadour lyric and the Italian "dolce stil nuovo" of Petrarch's time. Beatrice's poems to her lover Raimbaut d'Aurenga in *Life and Adventures* do very much the same thing. In fact, by challenging the conventional style of the *minnesang*, Beatrice turns into a female "lovesinger." With this double challenge to the conventions of medieval society, she becomes intolerable to her husband and courtly society and her husband burns her poems, making Beatrice decide to leave the Middle Ages.

Both Dante and Petrarch are figures who break with the literary conventions of their time through their love poetry to women. Although the literary treatment of women in Dante and Petrarch in many ways confirms the existing stereotypes of women, Morgner emphasizes those aspects of their work that break significant boundaries. It is no surprise, for example, that Morgner lets Morolf quote the passage from *The*

Divine Comedy that shows Beatrice active, guiding and teaching Dante on his journey through paradise.[29] Through the names for her characters, Morgner alludes to the literary tradition to indicate certain turning points in the (male) literary canon. But it is not only the names of the two main characters that establish connections between different characters through allusions to the literary tradition.

Wenzel Morolf's philosophical musings establish a connection to Beatrice because they occur after he has seen her fall to her death, leading him to talk about Dante, but his own name also connects him to Laura via the intertext of "Salman and Morolf," a medieval epic [Spielmannsepos].[30] In the Salman figure of the medieval epic, the biblical tradition of wise King Solomon and legends from the Talmud and the cabbala (with Solomon a demonic king who enters into dialogic competition with his brother) are combined. By choosing the name Salman for her main character, Morgner explores a highly ambiguous figure in literary tradition and history. Beatrice is part of the text's allusion to "Salman and Morolf," not only because Laura and Beatrice parallel the sibling relationship in the epic, entering into dialogues to connect to one another and understand the world, but also because Beatrice's story is similar to an early version of the story of "Salman and Morolf" in which the unfaithful wife of Salman has herself put to artificial death to escape from her husband.[31] Similarly, Beatrice, in her

29   Morolf says: "New ideas don't arise from the rational intelligence, but from the artistically creative imagination. We ask Nature questions. Formulating such questions requires the greatest expenditure of imagination. Physics is an extremely sensual science [...]. The struggle with the unknown is always a sensual experience. For Dante, all battles that he fought intellectually were battles with the Pergalotta. In the *rime petrose*, Florence is the Pergalotta, he plunges into politics as into a love battle. In the *Divine Comedy* he himself is instructed – paradoxically by the immortalized Beatrice, whom he loved after her death in boyish ascetic excess for quite a long time – as follows: 'Only through the senses can intelligence grasp/ that which it will later elevate to rational thought'" (438).

30   It was Patricia Herminghouse who first pointed out the many texts that are quoted in *Life and Adventures*, such as the "Salman and Morolf" epic, Petrarch, Dante, and medieval Arthurian epics, in her essay, "Die Frau und das Phantastische," 248–66.

31   The sibling relationship is already present in the Talmud: King Solomon fights with the lord of ghosts Aschmedai, who is also his brother. In the Western

first life in the Middle Ages, enters into an eight-hundred-year-long sleep through the use of magic to escape her husband's prosecution for being a female minnesinger who embarrasses his court. These allusions render the relationship between Laura and Beatrice complex, pointing to their similarities and connections (in the allusion to their sibling relationship) and to their differences and separations (in the allusion to the escaping wife). Their relationship is that of sisters, but it also contains elements of competition and struggle. At times the two figures seem to merge, and at other times they are separated. Through other intertexts, all the female characters are connected and rendered ambiguous. There are four important female characters in *Life and Adventures*: Laura Salman, Beatrice de Dia, Valeska Kantus, and Vera Hill. A fifth figure, Bele H., only has a small appearance. She is closely connected to Beatrice, however, and she was also the main character and Scheherazade figure of Morgner's *Hochzeit in Konstantinopel* and the fictional author of *Die wundersamen Reisen Gustavus des Weltfahrers*.[32] All of these figures are connected through allusions to a network of intertexts.

One more intertext that works as a connecting device for the different female characters is Wolfram von Eschenbach's medieval

---

tradition Aschmedai becomes Markolf, the demonic brother of Salomon. In a dialogic competition, Salomon proves his wisdom over other demonic lords. From these traditions two medieval epics develop: the "Salman and Morolf" epic (a Spielmannsepos) (ca. 1190), and the "Spruchgedicht Salomon und Morolf" (fifteenth century). The "Spruchgedicht" uses the motif of the dialogic competition for its plot: the farmer Morolf beats Salomon and his didactic moral speeches in dialogue with his realistic, cynical wit. Salomon declares himself beaten and rewards Morolf. In a second story Markolf gets Salomon so angry that the king decides to hang Markolf. But again Markolf proves his wit by asking as a last favor to be able to choose the tree where he will be hanged. Of course he cannot find the right tree and is saved.

32   In *Life and Adventure*, Beatrice meets her in Split. Bele tells Beatrice that she met history in the legendary form of her dead grandfather, a story told in *The Wondrous Journeys of Gustav, the World Traveler*. Beatrice tells the reader: "I would have taken the woman for my mouthpiece, if she had not been night blind. She not only clung to me, however, while the two of us wandered through fifty dark cellar rooms, but also stepped on my toes" (193).

Arthurian epic *Parzival*.[33] Beatrice, like Parzival in Wolfram's story, goes on a quest [aventuire] to find the unicorn Anaximander, which, like the Grail, can redeem the world and provide truth and wisdom.[34] Parzival's father in Wolfram's text is Gahmuret. Gahmuret, on one of his crusades to the Orient, meets the black queen Belakane and has a son with her, Feirefiz, who is both black and white. Parzival has to encounter and then befriend his half-brother before he can find the Grail. As in the "Salman and Morolf" epic, another sibling relationship figures in *Parzival* – a mirror relationship, the sibling the alter ego of the main character – which is highly significant for the development and self-definition of the main character. Morgner's repeated use of this constellation to define her own characters in *Life and Adventures* shows how important the doubling of characters is for her text.

Belakane, the Oriental queen and lover of Parzival's father, is Bele H. in *Life and Adventures*. Gahmuret, Parzival's father, appears in two of the poems that Beatrice writes after her "vocal range" has been found. In one poem, "Seegang" ["Motion of the Sea," as well as "Going to Sea" or "Sea Walk"], Gahmuret is a Jesus figure who walks across the water to call out to his apostle Paul (who is Beatrice in the poem) and saves her from drowning when she begins to doubt her faith. In a second, highly erotic poem, "Dach" [Roof], Gahmuret is Beatrice's lover. Gahmuret, who helps Beatrice have faith in herself through love, emphasizes the significance of characters who move between different worlds, cultures (Gahmuret between the Orient and the West), and racial definitions (Feirefiz, Gahmuret's and Belakane's

---

33 Synnöve Clason points to *Parzival* as an intertext for *Life and Adventures* in her essay, "Mit dieser Handschrift wünschte sie in die Historie einzutreten." She focuses on the male figures in the Intermezzos and sees Uwe Parnitzke as another Parzival figure.

34 Anaximander, of course, is a reference to the pre-Socratic philosopher who anticipated some elements of modern developmental philosophy. Morgner explicitly says in the novel that she wants the reader to make the connection to the Greek philosopher. In bk 8, ch. 28, Laura mentions that she chose the name Anaximander because of a commentary of her philosophy teacher. And in bk 8, ch. 15, Laura says about Beatrice: "A woman who had read all the romances of Chrétien de Troyes ought to know who Anaximander was. The medieval chivalric romances were *Bildungsromane*, novels of development. Which were supposed to teach the courtly virtues of *maze* and *treue*" (190).

148

son, is both black and white) for the self-definition of Beatrice (and by implication all women). Morgner's technique of connecting, contrasting, and mirroring figures through intertextual relationships allows her to establish a metonymic chain of signifiers in Jacobson's definition of the term. One signifier points to the next and the chain of representation is never closed. Movement between texts and signifiers replaces definitions and reopens the problem of representation.

Beatrice is connected to the third main character of *Life and Adventures*, Valeska, through allusions to the Bible: both are prophet figures (Valeska wants to redeem the world with her "new testament," and Beatrice is repeatedly called a prophet). They are also connected to Vera Hill through Morgner's parody of the Parzival story. In Wolfram's version, Parzival has to undergo a long development to prove himself worthy of the Grail. Gurnemann, his uncle, is the person who first teaches him about knighthood. Gurnemann advises Parzival not to ask too many questions, a lesson that leads to Parzival's fateful mistake at the Grail castle. He neglects to ask Anfortas, the Grail king, about his deadly wound, which would have shown his sympathy and compassion for the suffering king. Because of Parzival's ignorance and negligence (really Gurnemann's fault), he has to leave the Grail castle and go through another cycle of learning and development.

Gurnemann in *Life and Adventures* is the physicist and boss of Vera Hill (and the friend of Wenzel Morolf [394]) and indirectly causes her death. Although he is one of the more supportive men in a male-dominated GDR society (especially true for the scientific community Vera has entered), he is the reason for Vera's accident because he does not understand her difficult position as a scientist and single mother. Vera has to use a shorter path on a tightrope to get to work in the morning, since otherwise she cannot manage her two jobs as mother and scientist. Because Gurnemann neglects to ask her about her difficulties and does not support her against the criticism of her neighbors, Vera loses her balance and dies. A connection between Vera and Beatrice is established not only through the allusion to *Parzival*, but also through her strange and highly metaphorical death from losing her balance, a death that is later repeated by Beatrice, who loses her balance while cleaning Laura's windows. The status of woman as a tightrope dancer between different realities and discourses, affected by all of these discourses and outside of them at the same time, assuming a place on the borderlines (tightropes) of different definitions, is Morgner's metaphor for woman.[35] Their place is a nonplace and their identity a nonidentity.

The Concept of Difference

In addition to Morgner's refusal to define a positive and stable female subject based on a positive "female essence" that is different from men's, her texts consciously destroy the concept of difference as such. Her main techniques are mimesis and masquerade. In fact, *Life and Adventures* is full of people who cross-dress and change gender positions: the "feminine" man Benno, who turns into a male Scheherazade figure at the end of the novel; the "masculine" woman Laura, who ironically behaves like a typical male in the story "Kaffee verkehrt"; Beatrice herself, who when she enters the GDR thinks that she awoke at a time when conditions for women had improved and accordingly acts unfettered, which is perceived as typical macho behavior by the men she meets; or Valeska, the woman who pretends to be and looks like a man after having gone through a sudden sex change, and who from that time on oscillates between the sexes. All these figures defy the notion of gender difference as sexual difference. In fact, the story of Valeska Kantus proves that sexual differences are not natural, but are constructed by various cultural "technologies of gender" (De Lauretis's term), which include the power to control social meaning and to produce representations of gender. The penis, Valeska finds out, is a "scepter of power," a "privileging uniform" ["Herrschaftszepter" (428), "privile-

35 Another metaphor for woman that is repeatedly used in Morgner's texts is that of the woman as a traveler, a person in constant movement. Almost all of Morgner's main characters are travelers: In *Wedding in Constantinople*, Bele H. decides on a trip to Constantinople that she cannot stay with her fiancé. In *The Wondrous Journeys*, Gustav is a "world traveler." In *Gauklerlegende* the heroine meets Rade, a traveling buffoon. In *Life and Adventures* Laura is a trolley car driver and in *Amanda* the snake Arke has to travel the world to help Beatrice to find her lost tongue.

gierende Uniform" (429)]. Her new male prerogatives are based on a political interpretation of a little difference between men and women rather than a natural superiority of the male sex. The difference between man and woman is unmasked as an artificial distinction between two arbitrary categories (that of "man" and that of "woman"), which operates in patriarchal societies to lock women into the position of objects of male desire. The text shows that definitions of gender difference are a matter of societal negotiations rather than essential differences; they *de*fine and *con*fine people. With our traditional gender categories shown to be arbitrary, the concept of difference itself is criticized or at least questioned. In the last instance, the notion of difference only makes sense when it is defined in relation to a specific historic and political situation.

Morgner does not deny that differences exist between men and women and between individual persons, but she shows that these differences are always operative in specific political situations and can never be fixed categories. Valeska Kantus, for example, consciously decides to keep her male body without giving up her female past, since in her specific historical situation (the GDR of the 1970s), this strategy allows her to gain experiences that she can reveal to other women as her "gospel." Since Valeska believes it is time for women to question the supposedly natural subordination of the category "woman" under the category "man," she makes the "pragmatic" decision to write down her story to encourage women to develop "faith in themselves" and to try out similar "temporary sex changes" (465). In view of women's lack of "geistigem Fanatismus" ["intellectual fanaticism/fervor"] (169), this is the appropriate strategy for Valeska, since her experiences might help women to question and redefine their female identity. Valeska's statement that she would also have herself crucified if that would convince women to act, indicates that Valeska understands her "gospel" as a pragmatic political strategy that is fit for the present historic and political circumstances, not as another fixed and universal truth (465). In fact, she calls her actions "friedenserpresserische Mittel" [means that can extort peace] that are appropriate at a time "of danger that humanity will destroy itself through wars" (465). It is Valeska's goal to encourage women to try out a similar sex change to understand how the concept of difference operates in a specific historical situation. She does not set out to define the concept of difference abstractly to affirm women's difference and celebrate some kind of feminine essence – a kind of "difference from." Instead, she insists on this concept as a relative category and an ideological construct that needs to be analyzed and put to political use in a specific political situation.

In Morgner's text, "reality" itself becomes a network of different discourses. Many critics have pointed out that Morgner uses the fantastic as a subversive strategy.[36] But even more radically, Morgner forces her readers to accept that the opposition between reality and fiction does not work for her text at all. Fantastic figures like the mermaid Melusine work together with "realistic" figures like East German workingwoman Laura Salman; fantastic events like movements through time and history or sex changes occur consecutively with realistic descriptions of everyday events; and texts on radically different levels of realism are treated equally. Fairy tales, legends, and myths acquire the same reality in *Life and Adventures* as legal and historical documents, or interviews and so-called "factual documents." Texts that are prominently designated as "documents," "witness reports," or "true stories" are shown to be something different. For example, in "The gist of Laura's notes on the trobadora's memories of the real Raimbaut d'Aurenga, who doesn't correspond to reality", the "real Raimbaut d'Aurenga" turns out to be an ideal model of the nonpatriarchal man (bk. 1, ch. 18). "Real" thus represents an ideal that makes sense to Beatrice rather than designating actuality. The borderline between "truth" and "fiction" is consciously brought into flux. Moreover, the same words that Beatrice had put into the mouth of her ideal lover Raimbaut in Book 1 are repeated by Benno later in the novel when he introduces himself to Laura in his "third information visit" (bk. 10, ch. 17). Thus, it becomes impossible to distinguish fact from fiction, truth from lies, original from imitation, and the reader is constantly made aware of this impossibility.[37] Our so-called

36   Compare, for example, Patricia Herminghouse's important article on Morgner, "Die Frau und das Phantastische," 248–66.
37   Morgner plays with the term "document" from the very beginning of the novel in "Vorsätze" [Foreword]. Morgner, who appears as a character in this prologue

"facts" are in the last instance nothing but parts of different texts. Reality as a concept that is pre-textual is constantly put into doubt.

Another strategy Morgner uses to show that our concept of reality is a construct and a particular interpretation of certain events can be observed in Valeska Kantus's "Hadische Erzählungen," which she writes on the back pages of a scientific treatise about the artificial production of protein.[38] She calls her fantastic counteressays, which discuss Valeska's position as a female scientist in a male-dominated scientific community, "Paralipomena [Greek: "left-out material"] for a Man" (225). In defiance of a bad reality that makes it hard for her to do research as a female scientist, since she always has to do a second shift at home, she writes "margin notes" that question the authority of our traditional scientific discourse by adding her own version of the facts to those of a male scientific discourse. In close proximity to Jean François Lyotard, Valeska points out that "doing science" involves its own kind of legitimization.[39] It means that certain narratives about reality are permitted while others are not. To explain why she hides her own magical abilities, Valeska says, for example:

> Because doing magic is classified among the successful but industrially not exploitable laboratory experiments. With fairylike abilities you can at best perform in the circus nowadays. Valeska wanted a scientific career. In an institute that employed 157 scientists, among them 11 women. Clemens read with colored pens and a ruler. Valeska devoured. He preferred books that put the world in

calls the manuscript she has bought from Laura "Dokumente" [documents] and "Zeugnisse" [witness reports]. In the "Bauplan" [construction plan] at the end of the novel, the following words are examples of how Morger plays with the concept of " truth" vs "fictions": "document" (8: 15), "protocol" (1: 11, 18), "proofs" (1: 15), "descriptions" (1: 1, 2: 11, 4: 3, 5, 17, 8: 26), "descriptions of true events" (1: 27), "Aufzeichnungen" [manuscripts] (2: 5, 6), "eidesstattliche Erklärung" [sworn statements] (4: 6), "report" (4: 9, 10, 7: 2, 10: 19), "witness reports" (8: 25, 11: 19), "Billanz" [summary report] (11: 25), "Meldung" ["announcement"] (12: 34), "Übersicht" [list of content] (1: 13, 26), "interview" (1: 11, 8: 2, 11: 2), "business negotiations" (8: 6), and "speech" (10: 8, 11: 8, 11) are only some examples.

38 This is obviously a reference to E. T. A. Hoffmann's *Kater Murr*. Patricia Herminghouse and other scholars have pointed out the many allusions to texts by authors of the Romantic period, especially to E. T. A. Hoffmann and Jean Paul.
39 Compare Lyotard, *The Postmodern Condition*.

order. She preferred books that described how to make a world. [...] A female scientist who is unmasked as a fairy would logically, in view of the often cited fact that women's brains on average weigh less than men's, cast suspicions of mysticism on her female professional colleagues also. (229–30)

Valeska has to disguise her magic and can only talk about it on the back pages of scientific treatises, because her forms of knowledge are not legitimate in the scientific community. In Valeska's narrative, Clemens's thinking, which aims at "ordering the world" and treats nature as something outside of the self, is legitimate. In contrast, Valeska's scientific work, which aims at "creating the world" and includes the subject in the process of analysis, is not allowed because the scientific discourse in Valeska's institute is based on the clear separation between researchers and their object (nature). Not only are Valeska's reading practices and her recourse to magic excluded from the scientific legitimization, but so are the narrative forms she uses to talk about nature. Valeska's description of the dandelion (which follows the quoted paragraph after one more front-page paragraph about the digestion of protein) is a good example. Valeska's discussion of the chemical components of the dandelion's leaves is a first-person narrative written from the point of view of the dandelion:

> The young leaves, rich in vitamins A and C and bitter substances, are harvested by the retired Herr Nussek as a wild vegetable. After that they pass through a basket, bowls, mouths, stomachs, and intestines. The retiree drinks infusions of my leaves and roots when he's lost his appetite, has indigestion or liver disorders; whosoever eats my flesh and drinks my blood will abide in me and I in him. [...] Sometimes I'd like to be a plant, for example, a dandelion, or lesbian. (233)

Clearly, Valeska's narratives on the back pages break with the conventions of scientific discourse, since she does not treat nature as an object that the scientist talks *about* but instead understands it as a subject with whom the researcher enters into dialogue.

Later in the novel, the reader finds out that Rudolf Uhlenbrook, the author of the front pages of Valeska's "Hadische Erzählungen," is Valeska's partner and the father of her son. Both Rudolf and Valeska talk about the same scientific theory, but Valeska's back pages include the story of the *production* of the scientific theory as part of the scientific narrative. The scientist's personal situatedness (the narrative of

154

Valeska's marriage and divorce from Uwe, the circumstances of her abortion, her relationship to Clemens, her position as a female scientist in a scientific institution dominated by men, and her new life in a "family of women and children" with Rudolf as the visiting father) are for Valeska important elements in the history of the scientific treatise. While Rudolf concentrates on the scientific results on the front pages, Valeska talks about the authors' personal contexts of the theory on the back pages. Through Valeska's strategy of pointing out that the scientific discourse functions through the selection of certain forms of knowledge as pertinent and the exclusion of others as unscientific, her marginalia deconstruct the scientific process of legitimization as producing the *only* adequate model of some outside reality. For Valeska, in contrast, scientific discourse is *one* possibility of constructing a narrative about reality. In this sense, Valeska's tales are not counterimages (218), as Uwe maintains, but part of Valeska's reality. Without the recognition that her own position as woman and scientist is one of constant tension, she would not be able to deal with the everyday contradictions in her life:

> He [Uwe] said, "Fantasy is an escape, a sign of capitulation." I [Valeska] said, "On the contrary, it's a sign of sovereignty. Indeed, of sovereign treatment of the stuff of reality, as children do when they draw pictures, for example. [...] in principle, I have to accept my situation as it is. And I do, no one can step out of history, I'm coming to terms with it. But not passively. That would be the end of me. Without the suspense that I create on the backs of manuscript pages to refresh my body and soul, I'd be a dead loss as a scientist. My optimism, my cheerfulness live on this suspense between the poles of reality and Communism; without this suspense I would lose the ability to love men." (225–6)

Valeska shows that the position of the scientist influences his or her scientific results. It determines the kind of questions the scientists asks and shapes the way he or she conducts research.

At the same time, Valeska points out that scientific discourse is not free from ideology. She criticizes the gender roles assigned to men and women in science. Although scientific representations are supposedly a reproduction for subjectivity, of an objectivity that lies outside it (Jameson's phrasing), Valeska's narratives point out that in this reproduction, neither scientists nor their object (nature) are gender neutral. For women like Valeska not to adapt to a male scientific discourse, and therefore "be suspected of being mythical," means to be thought of as part of nature. When Valeska begins to perform scientific miracles for Clemens by letting him taste from her flesh during their lovemaking and then replacing it with artificially produced meat, Clemens is encouraged in his tendency to "mythologize woman" (230). Valeska explains that this male tendency "to mythologize woman" means to believe in "the division of labor between human beings and nature," i.e. in this ideology, human beings are men and nature is woman (230). The ideology that is at the foundation of science even today, Valeska points out, is one of man's domination over nature.

Thus, Valeska's "Stories from Hades" point out that science has a flip side to it. Her questions that compose the "back side" of science are those of scientific legitimization. Why are certain language games permitted in scientific discourse and others not? What "master narrative" (Lyotard) is the foundation for our traditional form of scientific discourse? What kind of ideology is functional in the shaping of the specific rules of scientific discourse? Valeska does not say that science is false or has to be abandoned; instead, she wants to show that other perspectives are possible. In this sense, Morgner operates in close proximity to Lyotard, who also criticizes what he calls our "meta-narratives" for their exclusiveness.

Entering History

Morgner not only thinks about the ideological foundations of the discourse of the natural sciences, however. History, as another narrative with specific linguistic rules and a specific "grand récit" at its basis, is repeatedly questioned in its traditional role. One example is Beatrice's description of Diocletian's palace in Split. Her travel log contains observations that are very different from the descriptions of the palace in travel guides. Beatrice does not talk about the sculptures, Romanic bell tower, or the emperor's mausoleum, but concentrates instead on what she calls the "infiltration of the tyrant's fortress" [die

156

Unterwanderung des tyrannischen Baus] (199) by the Salonites in the seventh century. She writes:

> Diocletian had had the palace built in ten years and moved into it in 305 A.D., after he supposedly had voluntarily renounced the Roman throne. His retirement seat was originally a combination of luxurious villa, Roman army camp, and Hellenistic fortress. In 615 A.D., when Avars and Slavs destroyed the once mighty Salona during their advance to the sea from the North, the homeless Salonites sought refuge within the solid walls of Diocletian's palace. At first, the palace's spacious cellar rooms served as the Salonites' dwelling place. Later they continued on through the institutions of the edifice by transforming the representative imperial premises into apartments. In the style of the respective historical period. New buildings were erected too, wherever there was space. In the course of centuries, honeycomb was joined to honeycomb. (200)

Instead of speaking about emperors, military victories, and other historical "accomplishments," Beatrice is interested in a process seldom described in history books. The "major figures" of the past do not interest Beatrice, as in traditional historical writings; she is interested in the process of "rewriting" [Überschreiben] reality through narratives about it. While the traditional accounts of the palace's history emphasize the beautiful and monumental aspects of the palace, Beatrice is fascinated by what she calls the "practical" and "human" aspects of the palace's history. She says, for example:

> I paid and entered the palace through the south gate. Which is avoided by photographers of postcards and art books. Because it is the least profitable, museum-wise. The entire south face of Diocletian's palace is the least profitable, museum-wise. The palm trees in front of the south face are perhaps supposed to soften the impression of irreverence, but in fact they intensify it. These trees, withered by heat and street dust, are useless for idylls. [...] History is located behind the palisade. In a natural, almost human manifestation. (198–9)

Beatrice is most impressed by the traces of everyday life visible in the less monumental and sometimes even ugly details of the palace. Her narrative about Split is formed from the bottom up, not the other way around, as in the accounts that we are used to. She concentrates on those details that tell small, local stories about everyday events. The contrast between historical narratives in travel guides and Beatrice's own narrative about the palace emphasizes again that history is a construct. In fact, Beatrice treats history as a palimpsest, as a text that contains different layers of writing.[40] The palace seems to illustrate this concept perfectly: the building itself shows that in the course of history, different people used it for different purposes. All added the stories of their own realities to the building by leaving their inscriptions in the structure of the monument. Stories are written on top of earlier stories and traces of different pasts can be found in the structure of the building. The past persists as an encoded message (for example, the traces of a variety of different events in the structure of a building like the palace) to be read or ignored. As Leslie Adelson puts it in her book *Making Bodies, Making History*, "*[W]hich* messages we choose to read and *how* we decode by encoding them in our own tongue depend on which questions we ask of our present in selecting our history from among many."[41] As in much recent scholarship, history is perceived as a dynamic construct, in flux and subject to constant revision; it becomes a mediation of signs interpreted as messages from the past.[42] In this sense, the "infiltration of the tyrant's fortress by the Salonites" also functions as a metaphor in Beatrice's report for a new way to think about history. Just as the Salonites used those aspects of the building that served their interests and did not let the monumental and beautiful elements of the palace prevent them from constructing their own reality, Beatrice wants women to use those historical traces that might help them to construct their own version of history.

In this sense, the "infiltration of the tyrant's palace by the Salonites" also functions as a metaphor in Beatrice's report for a new way of thinking about history. Just as the Salonites used those aspects of the building that served their interests and did not let the monumental and beautiful elements of the palace prevent them from constructing their own reality, Morgner wants women to appropriate history and

40 As a technical term, palimpsest is a parchment or tablet used one or more times after earlier writing has been erased. The French narratologist Gérard Genette turned palimpsest into a metaphor for intertextuality in his book *Palimpsestes* (Paris: Seuil, 1982).

41 Leslie A. Adelson, *Making Bodies, Making History: Feminism and German Identity* (Lincoln: University of Nebraska Press, 1993), 26.

42 Leslie Adelson gives a detailed discussion of this concept of history in *Making Bodies, Making History*; see especially chapter 1.

leave their own traces. To decode women's barely visible messages in the monumental versions of official history, we need to distance ourselves from the official patriarchal historical discourse, or as Morgner puts it, we need to exit history temporarily. With this critical distance, women might be able to discover other, unspectacular, almost invisible traces as they might be left by different disadvantaged groups in history. This way of looking at history from a different perspective, which is at the same time a type of rewriting of history, is so important because "nobody can do without the support of history," as Bele H. explains to Beatrice (202) and as Morgner herself argued in front of the Writers' Union in 1974:

> The great Greek culture originated in a slaveholding order. The present culture's great accomplishments in the arts, the sciences, and in technology are based on an order in which women have the status of slaves. This basis-function of women has gone totally unnoticed, but it has nevertheless been historically formative, and not only indirectly. If women are currently starting to want to be people, i.e., to appropriate nature – first of all their own –, they need knowledge of their own history for a head start and for the will to resist. To reverse, after economic expropriation, the historical as well, to make those who uphold our state aware that their legendary history is a head start, that, in my opinion, is the great task of literature.[43]

Again, it is a taking-seriously and a making-visible of concrete traces of women's lives that have been suppressed in a male-dominated historicism. Against the great "accomplishments" and the "fame" of a male-centered historicism, Morgner talks about women's "geschichtsbildende Basisfunktionen" [the function of shaping history through images].

At more than one point in *Life and Adventures*, Morgner compares women's efforts to become subjects and "enter history" to the activity of an archeologist, as the "excavating of women's vocal range" [das Freilegen der eigenen Stimmlage]. The second chapter of book 2, for example, is called "Beatrice's vocal range is uncovered" [Beatrizens Stimmlage wird freigelegt]. The narrator tells us: "Finally she realized that she could no longer compose scholastic cansos, those imitations with disguised tenor, baritone, bass. Imperceptibly, perhaps

43   Morgner, "Rede auf dem VII. Schriftstellerkongreß," 112–13.

on the brutal paths of humiliation, her own vocal range had been uncovered" (58). Morgner does not call for the *voice* of Woman that needs to be found. She does not promote the search for the *one* meaning of history, for the cause and effect of certain historical events. Instead, she speaks of women's *vocal range* that needs to be uncovered. The first translation of "Stimmlage" in German is "pitch" or "register" of the voice. "Lage" can also mean layer, position, situation, or condition. Together with the verb "freilegen," a verb that is mostly used for the activity of an archeologist, Morgner creates a range of possible meanings and associations here that describe the novelty of the process involved in rethinking our everyday reality from women's perspectives. At the same time, Morgner's choice of words evokes Foucault's concept of historical science as an "archeology of knowledge."[44] The process that Morgner describes is the search for the possibility of different layers of meaning inside our traditional historical narratives. There might not be one voice of women in which to speak; instead it is important that we experiment with different possibilities of speaking.

The breaks in the traditional discourse that can be discovered in the structure of the palace in Split might allow for different, nontraditional possibilities of thinking. We might be able to think about a different kind of historical discourse, one that might include the history of women into its logic. Beatrice says in her report about Split:

> In Split I comprehend a woman's skin. In contrast to her brothers, who sit in university chairs thinking about the world, she tastes of it. That is why Laura is crossed by streets and tracks and rivers which deposit objects in the fabric of her body, animate objects and inanimate ones. [...] How many Lauras does the world structure of today need in order to be marbled with Lauras? (202–3)

Just as the palace contains inscriptions of different pasts in its structure, so does history leave its inscriptions in women. Beatrice makes clear that the way we conceive of history directly influences our thinking. On the one hand, we are part of this history and cannot think outside of these structures; on the other hand, we are also agents of history and can choose which messages of the past we want to read

44   Cf. Michel Foucault, *The Archeology of Knowledge*, S. Smith (trans.) (New York: Harper & Row, 1976).

and use. Beatrice compares women to the Salonites who infiltrated the palace of Diocletian because women – their stories and their living conditions – represent "breaks" in the great narratives of our patriarchal culture. Just as the palace's monumentality was undermined by the traces of the Salonites' everyday activities, women's realities disrupt the smooth representation of patriarchal history as a history of monuments. If we succeed in reimagining and rewriting our historical narratives from the different perspectives of women, our world building might in fact become infiltrated like the Diocletian palace or "marbled by Lauras," as Morgner says. The effort to add women's stories to our traditional historical narratives does not simply involve a recovering of women's unwritten histories; it also means uncovering and rethinking the structures and ideological foundations that are at the basis of our traditional accounts of history.

The deconstructive strategies in the quoted passage from *Die wundersamen Reisen* from 1972, the artistic play with intertexts in *Life and Adventures*, and the radical questioning of prevailing notions of the stable and unified subject or a given reality "out there" show that Morgner's discourse is markedly different from most other feminist texts of the 1970s. While other feminist texts from that time defined gender difference as sexual difference in order to criticize the male practice of excluding the feminine perspective, to define a distinct female tradition, and to create social spaces in which sexual difference itself could be affirmed, Morgner, by contrast, does not rely on the notion of sexual difference or "authentic experience." On the contrary, Morgner's text deconstructs the metaphysical grounds of concepts like "Nature," the "Subject," the "Author," "Science," "History," and "Reality" writ large; Morgner's close affinity to postmodernism is evident.

As a postmodernist text, Morgner's 1974 novel ties in to key questions about the differences between and the intersections of postmodernist and feminist theories, questions that were not debated until the early 1980s. The contribution of a text like *Life and Adventures* to the debate on postmodernism is all the more surprising because since Morgner's novel was written at a time when GDR literature was supposedly just starting to catch up with literary modernism.[45] No

---

45   Emmerich, *Kleine Literaturgeschichte*, 284.

wonder, then, that the postmodernist elements were overlooked in the early responses to the novel. While there was little doubt in the secondary literature on *Life and Adventures* that Morgner's text displayed a feminist consciousness (even if Morgner did not agree with the definition "feminist" for herself), the question of whether her aesthetic strategies succeeded in making a political impact led to disagreement among critics. Similarly, in the debate about postmodernism, questions about the critical potential of postmodernist texts, the political nature of postmodernism itself, and the usefulness of an alliance of postmodernism and feminism have been at the center of interest.[46] Let me now suggest some ways that a text like Morgner's *Life and Adventures* has unwittingly contributed to this debate.

The Postmodernism Debate

The connection between postmodernism and feminism has provoked much discussion. One of the main charges made against postmodernism by critics in the tradition of Frankfurt School critical theory, such as Jürgen Habermas and Fredric Jameson – although for different reasons – has been that postmodernism as a cultural phenomenon does not preserve a critical potential and as such is politically irrelevant or even dangerously neoconservative.[47] The charges of a lack of histori-

---

46   I would argue with Susan Suleiman and Andreas Huyssen that while it is possible to read postmodernism chiefly as a formal category and to oppose it as such to modernism, such an effort is of limited interest. A postmodernist practice in the arts has provoked controversy when it was understood as a cultural intervention rather than an object of descriptive poetics. The debate on postmodernism that has been going on since the 1980s is a debate about postmodernism as a cultural category. See Susan Rubin Suleiman, "Feminism and Postmodernism," in Ingeborg Hoesterey (ed.), *Zeitgeist in Babel: The Postmodern Controversy* (Bloomington: Indiana University Press), 111–30, esp. 113; and Huyssen, "Mapping the Postmodern," 9.

47   In a debate with Jean-François Lyotard, Habermas identified the notion of postmodernity with French poststructuralism, which he attacked as the (neo)-conservative position of those who believe that modernity has failed and that the

cal consciousness and political relevance cannot be made against feminism, a movement that by definition is political, with its goal of improving the position and status of women in society. Moreover, from the beginning, the reexamination of history from a feminist perspective has been of utmost importance for feminist critics. Feminism, unlike *post*modernism, is said to have its foundations in the discourses of modernity, and is usually defined as part of modernity's more general emancipatory project. If one looks at the terms of the debate on postmodernism, then, there seems to be a myriad of differences between the two movements.

These basic differences between feminism and postmodernism have been challenged, however, not only by artistic practices that use postmodern strategies to support feminist goals, but also by theorists who began to examine the political implications of the intersection of a "feminist critique of patriarchy and a poststructuralist critique of representation."[48] Critics like Craig Owens, Hal Foster, Andreas Huyssen, or

utopian impulses it gave rise to should therefore be abandoned. But modernity or "the project of Enlightenment," Habermas argues from the point of view of his own emancipatory philosophy of rational consensus, is not an obsolete project, only an unfinished one. What should be rejected, in Habermas's opinion, is not modernity, but the neoconservative ideology of postmodernity. (Compare his famous Adorno-Preisrede from 1980, translated as "Modernity versus Postmodernity," *New German Critique*, 22 (1981), 3–14.) While Fredric Jameson, unlike Habermas, deals with postmodernism as something that has to be reckoned with, he similarly comes to a negative evaluation of postmodernism, a term he equates with postmodernity. Jameson argues that as a typical outgrowth of a late capitalism, postmodernism lacks historical consciousness and is unable to preserve critical distance. He charges that postmodernism does not only replicate the logic of late capitalism, but reinforces and intensifies it. Postmodernism's intertextuality, in his view, is "a field of stylistic and discursive heterogeneity without a norm" and "a blank parody, a statue with blind eyeballs" ("Postmodernism, or the Cultural Logic of Late Capitalism," 65). While many have pointed out that both Habermas and Jameson have raised important questions, and that the argument of both critics is more complex than has usually been stated in the rather heated debate on postmodernism, I will admit to similarly simplifying both of their arguments here for the sake of brevity.

48   Craig Owens, "The Discourse of Others: Feminists and Postmodernism," in Hal Foster (ed.), *The Anti-Aesthetic: Essays on Postmodern Culture* (Seattle: Bay, 1983), 59.

more recently Linda Hutcheon, all placed feminist issues at the center of the debate on postmodernism and emphasized the common interests of both movements.[49] Andreas Huyssen spoke of a new "postmodernism of resistance" created by the women's movement, the ecology movement, anti-imperialism, and a growing awareness of "other, non-European, non-Western cultures."[50] Linda Hutcheon, in *Politics of Postmodernism,* pointed to the overlapping agendas between postmodernism and feminism. While there are other voices that have suggested the political potential of postmodernist works, the feminist aspect of postmodernism allowed for a new, more politically acute view of postmodernism itself.[51] In fact, the debate on postmodernism has been greatly enriched by the discussions about the possible usefulness of postmodernist strategies for the political purposes of different marginalized groups. These discussions have allowed for a reevaluation of the critical potential of many postmodernist texts.

While the tendency to point to common interests between postmodernism and feminism seems unusually harmonious in the debate on postmodernism, there have also been warning voices from feminist critics that underscore the complexity and problematic nature of the argument. For many feminists, the main concern with the connection between postmodernism and feminism is the political status of the "decentered subject" in postmodern texts, a concept that seems to question a theory of personal agency.[52] Such a theory of agency,

---

49   Compare, for example, Andreas Huyssen's remarks: "The ways in which we now raise the questions of gender and sexuality, reading and writing, subjectivity and enunciation, voice and performance are unthinkable without the impact of feminism, even though many of these activities may take place on the margin or even outside the movement proper" ("Mapping the Postmodern," 220).

50   Ibid., 52.

51   Susan Suleiman sums up this shift in the debate on the status of postmodernism in the following ironic way: "In short, feminism brings to postmodernism the political guarantee postmodernism needs in order to feel respectable as an avant-garde practice. Postmodernism, in turn, brings feminism into a certain kind of 'high theoretical' discourse on the frontiers of culture, traditionally an exclusively male domain" ("Feminism and Postmodernism," 116).

52   Wolfgang Welsch has pointed out that the transformation of our conception of the subject is at the center of the debate on postmodernism. The criticism of the subject has been rejected, he maintains, because it seemed to lead to a weakening

however, is necessary for feminism (and any other political movement) to guarantee the possibility of political change. Although interested in a deconstruction of (mis)representations, feminists cannot stop there. They need to develop a theory of positive action, create spaces of discourse, rewrite cultural narratives, and define the terms of a different perspective – a view from "elsewhere." What Teresa de Lauretis calls the "twofold pull in contrary directions" of feminist theory becomes visible precisely at the intersection between postmodernism and feminism. She calls this tension "the critical negativity of its theory, and the affirmative positivity of its politics."[53] That is, feminist theory has to be interested in a radical critique of dominant discourses on gender, but on the other hand, it also has to develop a theory of positive political action, thereby necessarily having to rely on restricting definitions itself.

The tension between a critical deconstructive impulse and the need for a positive theory of political action noted by de Lauretis is already present in Morgner's texts. *Life and Adventures* explores the contradictions between these two tendencies in feminism and offers suggestions for a political practice that takes this dilemma into account. Morgner's parody of the discourses of different feminist groups – not only in East Germany, but also in the West, where feminist debates could take place more openly – proves her interest in the definition of woman and the consequences such a definition might have for the political strategy of different feminist groups.

The first feminist position depicted in *Life and Adventures* is represented by Persephone and Demeter, who have been dethroned by God and the devil and spend their lives in a bunker singing matriarchal revenge songs. These two goddesses, who are the first women

of the autonomous subject and the responsible citizen, the basis for any political criticism until today. Welsch argues, however, that the postmodern criticism of the subject does not necessarily lead to the "death of the subject," as has often been maintained, but on the contrary needs to be understood as the criticism of a certain type of subject. For Welsch, the challenge that presents itself to us today is to come to a different conception of the subject, a subject that would be able to deal with the plurality of our modern reality. Welsch calls this new type of subject the "vielheitsfähige Subjekt" ("Subjektsein heute. Überlegungen zur Transformation des Subjekts," *Deutsche Zeitschrift für Philosophie*, 39:4 (1991), 347–65).

53   De Lauretis, *Technologies of Gender*, 26.

to give Beatrice advice, represent a separatist wing of feminism whose goal is to overturn patriarchy so that women can assume power. Persephone's radical separatist feminism is quickly rejected by Beatrice as a strategy that only reverses power structures rather than questioning them:

> But just as it had eight hundred and eight years ago, a holding cell landed suddenly at her [Beatrice's] feet. It was made of concrete, cube shaped, about eight cubic meters in size. […] A song in two-part harmony rang out thorough the vents. As she had done so long ago, Beatrice followed the instructions for removing the iron poles from the hooks. The door was pushed open from the inside – the same as before. And the song swelled with that zealous resolve which Beatrice always found offensive. But she masked her aversion with a smile and listened to several programmatic songs. The first part was sung by the divine daughter, the second by the divine mother. Mouths agape, eyes turned inward, Persephone and Demeter were actually singing the same old songs of revenge and prophesying the reinstatement of the matriarchy. […] Beatrice was informed hypnopedically by her sister-in-law of the goddesses' reactionary endeavours and quickly decided in favor of the third order. Which was to be neither matriarchal nor patriarchal, but human. (15–16)

The bunker and the goddesses' "inward view" are indications of their inability to look beyond their immediate political goals. By focusing only on their own agenda and on women, they merely replace one center (men) with another (women), without being able to analyze the mechanisms and structures that lead to the marginalization of different groups in society. Because this strategy leads to a reversal of power structures rather than a questioning of these very structures, Beatrice decides to support the "third order which was to be neither matriarchal nor patriarchal, but human."

Beatrice's sister-in-law, the mermaid Melusine, who believes the primary goal for women to be the overthrow of capitalism, represents a second group of feminists for whom the first step is a socialist revolution, after which women's struggle for equality will be easier, if not automatic:

> The agitprop art is to be produced for capitalist relations, the overthrow of which is the focus of Melusine's illegal activity. Battle cry of the requisite protest songs: A woman today who can afford to have character must be a socialist. (105)

166

Melusine and Laura, a GDR working woman who is also a loyal socialist (although she is the first to admit that reforms of "real existing socialism" in the GDR are overdue), are convinced that Beatrice lacks pragmatism, without which political change will be impossible. They scold her for her absolutism and for her seemingly naive belief in fantasy, poetry, and magic as the only means to change society truly. Although Beatrice's position constantly challenges the customs and "normal" beliefs of the people she meets, Laura wants her to become more politically active. She suggests that Beatrice move to Berlin, become the editor of a women's magazine, and work practically toward the emancipation of women.

Since Laura advocates a feminism that allows women to act and make political decisions, she is convinced that magic, subversive as it may be, is a "private solution for cowards." Laura emphasizes that women cannot escape personal responsibility for their actions and need to develop a practical and realistic political strategy. She says:

> Accepting the realities wouldn't have to mean wholesale affirmation, she continued. In any case, the process of life demanded pride, realpolitik, a talent for improvisation. And consisted of the ability to struggle through. Miracles, okay, but no private ones for slackers. (114)

Beatrice, on the other hand, argues that in a "hopeless situation," "miracles" can be necessary for women to gain a subject position from which to speak. Women might have to leave history temporarily to be able to analyze the foundations of our concept of history and reality "from the outside." While Beatrice knows, of course, that such a movement is only possible with the help of miracles, she nevertheless pleads for a critical analysis of the foundations of our culture:

> Beatrice called Laura squeamish. Facing realities could only be judged a sign of strength if you had good luck. "A person who is condemned to life imprisonment and doesn't make plans to escape is not proud but cowardly. Didn't you also bewail the lack of solidarity among women? That's natural among those who have been humiliated for millennia. Their hope of escaping from a hopeless situation could only be based on miracles, that is, on individual actions. I have exited history because I wanted to enter history. To appropriate nature. First of all, my own. Tackle the making of humanity head-on. The end justifies all magical means. Prosit." (114–15)

Just like Bele H.'s position in *Die wundersamen Reisen*, whose words Beatrice repeats almost verbatim, Beatrice points out that the metaphysical grounds of core concepts of our Western culture are really part of a male ideology that excludes women. In this sense, Beatrice represents the view from "elsewhere," a third feminist position. In fact, Beatrice's strategies are very similar to deconstructive reading practices. Yet from Beatrice's position, any *practical* political action seems difficult, since these actions require different concepts and definitions that again would be subject to deconstructive readings.

On the one hand, the depictions of these different women parody debates among feminist groups in the two Germanies at the time. It reveals the closed-mindedness of certain groups of feminists who fought each other, rather than the circumstances that led to their oppression. On the other hand, the depiction of different camps of feminists is not only humorous, but also philosophical and political in nature. On her journey through time and history, Beatrice oscillates between these last two positions: Laura's pragmatism, which seeks concrete political results based on a fixed subject position, and Beatrice's own more deconstructive movement, which radically questions its foundations. Since a deconstruction of the concept of feminine identity is included in this process, any concrete positive political action is difficult. Through the debates between the women, which include multiple switches in positions, overlappings, and contradictions, the reader understands that it is not only the definitions of men and a patriarchal society that have serious consequences for women's position and status in society, but also self-definitions formulated by different women and feminist groups. These definitions are necessary to be able to act politically, but they are also restricting and exclusive.

The text never makes clear what the definition of woman should finally be. At first it seems that Beatrice, after returning from her unsuccessful attempt to find the unicorn Anaximander, whose horn could save the world and solve all problems, resigns herself to the existing conditions and adopts Laura's pragmatism, becoming more and more like her friend. But this assimilation of the two women is depicted as problematic and full of contradictions. When Laura realizes that Beatrice is becoming like herself, she warns her: "[D]o you want to double me? Do you want to render yourself superfluous?" (415). Laura, having tried to educate Beatrice to become more realistic, understands that Beatrice's position is an important element in women's struggle to gain subject status. Both of these roles are needed: the pragmatism *and* the miracles that serve as a deconstructive element that challenges the foundations of what we call "reality."[54] In fact, Laura and Beatrice seem to switch roles: while Beatrice becomes concerned with everyday life (and dies from it while cleaning windows), Laura falls sick with "Fernweh" and is finally elected to the Round Table of the Queen of Sheba in Beatrice's place. Laura finds the utopian man Benno in the end, but instead of engaging in a traditional heterosexual marriage, they switch gender roles in their partnership. While Laura mourns the loss of her friend and alter ego Beatrice, Benno assumes the role of Scheherazade, telling nightly stories in Beatrice's style to save, i.e. justify, his existence. While it seems at first that the Beatricean element is dropped in the end, the irony of the ending, together with Benno's repetition of the very first words of the novel – "[O]f course this land is a place of wonders" – encourages the readers to begin the dialogue anew, a task that Morgner herself took on in *Amanda*, the second part of her *Salman* trilogy.[55] Neither Laura nor Beatrice is

54 Angelika Bammer makes a similar point in her discussion of *Life and Adventures*. She writes: "If the Lauras of this world are not to be stuck forever coping with dirty diapers, polluted cities, and oppressive relationships, they must also be able to imagine that alternatives exist. They must periodically 'step out of history' to prevent the future from being exhausted by its own past. [...] Beatrice's fantasies are as important as Laura's productivity. Beatrice thus embodies Morgner's challenge to the productivist ideology of a state that denies the usefulness of fantasy even as it acknowledges its power by censoring it" (*Partial Visions*, 111).

55 *Amanda. Ein Hexenroman* appeared in 1983. Beatrice's story is retold again by Beatrice herself, because the trobadora who has been resurrected as a siren claims that Irmtraud Morgner made mistakes in her version of the story, not only because Morgner did not know all the facts, but also because her novel smacks of self-censorship. I disagree with Biddy Martin's interpretation of the ending of *Life and Adventures*. Martin maintained that Beatrice's death meant that the subversive elements that this figure brought to the text were finally dropped ("Socialist Patriarchy and the Limits of Reform"). Martin's criticism of the novel's "final domesticity," represented by the heterosexual marriage between Benno and Laura, neglects the irony in the final scene in which Benno

ever confined to fixed roles; they travel between ideologies, trying out possible roles and subjectivities like costumes without remaining locked into definitions of their own subject positions. The attempt to define one's own role and become a subject turns out to be a never-ending *process,* rather than a teleological path with a fixed ending. Although the attempt to define oneself is necessary for women, any definition can only be a temporary one based on concrete political needs at a specific time in history.

The New "Subject of Feminism"

Much like Teresa de Lauretis's suggestion of a new "subject of feminism," a subject whose definition or conception is in progress, a subject that is "at the same time inside *and* outside the ideology of gender, and conscious of being so, conscious of that twofold pull, of that division, that doubled vision," the text's subjects are both inside *and* outside the ideology of gender.[56] While the novel demonstrates how dominant representations of women affect all of the figures, new subjects are constructed through the process of moving inside and out-side of different discourses, showing that women are more than ide-ology. These characters move from the governing representations of women (in their male-centered frame of reference) to those spaces that

tells the first of his thousand and one stories in Beatrice's style. The "solution" he talks about is obviously an ironic fantasy (in the renters' communal activity of pulling weeds in front of their doors or Beatrice's strategy of dropping leaf-lets with her "golden words" out of planes of the GDR airline "Interflug," for example). Morgner herself emphasized the suspicious irony at the end of the novel in an interview with Doris Berger. To Berger's question of why she decided to write a second part to *Life and Adventures* in which she openly "corrected" certain statements in the first novel, Morgner answered: "Well, the end, the supposed happy end of *Beatrice* was of course suspicious. I mean, one had to unravel that, one had to dig deeper and ask: what happens then? This issue was already forthcoming at the end of the novel" (Doris Berger, "Ge-spräch mit Irmtraud Morgner," *GDR Monitor*, 12 (winter 1984/85), 29).

56   De Lauretis, *Technologies of Gender*, 9–10.

this representation leaves out, spaces at the margins of the official discourse, unrepresentable in its dominant images, but nevertheless implied by it.

If Beatrice's quest is for self-definition and, ultimately, a definition of woman, then her journey demonstrates how this quest can only lead to a definition in the "space-off" of discourse. This "space-off," a term borrowed from film theory, designates the space not visible in the frame, but inferable from what the frame makes visible.[57] In *Life and Adventures*, these spaces include utopian and fantastic possibilities, such as Vera Hill's technique of tightrope walking, Valeska's strategy of changing her sex at will, or Laura's fantastic election to the Round Table of the Queen of Sheba, as well as more "realistic" options at the margins of society, such as female communes, women's friendships, joint artistic projects of women, and women's laughter.[58]

---

57 Ibid., 26.
58 Friendships and common projects among women repeatedly lead to significant changes and challenges of existing structures in GDR society in *Life and Adventures*. The community of women and children who live together as a new type of family in Valeska's "Hadische Erzählungen" not only leads to a radically new lifestyle for Valeska, but also to a new type of relationship to her parents, her children, and her lover. She says, for example: "Love lost its dogmatic system with the character of a natural event that overpowers the world with grand gestures. Events and objects approached their own value, by comparison. In friendly company there was variety, beautiful human community" (242). In her "Frohe Botschaft," Valeska's new sexual relationship to her girlfriend Shenya, which takes place after she has changed into a man, teaches her that heterosexual relationships can function without the subjugation of women. She is astonished to find that "the apparatus, tried out for the first time, had functioned without feelings of dominance or visions of subjugation" (456). Because of these experiences she demands from her lover Rudolf a new type of relationship based on true equality. Valeska says that they now can have a relationship that can do without "the images that they had made of each other and that others had made for them. Then they knew that they loved each other. Personally – miracle of all miracles" (464). Only after Rudolf has loved her without even noticing her new male body does she switch back to her female body during the time of their lovemaking. In fact, homosexual or heterosexual love is a question of choice for Valeska. Valeska seems to have learned through the experience of her miraculous sex change that the outer appearances of the lovers' bodies are unimportant as long as the structure of their relationship is one that is radically different from oppressive heterosexual relationships in a patriarchal society.

Through a constant effort to rewrite and reexamine these options, they are shown to be *possibilities* for women, with none offering a definite answer or solution. In fact, the movement between discourses, the process of being inside a certain discourse and constantly moving outside it at the same time, is the movement that Beatrice and Laura demonstrate in their quest. In the last interview before her death in 1990, Morgner stated:

> One has to be able to observe oneself. Oneself and language. Its possibilities. The ambiguity of a word is comparable for the writer to the ambiguity of her self. The ensemble of characters that I create – like a dramatist – is nothing but the splitting of that which one calls I. The main characters of my novels are different sides of my own self. Like fire, one consumes oneself.[59]

What we call "subject" is not a fixed category in Morgner's texts. It is not only ambiguous and in flux, but facets of the subject are also con-stantly created and recreated through a process of masquerade and self-experiment that rekindles and opens up other possibilities.

The definition of woman advocated in *Life and Adventures* turns out to be a nondefinition, one that demonstrates the impossibility of such a project without negating the need for it. For Morgner, the prob-lem is not to discover women's nature and "authentic" voice, but rather to excavate, like an archeologist, the *voice range* of woman. The text points out that there is no *one* voice, one subject position for women, but rather a range of possibilities that are unlimited and never fixed. The characters do assume subject positions and different roles that allow them to act, but these definitions can never be fixed once and for all. On the contrary, they are only temporarily possible and constantly need to be redefined in response to concrete political and historical needs.

If it is true that one of Morgner's agendas is to construct a new kind of feminist subject, then the notion of agency also needs to be redefined. Morgner's new type of political agency in feminism would no longer be dependent on a relatively unified notion of the social sub-

---

59 Synnöve Clason, "Am Ende bleibt das eigene Leben. Ost-Berlin, 1990: Ein Gespräch mit Irmtraud Morgner – kurz vor ihrem Tod," *Die Zeit*, 6 November 1992, 6.

ject "woman," but instead represents an attempt to take the diversity of women into account. Sensitive to the complex nature of different definitions and self-definitions of women, such a new kind of feminist subject would be structured plurally; it would be a subject that promotes a new kind of political agency able to deal out of and with this plurality.

Morgner's radical questioning of the subject is consonant with other more recent attempts by feminist theoreticians to come to new definitions of feminist subjectivity. Teresa de Lauretis, Judith Butler, and Donna Haraway, among others, have all made suggestions in this regard. Butler argues for a Foucauldian critique of the subject that does not pronounce the subject's death, but instead claims that certain versions of the subject are politically insidious. Butler's goal is to reinscribe the subject outside the terms of an epistemological given. She rejects any attempt to define a universal or specific content to the category "women" and to use "identity" as a point of departure. Instead, she wants to use the term "women" as a site of "permanent openness and resignifiability."[60] From her point of view, only through releasing the category of women from a fixed referent does something like "agency" become possible. Only such a practice would expand the possibilities of what it means to be a woman. Donna Haraway's metaphor for a new kind of feminist subject is the cyborg. Haraway argues that what now becomes possible is a political practice that embraces a recognition of the multiple, pregnant, and contradictory aspects of both our individual and collective identities. Such a politics no longer requires essential criteria of identification, but we are beginning to see instead the formation of political groupings that rest on the conscious negation of such criteria. Haraway gives the identifying phrase "women of color" as an example for a postmodern identity constructed out of a recognition of otherness and difference.

Morgner's texts, it seems to me, display a sensitivity to the complexities of the problems involved in the attempt to arrive at a definition of woman. Her new kind of feminist subject is a concept that

---

60   Judith Butler, "Contingent Foundations: Feminism and the Question of 'Post-modernism'," in Judith Butler and Joan W. Scott (eds), *Feminists Theorize the Political* (New York: Routledge, 1992), 16.

constantly needs to be renegotiated and examined. Through her emphasis on the diverse and sometimes conflicting perspectives of the women
in the novel, the text acknowledges and also encourages its readers to see
that the premises from which Morgner is working as an author also
possess a specific location. *Life and Adventures* makes clear that women's writings cannot proclaim another kind of "truth" that would be
different from men's, yet somehow more objective and "real." In fact,
the alleged accounts of women's "true," "authentic" experiences in other
feminist texts of the 1970s are prominently missing. In this sense, the
text takes issue with those feminist positions that attempt to describe "a
woman's distinct perspective" and thereby postulate aspects of modern
Western culture as present in all or most of human history. With the
emphasis on the differences between individual women and the diversity
in experiences among different groups of women from different times
and places, the text criticizes attempts to come to a universal definition
of woman, as they tend to be on white, middle-class, heterosexist
experiences of women who live in Western capitalist states in the
twentieth and twenty-first centuries.[61] Although Morgner is conscious of
the fact that we need to define different agendas and political goals at
different points in history to be able to act politically, she promotes an
awareness that any of these definitions can only function temporarily and
in the context of specific political needs. In this sense, the new feminist
subject of *Life and Adventures* operates in close proximity to De Lauretis's "new subject of feminism," Haraway's cyborg, or Butler's category
of women as a "place of permanent openness and resignifiability."

In sum, *Life and Adventures* can be read as a feminist, a
postmodern, *and* a political text. But in a novel from the early 1970s,
written by a female author in the former GDR, the combination of
these categories questions not so much the political status of the text
itself as the terms and preconditions of the definitions we use to
approach it. In this more inclusive view, one of the clearly political

61   In fact, women with radically different experiences appear in the text: they come
     from the Middle Ages and modern GDR society, there are working-class women
     and noble ladies, women from socialist and capitalist societies, old and young
     women, lesbians and heterosexual women, and women from many different
     cultures (the United States, France, the Soviet Union, Yugoslavia, and Italy).

174

features of *Life and Adventures* is that the text experiments with positive definitions and, at the same time, encourages its readers to focus on discourse itself, not only on *what* is said, but also on *how* it is said, in *what* historical context, and in reference to *which* social and cultural situation.

Chapter IV
Dialogic Politics

Antipodean Artists and Tightrope Walkers

> At the central train station in Leipzig, Beatrice was greeted by the antipodean artist Orlando. He brought her three chrysanthemums and greetings from Madame Eos, the circus director. Since the trobadora's suitcase was too heavy for Orlando's arms, he hired a porter with a baggage cart. Orlando lay down on his back on the cart and raised his legs. When his shoe soles were vertically exposed to the sooty glass roof of the station, the artist told Beatrice to throw the suitcase toward his shoes when he gave the order. Beatrice did as she was told. Orlando caught the suitcase with the tip of his right foot, upended it, shifted it to the left foot and back again, and continued in this way to the exit. While the porter and Beatrice transported the cart across the stairs of the east hall, Orlando made the suitcase spin like a top. Performed balancing acts with his eyes blindfolded and other tricks until they reached the circus director's apartment across from the winter quarters. (*Life and Adventures*, 101–2)

The antipodean artist [Antipodenkünstler] Orlando is another figure who, like Beatrice, Valeska, and Vera, defies definitions and performs balancing acts on the borderlines between different concepts. He is a circus artist and a buffoon who balances Beatrice's baggage, her past and her material belongings, on his feet lying upside down on a cart. As an antipodean artist (Greek: with feet opposite), his feet are literally in an opposite position when they stick out in the air, and his way of carrying baggage is contrary to our "normal" walking posture. As a person who works with opposites, his art gives us new perspectives on opposing objects by letting them circle and be in flux. With the *Antipodenkünstler* Orlando, Morgner creates another metaphor for an unusual strategy to deal with opposites. By giving the observer a strange view on seemingly "normal" and "natural" concepts, Orlando questions the validity of our conventional perspectives and encourages their reexamination. Like most of the women in Morgner's text, he seems to be an allegory for the "new subject of feminism" discussed in chapter 3.

Orlando is not only between opposing concepts because he has a funny way of carrying Beatrice's luggage, but also because he reminds us of Virginia Woolf's character Orlando, from her novel of the same title, who is both woman and man.[1] Woolf's Orlando one day miraculously changes into a woman, and Morgner likewise creates a figure, Valeska, who finds one morning when she looks into a mirror that she has changed into a man. Valeska's sex change is of central importance in *Life and Adventures*, and Laura reads Valeska's "Gospel" as Beatrice's last will and testament. The transformations of both Orlando and Valeska happen without explanation as part of a fantastic plot that frustrates our expectations and our concept of "reality." Neither Orlando nor Valeska are particularly surprised by the miracle and preserve their male and female identity, respectively, despite their sex change. Of Orlando, Woolf writes:

> He stretched himself. He rose. He stood upright in complete nakedness before us, and while the trumpets pealed Truth! Truth! we have no choice left but confess – he was a woman. [...] Orlando looked himself up and down in a long looking-glass, without showing any signs of discomposure, and went, presumably, to his bath.
> We may take the advantage of this pause in the narrative to make certain statements. Orlando had become a woman – there was no denying it. But in every other respect, Orlando remained precisely as he had been. (137–8)

In their analysis of *Orlando*, Sandra Gilbert and Susan Gubar emphasize that Orlando changes gender as easily as one might change clothing, while remaining otherwise unaffected. The reason, Gilbert and Gubar maintain, "is not because sexually defining costumes are false and selves are true but because costumes are selves and thus easily, fluidly, interchangeable."[2] In fact, Woolf makes this point directly in her novel: "Thus, there is much to support the view that it is clothes that wear us and not we them; we may make them take the mould of arm or breast, but they mold our hearts, our brains, our tongues in their liking" (188). With Orlando's change into a woman, M. Keith Booker argues, "Woolf's book thus mounts a direct chal-

1   Virginia Woolf, *Orlando: A Biography* (New York: Harvest Book, 1956).
2   Sandra Gilbert and Susan Gubar, *Sexchanges. No Man's Land*, vol. 2 (New Haven: Yale University Press, 1989), 344.

lenge to conventional notions of identity and to the hierarchies with which those notions are associated."[3]

A similar challenge to conventional notions of identity is present in Morgner's novel. Valeska's first reaction when she notices that she has become a man is to burst into laughter. But just like Orlando, Valeska "was able to accept her reflection in the mirror" because, as the narrator explains, "Valeska had the advantage of having been trained to take great changes in one's own body in stride" (451). Like Orlando, she also remains as she had been despite her new gender, which she perceives as nothing but "a privileging uniform." For this reason, the narrator emphasizes, "the continuation of the gospel is narrated without a change of name. Also without a change of grammatical gender" (450).

The ease with which Orlando and Valeska accept their transformation and adjust to their new roles is in sharp contrast to the ways their environments respond to them after they have undergone the sex change. Both Woolf and Morgner get a lot of satiric mileage out of the depiction of the ways society treats Orlando and Valeska after they have assumed different gender roles. Valeska knows, for example, that as a man she can leave Rudolf's apartment building early in the morning without being suspected of coming from "work," as she would have been as a woman (424). And Orlando considers her position:

> She remembered how, as a young man, she had insisted that women must be obedient, chaste, scented, and exquisitely appareled. "Now I shall have to pay in my own person for those desires," she reflected; "for women are not (judging by my own short experience of the sex) obedient, chaste, scented, and exquisitely appareled by nature. They can only attain these graces, without which they may enjoy none of the delights of life, by the most tedious discipline. There's the hairdressing," she thought, "that alone will take an hour of my morning; there's looking in the looking-glass, another hour; there's staying and lacing; there's washing and powdering; there's changing from silk to lace and from lace to paduasoy; and there's being chaste year in and year out." (156–7)

The definitions of women's roles, Orlando understands, are not natural but artificial and restrictive; they require "the most tedious discipline." Valeska has similar experiences as a man:

3   M. Keith Booker, *Techniques of Subversion in Modern Literature: Transgression, Abjection, and the Carnivalesque* (Gainesville: University of Florida Press, 1991), 164.

Inspired by injustice, she swung her feet onto the pillow, then flung them over the edge of the bed, and came abruptly to her feet before the mirror. A site she was in the habit of seeking out for dressing and undressing. In her own room an Empire mirror had been installed for such occasions, the most expensive piece of furniture in her apartment. Rudolf's rented mirror cast unflattering images. Valeska was used to it. Which is why she always looked only fleetingly. She was unwilling to go along with the custom that demands eternal youth of women without technical amenities, from which a certain accommodation can be expected. (448)

Both authors point out that the gender roles for men and women are oppressive and far from "natural." The hierarchy that goes along with the definition of gender roles is shown to be arbitrary and detrimental for women's status as subjects, since they are only allowed to define themselves in relation to men. Through allusions to Woolf's novel in *Life and Adventures*, the reader understands that the role definitions for men and women have not essentially changed since Orlando's times. Valeska finds out that men are still the norm and women still have to define their own role in relation to this norm. On a visit with her girlfriend Shenya, Valeska realizes that gender roles shape our personality and constitute our identity:

Perhaps Shenya was only proud and not at all inclined toward being an extraordinary character; maybe her generic affiliation had forced it, little by little? Because Shenya too had probably not escaped constantly doubting herself, reflecting about herself, testing herself, resurrecting herself; that fosters human virtues such as modesty, tolerance, patience. Nothing forced Rudolf to doubt himself. His generic affiliation allowed him to be convinced that he was the norm. (457)

Women have a hard time claiming the status of a subject, because their restrictive role definition keeps them from developing self-confidence and independence. Like Woolf, Morgner emphasizes that the costumes we wear "mould our hearts, our brains, our tongues."

Both Orlando and Valeska are "spies" in the other sex's camp, like Tiresias, the Greek seer, who had also been a woman at one time. As such they provide insider information on the other sex and question traditional gender roles, a mission that is of crucial importance to Morgner, emphasized by the fact that she lets Valeska write down her experiences as her "Gospel." Yet both writers let their character's gender remain highly uncertain. After some time, Valeska in *Life and*

Adventures learns how to change her sex at will, and the narrator in *Orlando* writes:

> And here it would seem from some ambiguity in her terms that she was censuring both sexes equally, as if she belonged to neither; and indeed, for the time being she seemed to vacillate; she was man; she was woman; she knew the secrets, shared the weaknesses of each. (158)

Both Woolf and Morgner show their characters as persons who defy all definitions by vacillating between different roles and identities. Even Orlando's husband Shel, with whom Orlando has children, suspects Orlando is a man, just as Orlando suspects that Shel is really a woman. In *Life and Adventures*, Valeska's lover, Rudolf, does not even notice at first that Valeska has changed into a man and loves her "as a person" rather than as a woman, a behavior that convinces Valeska to truly believe in their love:

> Rudolf stood before her. Came in as usual. Kissed Valeska as usual. Took off his and her clothes as usual.
> Later it occurred to Valeska that she should be afraid. Later it struck Rudolf that the naked Valeska was disguised.
> At that, they realized that if necessary, they could do without the images that they had made of each other and that others had made for them. Then they knew that they loved each other. Personally – miracle of all miracles. (464)

True love for Morgner, a relationship between two persons who recognize each other as subjects, can only be thought of as a miracle since it requires the construction of a space outside the ideology of gender. Like Woolf, Morgner creates positive figures who defy traditional definitions by occupying a space in between gender definitions, figures that are more than one thing at a time, that have their place on the borderlines of discourse. Orlando and Valeska represent a different concept of identity, one that does not rely on binary oppositions as its foundation, but one that embraces differences. We come across many of these "tightrope walkers" and "balancing artists" in Morgner's novel. In fact, Valeska is not the only figure whose gender identity is in question: Benno, Laura, and Beatrice also vacillate between the sexes at times.[4] Beatrice, for example, has incorporated in her identity

---

4   See chapter 3 of this volume.

two years of a boy's childhood memory in her first life in the Middle Ages, because by accident she drank a magic potion that exchanged two years of Beatrice's memory with those of her lover Raimbaut.[5] Beatrice's journey is also a journey through time and history just like that of Orlando, who lives through four centuries.

Antipodean artists (Orlando/Valeska), tightrope walkers (Vera/Hill), world travelers (Beatrice/Laura), female Parzivals (Beatrice/Vera), female Faust figures with two souls in their breast (Beatrice/Valeska), prophets (Valeska/Beatrice), and rogues are the true heroines in *Life and Adventures*. They represent Morgner's attempt to construct a new female and feminist subject. All of these figures defy the notion of a simple female identity; they are figures that are "different" and represent difference by incorporating it into the definition of themselves, and all of them are constructed plurally. Their most important common characteristic is that they transgress boundaries and embody resistance to restricting conventions and definitions ("Customs" [Sitten] as Morgner phrases it). But these antipodean artists do not leave it at that. Instead, they search for new, differently structured definitions in order to be able to act politically. They seek new possibilities for dealing with opposites by recognizing that at least two voices – two worldviews – speak through them. In fact, Morgner creates a polyphony of voices in *Life and Adventures* in part by experimenting with Mikhail Bakhtin's theories of polyphony and dialogism in language. Not only do her texts use many of Bakhtin's key terms, but Morgner also quotes Bakhtin directly in *Amanda* to point the reader in Bakhtin's direction and to create a dialogue between her own feminist ideas and his theory of language.

---

5   Laura tells the story of Beatrice's past to Irmtraud Morgner in bk 1 ch. 15. The
     title of this chapter is "Wherein Laura delivers the proof demanded by I. M.";
     the passage that tells about the magic potion has the subtitle: "The Ahistorical
     Role of Mr. de Poitiers's Wife".

The Antipodean Artist Mikhail Bakhtin

The Russian language scholar and literary critic Mikhail Bakhtin began writing in the early 1920s, but it was only in the 1980s that the magnitude of his accomplishment began to be appreciated. Bakhtin viewed language as essentially dialogic, as a struggle between language systems within a particular sociohistorical context. For Bakhtin, to interact in language meant to engage in speech as citation, for any linguistic utterance involves adaptation of and response to prior speech. Every word, saturated in contextual meaning, becomes a word about the word of another addressed to someone else. In "Discourse in the Novel," Bakhtin explains, "The word in living conversation is directly, blatantly oriented toward a future answer word: it provokes an answer, anticipates it and structures itself in the answer's direction."[6] The words we use come to us already imprinted with the meanings, intentions, and accents of previous users, and any one of our utterances is in turn directed toward some other real or hypothetical user.

Bakhtin distinguishes at least five different types of dialogic relationships: what Bakhtin calls a "double-voiced discourse" arises between individual words (the word as someone else's semantic position, as the representative of another person's utterance); between whole utterances; between language styles or social dialects; in relation to aspects of our own previous utterances; and finally among different semiotic phenomena, such as images belonging to different art forms. In the relation between author and character, dialogism finds its most explicit expression in the novel. Bakhtin is interested above all in the novel – as both a noncanonical and a mixed genre, which allows the incorporation of extra-literary genres – because it most completely reflects the oppositional forces that characterize all language. In the novel, the author and the character approach the same theme through two different discourses, entering into a semantic bond based on the intersection of two embodied meanings. The dialogic in

6   M. M. Bakhtin, *The Dialogic Imagination: Four Essays*, Michael Holquist (ed.), Caryl Emerson and Michael Holquist (trans.) (Austin: University of Texas Press, 1987), 280.

the novel thus represents the struggle between opposing discourses arising out of different contexts. It disrupts the assimilation of differences sought in what Bakhtin calls the monologic discourses.[7]

The distinguishing characteristic of the Bakhtinian dialogic is its propensity for digression, a characteristic that provides its connection to the "carnivalesque," the second important notion in Bakhtin's theory of language. First developed in *Rabelais and His World* (completed in 1941, but not published until 1965), Bakhtin's concept of carnival not only describes a festive ritual in feudal times, but also designates a specific way to interact with reality.[8] Carnival offers recurrent disruptions of a seemingly stable order. It abolishes, for example, the distinction between spectator and performer and as a symbolic event, it reverses the hierarchical order of birth and death, high and low, male and female, and so on. Bakhtin developed his notion of the "carnivalesque" into a potent, populist, critical inversion of *all* official discourses and hierarchies in a way that has implications far beyond the specific realm of Rabelais studies. Carnival for Bakhtin is both a populist utopian vision of the world seen from below and a festive critique of the "high" culture through the inversion of hierarchy. Thus, Morgner's amusing play with the figure of the *antipodean artist* Orlando in her novel, whose trade it is to see the world upside down and question our traditional perspectives through an inversion of hierarchies, is a metaphor for Bakhtin's concept of carnival.

With the translation of Bakhtin's *Rabelais and His World*, Western scholars became interested in the notion of carnival and dialogism as a site of special interest for the analysis of literature and

7   Holquist explains: "A word, discourse, language or culture undergoes 'dialogization' when it becomes relativized, de-privileged, aware of competing definitions for the same thing. Undialogized language is authoritative or absolute" (*The Dialogic Imagination*, 427). Bakhtin says there are "centripetal," or centralizing, and "centrifugal" or decentralizing forces in any language or culture. "The rulers and the high poetic genres of any era exercise a centripetal – a homogenizing and hierarchizing – influence; the centrifugal (decrowning, dispersing) forces of the clown, mimic and rogue create alternative 'degraded' genres down below. The novel, Bakhtin argues, is a denormatizing and therefore centrifugal force" (*The Dialogic Imagination*, 425).

8   M. M. Bakhtin, *Rabelais and His World*, Hélène Iswolsky (trans.) (Bloomington: Indiana University Press, 1984).

184

symbolic practices. Since the late 70s and early 80s an increasing body of writing has emerged applying Bakhtin's theories of carnival transgression and dialogism. In literary and cultural studies, Bakhtin's notion of the carnivalesque has been understood not simply to denote ritual features in European culture, but as a mode of understanding, a model and an ideal.[9] An extraordinarily complex, contradictory, and at times even enigmatic figure, Bakhtin has been appropriated by the most diverse ideological currents. As Robert Stam points out, "[I]n political terms, we find Bakhtin the populist, Bakhtin the Marxist, Bakhtin the anti-Marxist, Bakhtin the social-democrat, and Bakhtin, the anti-Stalinist. There is a left reading of Bakhtin (Fredric Jameson, Terry Eagleton, Tony Bennett, Ken Hirschkop, Allon White/Peter Stallybrass, Graham Pechey) and a liberal reading (Wayne Booth, David Lodge, Tzvetan Todorov)."[10] Because of the intrinsic identification in Bakhtin's

9   Today, an increasing number of literary and historical studies use Bakhtin's notions as analytical and epistemological categories. In 1979, for example, Tony Bennett suggested that Bakhtin's study of Rabelais should hold an exemplary place in materialist cultural criticism (*Formalism and Marxism* (London: Methuen, 1979) 90–2). In fact, Bakhtin's influence has spread to many parts of the world, crucial Bakhtinian terms have gained wide dissemination, and the exegetical application of his ideas is proceeding apace. Robert Stam explains that in France, when his books on Dostoevsky and Rabelais appeared in translation in the late 1960s, Bakhtin was initially seen as a kind of protostructuralist working out of the formalist tradition. In two landmark articles, "Bakhtin, le mot, le dialogue et le roman" (1967) and "Une Poetique Ruinée" (1970), Julia Kristeva presented Bakhtin as a precursor of the most sophisticated literary theoretician of structuralism and poststructuralism. And in 1981, Tzvetan Todorov performed a major reevaluation of Bakhtin's oeuvre in his *Mikhail Bakhtin: Le Principe Dialogique*. In the Anglophonic world, Bakhtin was at first viewed largely as the theorist of carnival and ritual inversions of hierarchy; only recently, with the translation of numerous books by or about him, has Bakhtin come to be seen as a major theoretician of language and literature. According to Robert Stam, Bakhtin managed to foreshadow aspects of Lacan's "linguistic" reading of Freud in *Freudianism: A Marxist Critique* (1927), aspects of contemporary sociolinguistics (Pécheux, Halliday, Lakoff) in *Marxism and the Philosophy of Language* (1929), and aspects of cultural anthropology (Victor Turner and Mary Douglas) and historical ethnography (Emanuael le Roy Ladurie) in *Rabelais and His World* (written in 1940). Cf. Robert Stam, *Subversive Pleasures: Bakhtin, Cultural Criticism, and Film* (Baltimore: The Johns Hopkins University Press, 1989), 2.

10   Stam, *Subversive Pleasures*, 15.

categories with difference and alterity, and a built-in affinity for the oppressed and the marginal, Bakhtin has been often appropriated for the analysis of oppositional and marginal practices. Feminists especially have found Bakhtin increasingly useful as a resource in recent years, particularly because his theories of dialogism lend themselves to a critique of the kind of authoritarian discourse often associated with the patriarchal tradition.

While few scholars deny Bakhtin's appeal and the vitality of his notion of carnival, some have been skeptical of Bakhtin's overall project. Politically thoughtful commentators such as Terry Eagleton, Mary Russo, and Peter Stallybrass and Allon White have warned that one must not forget that carnival itself was and continues to be a sanctioned form of subversion, at times serving to sublimate and defuse the social tensions that might have led to genuine subversion. Since the political dimensions of carnival are complex, the politics of carnival cannot be removed from a specific historical context. Morgner was well aware of the problems of an ahistorical appropriation of Bakhtin's notion of carnival. In her novel *Amanda*, she quotes from Bakhtin's *Rabelais and His World* to show that carnival as authorized transgression can be used by authoritarian regimes to defuse existing tensions. In Morgner's novel, the (male) ravens of *Hörselberg* allow the witches, whom they control, an outlet for their aggressions in a yearly carnival spectacle to prevent them from organizing an uprising that would endanger the ravens' position of power. In her discussion of Bakhtin's ideas Morgner points to different ways of using some of his key concepts, without ignoring the dangers of their ahistorical use. For Morgner, Bakhtin's theories serve as catalysts in her search for solutions to her own concerns with ways to help women enter history and become subjects.

Aside from her insistence on a close historical analysis of every occurrence of carnival, Morgner uses Bakhtin's notion of the carnivalesque as one instance of a generalized economy of transgression and of the recoding of high/low relations across the whole social spectrum. In her comparison of the different ways in which the body is represented in the official culture of the GDR, on the one hand, and in women's writings, on the other, she criticizes cultural classifications of the body as well as structural oppositions of high versus low, which function to

186

establish identity in the official discourse of the GDR. Such a transposition of the notion of carnival reveals that its underlying structural features operate far beyond the strict confines of popular festivity and are intrinsic to the dialectics of social classification as such. An analysis of the way specific discourses exclude difference or the "Other" in order to establish identity of the self has been a major preoccupation of contemporary philosophical thought. The appropriation of Derrida's "differánce" and feminists' rethinking of the notion of gender difference are only two of the most prominent examples of this interest in difference. Bakhtin has become a focus of interest in this context because his writings concentrate on the possibility of encompassing difference simultaneously. Katarina Clark and Michael Holquist propose that Bakhtin "conceives of the old problem of identity along the lines not of 'the same as' but of 'simultaneous with.' He is thus led to mediate on the interaction of forces that are conceived by others as mutually exclusive."[11] Bakhtin's reevaluation of difference seems to have been one of the aspects of his thought that fascinated Morgner. The Russian thinker's ideas provide her with one more possibility for thinking of difference differently.

In this chapter, I will be tracing Morgner's use of Bakhtin's concepts of dialogism and carnival in *Life and Adventures*, and in particular, how Morgner incorporates his vocabulary of the "classical" and "grotesque" body in her exploration of high/low symbolism in GDR society in the 1970s. As I shall demonstrate, Morgner's use of Bakhtin can be tied to her feminist project of "helping women enter history." Morgner's goal is twofold: to develop strategies for a subversion of official (male) norms *and* to provide a utopian vision for a new definition of a subject of feminism. "The twofold pull in contradictory directions" of contemporary feminist theory, as diagnosed by Teresa de Lauretis, is visible in a different way in Morgner's incorporation of Bakhtin's notions of dialogism and carnival into her novel.

---

11   Katerina Clark and Michael Holquist, *Mikhail Bakhtin* (Cambridge: Harvard University Press, 1984), 9–10.

Creating a "Legendary Historical Consciousness"

Morgner's twofold project of subverting existing norms and creating differently structured identities shapes her treatment of history and the literary canon, projects for which Virginia Woolf serves as precursor and model. The need to subvert an overwhelming male tradition is clear from the start in *Life and Adventures*. Beatrice leaves the Middle Ages because she is not allowed to write love poems to a man in this "male world", in which a male voice range of "tenor, baritone and bass" is the norm. Even in modern GDR society, Laura feels the urge to leave history temporarily because she still perceives it as a "male sea of egotism" (23). Even today, women's role is to be passive and assume the status of an object. In the discussion in the beginning of the book between Irmtraud Morgner and Laura Salman about the importance of the historical figure Beatrice de Dia, the two women insist that "female role socialization drills these and other abilities [to be able to have an active relationship to the world] out of you" (24). The two women agree that the appearance of Beatrice de Dia represents an attempt to rewrite (male) history: "A typical case of a legend created for the purpose of correcting history, then. Why shouldn't a woman rewrite her past any way she likes. Nations and peoples have always done it" (25).

Since women have not been included in traditional historiography, they need to find ways of creating their own historical tradition by "rewriting" the past.[12] Morgner again and again empha-

---

12 For example, Bele H. states: "There she [Bele H.] took the floor again, to discuss in a tendentious manner Brecht's poem about the reading worker. 'Here the poet raises the question about creativity that are not found in books. About the slaves who built cities, for example, who left nameless but visible traces of their abilities: about men. I am waiting for the poet who could let a female worker who reads raise questions,' said Bele H. 'the slaves of the slaves, who could leave no visible trace of their abilities' [...] 'Nobody who strives for greater things can do without the assistance of history. This certainty of being rooted. Self-consciousness that creates awareness of tradition. Pride. A noble man who can lean on his family tree, for example, has an advantage over workers and women who believe they are standing alone'" (201–2).

sizes the importance of this project, which she calls "the creation of a legendary historical consciousness":

> Women have not yet entered written history in substantial ways, they are just beginning. The tradition of their ways of working can be felt, not measured. Legendary. (364)

Because women have been excluded from history as subjects, they exist only as traces of traces: as legends, which do not have the status of historical subjects. (It is always implicitly suggested of a legend that "this is not true.") Consequently, women have to try to find ways to read and represent history differently. Because women are inscribed historically only outside of "real history" (i.e. as "legends"), recuperating historical women means taking legends seriously. As long as women do not exist as historical subjects, the method of creating a "legendary historical consciousness" is a necessary step that involves a departure from our usual tools of analysis, or as Morgner puts it, the traces of women's actions are "felt not measured." The process of creating a "legendary historical consciousness" as a first step to help women enter history is thus a truly subversive act, since it involves a different reading and thinking process.

While Virginia Woolf's *Orlando* is perhaps the classic text of gender transgression in modern literature, it also raises the issue of history (both literary and general history), thereby indicating a relationship between history and gender. Woolf's other classic text, *A Room of One's Own*, is even more explicit when it comes to history. Like Morgner, Woolf suggests that women do not have a tradition they can claim for themselves:

> But whatever effect discouragement and criticism had upon their writing – and I believe that they had a very great effect – that was unimportant compared with the other difficulty which faced them (I was still considering those early nineteenth-century novelists) when they came to set their thoughts on paper – that is that they had no tradition behind them, or one so short and partial that it was of little help. [...] Perhaps, the first thing she would find, setting pen to paper, was that there was no common sentence ready for her use.[13]

13   Virginia Woolf, *A Room of One's Own* (San Diego: Harvest, 1957), 79.

The question of how women might be able to take up the pen and write despite the (relative) absence of a tradition of their own is one of the most important concerns for Woolf and Morgner. Woolf's *Orlando* serves as a model for Morgner since it turns the discourse of the male tradition against itself in an exemplary fashion. This feminist transgression through parodic appropriation of the male discourse has great potential, and Morgner uses it extensively. It functions by means of a dialogue with the past, in which two opposing voices struggle for expression. By representing and at the same time subverting an official language through parodic stylization, the official authoritarian discourse can be analyzed and criticized. In "Discourse and the Novel," Bakhtin argues:

> The novelistic discourse dominating a given epoch is itself turned into an object and itself becomes a means for refracting new authorial intentions. [...] The incorporated languages and socio-ideological belief systems, while of course utilized to refract the author's intentions, are unmasked and destroyed as something false, hypocritical, greedy, limited, narrowly rationalistic, inadequate to reality. In most cases these languages – already fully formed, officially recognized, reigning languages that are authoritative and reactionary – are (in real life) doomed to death and displacement. Therefore what predominates in the novel are various forms and degrees of parodic stylization of incorporated languages.[14]

Through parodic stylization, both Woolf and Morgner incorporate different languages (in Bakhtin's broad sense of the term) into their novels. Woolf, for example, lets her character find out that the works of the "great" authors of her time are not only less original than one might think, but also oddly disappointing and boring compared to the works of the marginalized female writers who are the heroines in *Orlando*. And Morgner makes clear in *Life and Adventures* that Raimbaut's "dark style" is pretentious and artificial compared to Beatrice's own poems. Ironically, Raimbaut's poems are celebrated while her husband burns Beatrice's poems:

> She [Beatrice] fell in love with Mr. Raimbaut d'Aurenga and composed many fine and beautiful songs for him, a few of which can be found in anthologies of old Provencal troubadour poetry. Next to the distinctive verses of Raimbaut d'Aurenga (French: d'Orange). He loved the game of playing with difficult

14   Bakhtin, *The Dialogic Imagination*, 309–12.

rhymes and the ambiguity of words. The game of playing with difficult rhymes and the ambiguity of words. The metric structure of his works reflects great refinement. Convinced of their exclusivity, the chronically indebted court constantly tried to find complicated words ending in -enga to rhyme with Aurenga, and showed disdain for all unaristocratic verse-artists. (6)

As Morgner points out in this passage, the motivation for Raimbaut's dark style is pseudo-objective. The narrator's entire characterization is consistent in tone and given from the point of view of Raimbaut himself, fused with his direct speech – for example in the designation "exquisite verses" and "extravagant fashion." At the same time, these words are permeated with the ironic intonation of the narrator. The little half sentences (such as "constantly in debt" and "he showed little respect for poets who weren't aristocrats") inserted into the seemingly objective description of Raimbaut's poetic production unmask his actual motivation as materialism, greed, and self-promotion. The passage thus has two accents and can be regarded as a typical hybrid construction in a Bakhtinian sense. Morgner, carefully and with great irony, points out that Raimbaut's style is representative of the officially recognized discourse of the time. The narrator tells us, for example, that Beatrice's husband Guilhem de Poitiers loved this troubadour because "Raimbaut extolled wealth and virtue as compatible, something his rivals more or less questioned" (30). Again, the ironic commentary of the narrator distances the author from the voice of official discourse and unmasks it as hypocritical, limited, and narrowly rationalistic. Although Raimbaut's "dark style" is in fact exclusive and pretentious, it is canonized because it serves the forces in power.[15]

Woolf employs similar techniques when she has Orlando meet the most prominent writers of the eighteenth century only to find their society oddly disappointing. Orlando ends up finding the company of Nell and her fellow prostitutes in the streets of London preferable to

---

15 Raimbaut's politically motivated elitism is emphasized again a little bit further down: "The troubadours disputed the issue in competing poems. Raimbaut in grandiose style as usual, in order to distance himself from his opponent and make his precious truths accessible only to a select few. The obscurities caused the highest listener, Sir de Poitiers, to nod off" (30–1).

that of such wits as Pope, Addison, and Lord Chesterfield. The preference for these marginal feminine figures over the greatest wits of the day in both Woolf's and Morgner's texts represents an inversion of hierarchies that sheds new light on our literary tradition. The unitary voice of the male tradition is unmasked as representative of an exclusive and authoritarian ideological position, with the voices of opposing characters (Beatrice and Orlando) opening up this mono-logic discourse for different possibilities of speaking.

Another strategy for subverting the male literary tradition is to reinterpret "great" figures of the male literary canon in order to claim them as predecessors for oneself. Woolf's favorite is Shakespeare, whom she sees as a figure of androgyny, a quality that Morgner has claimed for Goethe in many of her interviews.[16] By reading the texts of the "great" figures of the male literary tradition against the grain and thereby emphasizing aspects of their work, which are usually overlooked, Woolf and Morgner succeed in claiming them as models for themselves.[17] They show the voices of the "great" male figures to be intrinsically dialogic and reveal the unifying force of the male canon as suppressing the dialogic nature of poets' speech.

A third strategy for creating a literary tradition for women is to find female predecessors – a difficult task since both Woolf and Morgner are aware that most female writers have either been marginalized in the literary tradition or excluded altogether. Of course, Virginia Woolf herself is such a female precursor for Irmtraud Morgner; another one she names is Hrotsvith of Gandersheim. In addition to the few existing female writers, both authors also invent literary predecessors. These "legendary" female figures (as Morgner calls them) are the basis for the creation of a countertradition for women. Because no information exists about women in the books on the library shelves, Woolf calls for a rewriting of history in *A Room of One's Own*. Woolf is convinced that

16   For example, in a 1984 interview with Doris Berger, Morgner says, "I believe Goethe's genius consists among other things in the fact that he is an androgynous character. And that he is a man and a woman, i.e., a complete human being. His gender is almost unimportant" (Doris Berger, "Gespräch mit Irmtraud Morgner," *GDR Monitor*, 12 (Winter 1984/85), 33).

17   Morgner, for example, considers *Pandora's Box,* a little-known drama by Goethe, to be one of his most important works.

because information on women is hard to find, since "hard facts" about women's lives have been suppressed in historiography, it is necessary to use other means. Woolf points out that the presence of female writers often can only be felt: "For often one catches a glimpse of them in the lives of the great, whisking away into the background, concealing, I sometimes think, a wink, a laugh, perhaps a tear" (47). Woolf therefore creates an imaginary account of the life of Shakespeare's sister Judith, who thus becomes a fictional but *possible* precursor for women. In *Life and Adventures*, Morgner creates the figure of Beatrice de Dia in a similar fashion using her imagination to recreate the details of Beatrice's life, since few details of her life are known. "Legendary" figures such as Judith Shakespeare and Beatrice de Dia thus become the nondocumented "proofs" of women's historical accomplishments.

In addition to rewriting literary history by inserting personal details about imaginary female intellectuals, Woolf creates the episode of Orlando's friendship with Nell to take an additional shot at male scholars, who for centuries have had the privilege of defining a literary tradition. Noting that male scholars have concluded that "women are incapable of any feeling of affection for their own sex and hold each other in the greatest aversion," Woolf's narrator chooses "merely [to] state that Orlando professed great enjoyment in the society of her own sex, and [to] leave it to the gentlemen to prove, as they are fond of doing, that this is impossible" (220). Morgner makes similar ironic statements to prove that the supposed lack of solidarity and friendships between women is not a matter of "nature," but caused by the circumstances and living situations in which women find themselves:

> For she [Valeska] had once read enviously of historical friendships between men that, without being homosexual, were of a beautiful intensity: a mutual undertaking reinforced them. At best, an idea. Elaborating and defending it created bonds. That sort of activity between men and women was mostly short-lived, because it was threatened by sexual tempests. But friendships among women were even rarer than solidarity. In part, because friendships need time. The hobby of most women was the second and third shifts: housework, children. But Valeska and Shenya, despite the daily journey from the diverse acts of stooping that are indigenous to housework to those heights where ideas are to be found, had still summoned the energy for a great friendship. (463)

One is reminded here of Woolf's description in *A Room of One's Own* of browsing through the many volumes on women written by men. Woolf decries the lack of depictions of women's relationships in literature and suggests the radical potential of even so simple a sentence as "Chloe liked Olivia" (86). The depiction of friendships and dialogue among women in *Life and Adventures* and in *Orlando* is an important means for promoting female solidarity, on the one hand, and attacking male stereotypes of women, on the other. Indeed, the dialogic interaction between the genders in both Woolf's and Morgner's writing directly participates in a carnivalesque assault on strictly defined boundaries between the genders. Furthermore, the dialogic relationship between Woolf's and Morgner's texts creates a connection between two female authors (similar to that between the female characters in their texts) that is highly productive. It can show how an absent female tradition and history can be represented by recreating voices suppressed in the dominant male tradition.

Morgner emphasizes the importance of this point in her acceptance speech for the Hrotsvith of Gandersheim prize in 1985. Like Virginia Woolf in *A Room of One's Own*, Morgner talks about the material preconditions women need to be able to write: "Virginia Woolf points to these preconditions with the formula: a room of one's own and 500 pounds a year." Morgner praises Hrotsvith for her ability to "take the Zeitgeist at its word" in her sharp and honest analysis of her own times, revealing "its critical and heretical potential." For Morgner, Hrotsvith is "our contemporary" because she shows us how to escape the thought patterns [Denkgleise] of our times. In her closing sentence, she claims Hrotsvith as "a younger sister of Beatrice de Dia."[18] Woolf and Morgner both believe that the "sisterhood" among female authors, established through fictional dialogues with different voices of an "imaginary" female tradition permits women to leave a "male" history *and* to reenter a "female" history as subjects.

With *Orlando* and *A Room of One's Own* as intertexts, Morgner establishes a connection with an author who employs a dialogic struc-

---

18   Morgner, "Zeitgemäß unzeitgemäß Hrotsvith," *Neue deutsche Literatur*, 2 (1986), 126–8. Reprinted in Marlis Gerhardt (ed.), *Irmtraud Morgner: Texte, Daten, Bilder* (Frankfurt a. M.: Luchterhand, 1990), 70–2.

ture similar to that in *Life and Adventures*. A comparison of the strategies that both Woolf and Morgner use to establish a Bakhtinian dialogism in their novels presents yet another perspective on Morgner's political strategy as "dialogic politics."[19] The dialogism of *Life and Adventures* allows the author to criticize the authoritarian discourse associated with the patriarchal tradition *and* to establish and experiment with "other" perspectives. By immersing herself within different systems of languages, at once appropriating and interrogating them in a highly complex play of masquerade, Morgner creates new perspectives that might provide women with a basis for imagining and exploring their own different "voice range." Morgner's strategy makes it possible for women to distance themselves from the ideology of gender without negating the fact that we are always inside the ideology of gender.

Helen Fehervary has analyzed a similar use of masks in Christa Wolf's texts. Her thesis is that Christa Wolf conveys historicity in the form of masks. Fehervary explains:

> The mask is not an idea or story, as is myth, but the premonition of memory of a fact, a gesture, a person, an historical identity. It does not belong to the tradition of a progressive history, but to the tradition of the historical persona. The mask is the persona of authorship that hangs suspended between female subjectivity absorbed by myth and the absence of another system of language. In contrast to the literary avant-garde's perpetual construction, deconstruction and reconstruction of myth, the literary quality of the mask allows for the expansion and multiplication of one literary self into many: literature as reproduction, not production. [...] The mask is a form of relational being and

19   So far, relatively little attention has been paid to the dialogic or carnivalesque aspects in Morgner's discourse. Ulrike Sati, in her essay "Figuren im Gespräch," (Ulrike Sati, "Figuren im Gespräch: Irmtraud Morgners 'Leben und Abenteuer der Trobadora Beatriz nach Zeugnissen ihrer Spielfrau Laura,'" *Carleton Germanic Papers*, 18 (1990), 75–87) argues that Morgner uses the form of the dialogue throughout the novel to create a structure for the interaction of different figures and to keep the text open through the use of multiple perspectives. She interprets Beatrice de Dia as a metaphor for writing in the novel and thus a form of self-representation for Morgner. Monika Meier analyzes the polyphonic structure in the voices of the different groups of witches in *Amanda* (Monika Meier, "Konzerte der Redevielfalt: Die Walpurgisnacht-Darstellungen in der 'Amanda' Irmtraud Morgners," *Literatur für Leser*, 4 (1990), 213–27).

enables the stripping away of an isolated individual identity. It is the wish to participate in a body of affinities and not to become the summation of an individual or collective teleology. In this sense the mask is the subversive underside of myth and an alternative to mankind's progressive journey toward perfection.[20]

In her essay, "The Gender of Authorship: Heiner Müller and Christa Wolf," Fehervary mentions the affinity of Christa Wolf's *No Place on Earth* and Virginia Woolf's *Orlando*, as both authors attempt to construct "female authorship as an intersubjective expansion of the self" (57). In her book *The Dialogic and Difference*, Anne Herrmann builds on this idea in her comparison of Virginia Woolf and Christa Wolf's discursive strategies in constituting the female subject.[21] Herrmann has named this subject, which appears as epistolary addressee, novelistic heroine, and literary precursor, "an/other woman." Applying Bakhtin's theory of the dialogic to feminist criticism, she examines the relation between rhetorically and historically female subjects in their struggle for a voice critical of masculinist cultural forms. Herrmann creates a dialogue between Bakhtin's dialogic and Luce Irigaray's specularity to address the debate over the female subject in feminist critical theory.

The critical and hopeful power of masquerade has also been analyzed by feminist film theorists, who have problematized the female spectator by analyzing the vacillation between masculine and feminine as a function of looking. Most of this work has built on Laura Mulvey's famous essay, "Visual Pleasure and Narrative Cinema" (1975), which posits man as bearer of the look and woman as icon.[22] Woman as spectator, according to Mulvey, has two options: she either masochistically overidentifies with the female image or narcissistically becomes her own object of desire. Mary Ann Doane addresses this problem in "Film and Masquerade: Theorizing the

20   Helen Fehervary, "Christa Wolf's Prose: A Landscape of Masks," in Marilyn Sibley Fries (ed.), *Responses to Christa Wolf: Critical Essays* (Detroit: Wayne State University Press, 1989), 70–4.

21   Anne Herrmann, *The Dialogic and Difference: "An/Other Woman" in Virginia Woolf and Christa Wolf* (New York: Columbia University Press, 1989).

22   Cf. Laura Mulvey, "Visual Pleasure and Narrative Cinema," *Screen*, 16:3 (Fall 1975), 6–18.

196

Female Spectator" (1982). Her argument is that "the effectivity of masquerade lies precisely in its potential to manufacture a distance from the image, to generate a problematic within which the image is manipulable, producible, and readable by women" (87). Doane argues that womanliness as a mask can be worn or taken off, since masquerade creates a distance between oneself and one's image. The hopeful potential of masquerade is that it might help to understand the production of femininity as a position within a network of power relations in order to dislocate it.[23] Again we see that Morgner's interest in the exploration of carnival and masquerade echoes discussions among feminist theoreticians that became important in the 1980s.

The Montage Novel: Fictional Experiments

Laura's novelistic program in *Life and Adventures*, as expressed in the interview with the editor of the *Aufbauverlag*, shows that Laura, similar to Bakhtin, views all language, including aesthetic genres and literary language, as historical and ideological.[24] Bakhtin had postulated that language has at its core a ceaseless battle between centrifugal forces, which keep things apart and centripetal forces, which strive to make

---

23   For important contributions to feminist film theory, see also Annette Kuhn, *Women's Pictures: Feminism and Cinema* (London: Routledge, 1982); E. Ann Kaplan, *Women and Film: Both Sides of the Camera* (New York: Methuen, 1983); Teresa de Lauretis, *Alice Doesn't: Feminism, Semiotics, Cinema* (Bloomington: Indiana University Press, 1984); and Mary Ann Doane, *The Desire to Desire: The Woman's Film of the 1940s* (Bloomington: Indiana University Press, 1987).

24   Bakhtin states in "Discourse in the Novel": "We are taking language not as a system of abstract grammatical categories, but rather language conceived as ideologically saturated, language as a world view, even as a concrete opinion, insuring a *maximum* of mutual understanding in all spheres of ideological life. Thus a unitary language gives expression to forces working toward concrete verbal and ideological unification and centralization, which develop in vital connection with the processes of sociopolitical and cultural centralization" (*The Dialogic Imagination*, 271).

things cohere.[25] Bakhtin's conception of language is enabled a priori by an almost Manichaean sense of opposition and an existential struggle, as Holquist points out. In fact, Bakhtin's conception of language as a duel between opposing forces stresses the fragility of language and its ineluctably historical nature. In addition to the philosophical argument that language is dialogical by its very nature, Bakhtin maintains that dialogism is at the same time a historical phenomenon, generated by a confrontation between social conventions of style and genre.[26] Bakhtin thus views dialogism and heteroglossia as both historically instantiated *and* normative concepts. There is some ambiguity in Bakhtin's terms and a change in emphasis in the course of the development of his ideas has caused difficulties of interpretation. As Ken Hirschkop has pointed out, however, there are good reasons for Bakhtin to want to have a foot

---

25   Bakhtin in "Discourse and the Novel": "But the centripetal forces of the life of language, embodied in a 'unitary language,' operate in the midst of heteroglossia. At any given moment of its evolution, language is stratified not only into linguistic dialects in the strict sense of the word (according to formal linguistic markers, especially phonetic), but also – and for us this is the essential point – into languages that are socio-ideological: languages of social groups, 'professional' and 'generic' languages, languages of generations and so forth. [...] Alongside the centripetal forces, the centrifugal forces of language carry on their uninterrupted work; alongside verbal-ideological centralization and unification, the uninterrupted process of decentralization and disunification go forward. [...] Every utterance participates in the 'unitary language' (in its centripetal forces and tendencies) and at the same time partakes in the social and historical heteroglossia (the centrifugal, stratifying forces)" (*The Dialogic Imagination,* 272).

26   For Bakhtin, the development of the genre of the novel shows the basic nature of all language most clearly. He says in "Discourse and the Novel": "At the time when the major divisions of the poetic genres were developing under the influence of the unifying, centralizing, centripetal forces of verbal-ideological life, the novel – and those artistic prose genres that gravitate toward it – was being historically shaped by the current of decentralizing, centrifugal forces. [...] In the majority of poetic genres (poetic in the narrow sense), as we have said, the internal dialogization of discourse is not put to artistic use, it does not enter into the work's 'aesthetic object,' and is artificially extinguished in poetic discourse. In the novel, however, this internal dialogization becomes one of the most fundamental aspects of prose style and undergoes a specific artistic elaboration" (*The Dialogic Imagination,* 284).

in the camps of both philosophy and empirical-cultural analysis.[27] The latter entails the specific analysis of historical phenomena, while the philosophical edge of the same concepts makes it possible to approach those historical objects critically. By viewing language as a form of social exchange, Bakhtin can postulate that language is susceptible to political and moral evaluation; language becomes an activity that can be criticized and even improved. This form of dual definition provides an implicit critique of monoglossia, and monoglossia appears as a systematization of language, which prevents it from living up to its natural potential, from realizing the kind of social interaction that it should.

Like Bakhtin, Morgner insists on a historical analysis of language in combination with a normative demand in order to criticize an official discourse, which she sees as authoritarian, exclusive, and monologic. Morgner lets Laura criticize the "orthodox form of the novel," referring to a socialist realist conception of literature that ironically takes as its model the great realist novel of the nineteenth century from the bourgeois individualist tradition. Laura claims that the times for the "orthodox novel" are over, and she gives three reasons: first, it is no longer adequate for our modern reality, "in view of violent political movements throughout the world and an appalling information explosion" (175); second, it suppresses the experiences of ordinary women whose life rhythm, "which is socially and not biologically conditioned," is constantly "diverted by the interruptions of household responsibilities" (176); and third, it does not allow space for contradiction and opposition, since this type of novel, like socialist societies in general, "has a tendency to totalize" (176).

As an alternative, Laura offers the editor of the *Aufbauverlag* her own concept of the novel, which she claims to be Beatrice's work. This "new novel of the future," which she calls "operative montage novel," is – in contrast to "the orthodox novel" – dialogic in the Bakhtinian sense, since it allows for opposing voices to be heard: "The operative montage novel is an indestructible genre. [...] An absolutely ideal genre for interventions" (175) [Der operative Montageroman ist ein unverwüstliches Genre. (...) Ein geradezu ideales Genre zum Reinreden,

27   Ken Hirschkop and David Shepherd (eds), *Bakhtin and Cultural Theory* (Manchester: Manchester University Press, 1989), 1–38.

(170)]. It can deal with and represent in its structure the interruptions, contradictions, and differences that are everyday realities for women. Morgner lets Laura explain, "Lack of time and unforeseeable interruptions force her to quick drafts without leisurely fine-tuning" (176). Laura is talking about a novel composed of short prose pieces, just like *Life and Adventures* itself. The language and form of this new novel are themselves its content, because they reflect the material living conditions of the author. Laura explains:

> An ensemble of short prose brings the life movement of the epic "I" clearly into the book with no need to frame it with respect to content. Truth about life in books cannot exist wthout the author's belief in himself. A mosaic is more than the sum of its stones. In the composition they have a strange effect with and against each other under the eye of the viewer. Reading should be creative work: pleasure. (176)

The polyphonic novel Laura envisions incorporates the different "priorities and shadings [Tonarten] of day-to-day politics" (175). Like Bakhtin, Morgner favors this type of novel for its ability to reflect "more deeply, more essentially, more sensitively and more rapidly, reality itself in the process of its unfolding."[28] Morgner's "operative montage novel" thus corresponds directly to Bakhtin's open novel type.

Laura promotes a Bakhtinian type of dialogic novel not only because of its subversive potential, but also because it allows both the author and the reader to experiment with different possibilities. Bakhtin had postulated: "The idea of testing the hero, of testing his discourse, may very well be the most fundamental organizing idea in the novel."[29] The novel is composed not only of extended arguments (as Bakhtin points out in his analysis of Dostoevsky), but also of arguments punctuated with events, which test the ideas, submitting them to a kind of fictional experiment. Such narrative probing distinguishes the novelistic testing of the hero from a kind of purely argumentative resolution of disputes since the novel's procedures can present arguments in the form of a "fictional experiment." In "Epic and the Novel," Bakhtin claims "laughter delivers the object, so to speak, into the fearless hands of investigative experiment – both scientific and artistic – and of a free

28   Bakhtin, *Dialogic Imagination,* 7.
29   Bakhtin, "Discourse in the Novel," ibid., 388.

200

experimental fantasy serving the aims of this experimentation."[30] This type of fictional experiment, Bakhtin was convinced, reveals the import and significance of ideologies more adequately than pure verbal disputation.[31] Like Bakhtin, Morgner lets Laura emphasize the experimental and dynamic nature of the genre in her dialogue with the editor of the *Aufbauverlag*: "Writing is an experimental process. Short prose is compressed air, in concentrated and very intense form" (176). Her new type of novel is able, Laura claims, to test verbal arguments through fictional experiments that are very similar to scientific experiments. In fact, Morgner repeatedly compares artistic and scientific imagination in *Life and Adventures*. Many characters are both scientists and poets (Laura, Valeska, Vera, and Wenzel Morolf), and Morgner lets them argue repeatedly that the task of both the scientific and the poetic approach to the world is to question and investigate reality. Bakhtin's and Morgner's ideal dialogized narratives are "hypothetical" in a scientific sense. The comparison of poetic and scientific experimentation is significant because it alerts us to an inevitably scientific moment in the pursuit of self-knowledge through discourse. It shows that the goal of the process is to arrive at a more adequate knowledge of the historical and material world.

The dialogic thus must be understood as a strategy to approximate a *possible* explanation of the truth, which is established or challenged through a series of trials. There is no ultimate "truth" that can be discovered for all historical situations, but the process of experimentation nevertheless allows author and reader to test particular ideologies at specific times in history. Such a claim is

---

30 Bakhtin, op. cit., 23.
31 In "Epic and the Novel," Bakhtin remarks on the "simultaneous birth of scientific cognition and the modern artistic-prosaic novel form," a comparison made more specific when he claims they are linked by the notion of an "experimental" approach to reality. He emphasizes that the novel, by destroying epic distance through dialogues between different voices or through irony and laughter, "began to investigate man freely and familiarly, to turn him inside out, expose the disparity between his surface and his center, between his potential and his reality. A dynamic authenticity was introduced into the image of man, dynamics of inconsistency and tension between various factors of this image; man ceased to coincide with himself, and consequently men ceased to be exhausted entirely by the plots that contain them" (*The Dialogic Imagination*, 35).

different from the proposition that all languages, narrative paradigms, or generic structures are necessarily subjective and partial. In fact, the belief in the social-historical dimension of all linguistic structures that need to be tested in particular textual experiments prevents such a thoroughgoing relativism.[32] Again, the twofold goal of Morgner's writing is apparent in her insistence on the experimental nature of her writing. She promotes a subversion of authoritarian forms of discourse *and* a reconstruction of positive models through textual experiment.

Not only are scientific cognition and the modern novel linked by the notion of an experimental approach to reality, but the fictional experiments are created by, and create in turn, a dialogue with the reader "under the eyes of the observer," for whom "reading should be creative work," as Laura emphasizes. She insists: "You can only write short stories with the consent of the readers. They have the job of completing the total. The genre is based on the reader's productivity" (176). Such an aesthetic practice as Laura describes not only democratizes the relationship between author and reader, but the reader is also part of the critical project that both Morgner and Bakhtin want to encourage. Bakhtin explains in "Epic and the Novel":

> For the first time in artistic-ideological consciousness, time and the world become historical: they unfold albeit at first still unclearly and confusedly, as becoming, as an uninterrupted movement into a real future, as a unified, all-embracing and unconcluded process. [...] But the novel has a new and quite specific problematicalness: characteristic for it is an eternal re-thinking and re-evaluating.[33]

For Morgner, the process of rethinking and reevaluating that is set in motion in the novel allows author and reader to find ways to change the "customs" in their society. While the law grants equality to women in the GDR, people's consciousness and the social conventions by which men and women interact have not kept pace. Therefore a thought process, a process of reevaluation, needs to be set in motion. Morgner wants to encourage this through a Bakhtinian type of "creative" or "active" understanding in the reader, which Bakhtin describes in "Discourse and the Novel" in the following way:

32   Ken Hirschkop makes this important point about Bakhtin in his introduction to *Bakhtin and Cultural Theory* (26–7).
33   Bakhtin, *Dialogic Imagination,* 30–1.

Responsive understanding is a fundamental force, one that participates in the formulation of discourse, and it is moreover an *active* understanding, one that discourse senses as resistance or support enriching the discourse. [...] Therefore his orientation toward the listener is an orientation toward a specific conceptual horizon, toward the specific world of the listener; it introduces totally new elements into his discourse; it is in this way, after all, that various different points of view, conceptual horizons, systems for providing expressive accents, various social languages come to interact with one another. [...] The speaker breaks through the alien conceptual horizon of the listener, constructs his own utterance on alien territory, against his, the listener's, apperceptive background.[34]

Morgner shows how a woman writer has to construct her utterance on alien (male) territory and against her (male) listener's apperceptive background in the amusing sixth chapter of book 4, "Wherein Irmtraud Morgner tries by means of a solemn oath to persuade certain male readers to keep on reading." In this chapter Morgner alludes to the difficulties the female author faces in regard to her male readers' reaction, while conducting one of the fictional experiments that Bakhtin valued so highly. The author Irmtraud Morgner creates a fictional dialogue with a resistant male reader. She explains in this chapter that she supposedly feels compelled to write a letter to her male readers to convince them to go on reading, despite their distrust of Beatrice de Dia's feminist agenda (98). With great irony, she assures her male readers "that the physical Beatrice de Dia was a woman who matched today's ideal of beauty completely," her measurements being "92, 61, and 90 centimeters." Therefore her feminist "truths" cannot be interpreted as stemming from a "physical defect" (98). This assurance is necessary, as Irmtraud Morgner points out in her letter, because men tend to interpret women as "monolithic beings" and "trace all their cares, problems, and suffering back to one single defect" (98). And she goes on to say – again openly anticipating the thoughts of her male readers – "and this single optimal defect is of course yourself. Gentlemen, bluntly stated: Your middle part" (99). In this passage, the author mimics the voice (i.e. the thought patterns) of men in order to anticipate and make fun of possible objections or prejudices. The author closes her letter with the following greeting:

34   Ibid., 281–2.

In the hope that my pragmatic explanation makes you, gentlemen, inclined to grant the right of existence not only to the works of the hunchbacked Herr Kant (Immanuel) and similar eminent authorities, I remain with socialist greetings, Irmtraud Morgner. (213)

Morgner suggests that Freud's theory of women's penis envy motivates her male readers not to respect Beatrice's experiences. At the same time, she emphasizes that any discourse anticipates and structures itself in resistance to or in support of the reader's voice. In her comic pretense of taking her male readers' point of view into account, she emphasizes that both voices – that of the reader and that of the author – exist not in a vacuum, but in a concrete socioideological setting. Both author's and reader's voices are always influenced by specific ideological forces.

Morgner subscribes to Bakhtin's thesis, which claims that languages, including literary languages and genres, have an ideological, material basis. Unlike Bakhtin, who was not interested in issues of gender, Morgner introduces gender into the equation. Bakhtin thus serves as a resource, particularly because his theories of dialogism lend themselves to a critique of the kind of authoritarian discourse associated with the patriarchal tradition. While Bakhtin's theories allow feminists to think about language and gender in ideological terms, works like *Orlando* and *Life and Adventures* illuminate the feminist potential in Bakhtin's work by bringing gender and its connection to language so prominently into view.

Like Virginia Woolf, Irmtraud Morgner proposes that conditions in the modern world demand new literary forms. Both authors were convinced that women writers needed to seek new modes of expression that went beyond what Woolf, in *A Room of One's Own,* called the "man's sentence" of "Johnson, Gibson, and the rest" (79). In view of the achievements of the great nineteenth-century women novelists, Woolf continues, "There is no reason to think that the form of the epic or of the poetic play suits a woman any more than the sentence suits her. But all the older forms of literature were hardened and set by the time she became a writer. The novel alone was young enough to be soft in her hands" (80). The notion of the novel as a young, open-ended, and evolving genre is reminiscent of the model of the novel put forth by Bakhtin. Because it allows for an experimental approach to reality, a dialogized narrative is the ideal genre for women who do not have models or proper literary traditions. Because experimentation with different artistic structures is of crucial importance for women, both Woolf and Morgner take recourse to dialogized forms of writing.

Dialogism: Excavating Women's Vocal Range

The artistic development of Morgner's title figure represents one of those fictional dialogic experiments in a Bakhtinian sense. Morgner shows Beatrice de Dia's development as a speaker and writer in a series of fictional trials in which different possibilities of writing for women are tested. Her development moves from poetry to prose, in the direction of increasingly dialogized texts. In the beginning of her career, Beatrice writes medieval "scholastic cansos." But she has to leave the Middle Ages as soon as she develops from a *minnesinger* into a lovesinger, thereby breaking with the gender conventions of her time.[35] In Paris and during her early months in the GDR, she starts writing highly dialogic poems, which move further and further toward novelization, in a Bakhtinian sense. After she returns from her unsuccessful quest to find the unicorn Anaximander, she writes only prose pieces that become more and more dialogized. The story of Beatrice's development as a writer therefore represents a fictional testing of Morgner's thesis – as Laura had stated it in the interview with the editor of the *Aufbauverlag* – namely, that women, if they succeed in being true to themselves, will automatically write "dialogical texts." I would like to look at Beatrice's development more closely to show what Morgner understands by dialogical texts.

Beatrice realizes that she cannot write scholastic cansos any more when she understands that this language represents one specific point of view of the world: a male ideological system that she, as a female

35 Laura explains to Irmtraud Morgner in the eleventh chapter of book 1 that Beatrice had to leave the Middle Ages when she began to write love poems, since from that point on she refused to write merely role poems, but began to assume the position of a subject, a role not allowed for her (26–8).

troubadour, is not part of (*Life and Adventures*, bk. 2). In the words of the narrator: "Finally she [Beatrice] realized that she could no longer compose scholastic cansos, those imitations with disguised tenor, baritone, bass" (56). That same night Beatrice writes the poem "Seegang" ("Water or Sea Walk," which means both "Walk by/on the Sea" and "Motion of the Sea"), which clearly transcends the tradition of the scholastic canso. In its poetic language, however, it preserves elements of what Bakhtin describes as "the unitary language of poetry." In her poem, Beatrice creates a double-voiced discourse: it contains the norms of the traditional poetic language as well as another language that cannot clearly be defined yet. Just as the ambivalent title of the poem combines certainty (a walk by the sea, with "sea" as a traditional metaphor for "truth," "life," and "essence") with uncertainty (the vacillating movement of a ship in rough seas), so the structure of the poem contains two contradictory voices brought into dialogue: the voice of the medieval canso and modern poetic language, which challenges the rigidity of that form. On a second level, dialogue is created between two further voices struggling for expression in the poem: the biblical narrative of Jesus and Peter, on the one hand, and a female "I," on the other. The female voice in the poem speaks from inside the structure of the biblical narrative as the apostle Peter turns into the poetic "I" of the text:

Water Walk

And my ship
was in midlake
rolling
and heeling in the waves,
and the wind chased wispy clouds.

But in the seventh night
Gahmuret came across the lake.
Slowly,
his hair resolute against the wind.
When I saw him
walking across the water,
I gave a start.

He said:
"It is I, don't be afraid."

206

I said:
"If it's you,
then call me to come to you
on the water."

"Come," he said.

And I climbed out of the ship
and stepped onto the water
and went toward the wispy cloud
that he had just smoked.
He was standing behind the cloud.

As the cloud was swept away
by a squall
and his mouth was naked,
I cried for help
and sank into the waves.

But Gahmuret bent down
at once
and pulled me from the water
of which I had drunk plentifully,
my hair was soaking wet,
and he said:
"You of little faith, why do you doubt?"

And we boarded the ship,
and the wind died down. (57–8)

This female "I" of the poem sinks into the waves because she can no longer see the Gahmuret, the Jesus figure, behind a cloud of smoke. She then notices that "his mouth was naked," that Jesus's words (a male voice) cannot be a model for her own voice any longer. After Gahmuret has criticized her for her lack of faith in herself with the words of Matthew 14:31, he saves her and the wind dies down. In Beatrice's poem, the voice of Peter changes into a woman's voice. The lack of faith is not a lack of faith in God, but a lack of self-confidence and faith in her own creative abilities. The biblical narrative is still clearly recognizable in Beatrice's text, but it is brought into dialogue with an opposing voice that competes for expression.

On a third level, other dialogues are created between Beatrice's poem and related passages in the novel that are structurally similar in their use of biblical intertexts. There are many references to the Bible in *Life and Adventures* and almost always the language of the Bible is brought into dialogue with a female voice as in "Water Walk." The voice of an official biblical language can be heard most clearly as an intertext in Valeska's "Gospel" (book 12), which talks about Valeska's miraculous sex change and her realization that women need to define themselves as subjects. After a successful experiment at the chemical lab where Valeska works as a scientist, she one day "encountered something on the way home that she interpreted as a vision [das befremdliche Gesicht]. Disconcertingly, it was her own face" (443). Valeska sees herself as an active autonomous person for the first time:

> The lighting lay misty over the water, upon it in dove blue and pink patches that were rocked up and down and against each other, also mixed together by the waves. Such water on flat, limestone-covered earth; dazed by pastels, light on her feet, Valeska stepped onto the sea and made her way through the fishy boats. Yes, miracles! Paths of least resistance. Walks over water instead of corpses. Quick relief. A different kind that takes generations could be of no interest to Valeska during this night. For she could not banish the belief, which had come to her on the way home, that she was a scientist who could not be replaced at any time. (444–5)

The reference to the same biblical passage of Jesus's walk on the sea connects Valeska's story to the scene in which Beatrice attempts to "uncover her own voice range"; the two passages enter into a dialogue and explain each other. The reader understands that women's lack of self-confidence (what Morgner calls "lack of fanaticism" [Mangel an Größenwahn] elsewhere) prevents them from becoming subjects.

In both Beatrice's poem and Valeska's story, the biblical language functions as one partner in a dialogue with a female voice. Both voices represent a specific ideology competing for expression. The reader is encouraged to look for structurally similar passages in the novel that continue the dialogue, one set into motion by Morgner's technique of rewriting the same stories in different voices.[36] Sometimes the dialogue

36   The use of similar intertexts is not the only structural similarity in *Life and Adventures*. Morgner also repeats statements or stories told by one character in the

208

in these passages displays an opposition or competition between two or more different voices, sometimes they are variations of each other, and sometimes they mirror each other. Women's attempts to bring their own voices to bear, a process for which "there do not yet exist any models," is explored in all of these passages. Models for women's vocal ranges are continually tested and experimented with throughout the book, while the readers will start to look for relationships between stories and map out networks of voices in the text.

As I have indicated earlier, the first poem that Beatrice writes after her vocal range has been found already shows a variety of techniques that Morgner uses to create a dialogic structure in her novel. Dialogism is created through the stylization of different literary languages (styles or genre conventions); by bringing a character's voice into dialogue with the narrator's voice; or in exchanges between narrator and implied reader. It can be created by way of different intertexts; between structurally similar passages (e.g. different passages that use similar intertexts); or between passages that are thematically similar.

Beatrice writes two more poems to her lover, Alain, in Paris, both of which parody the medieval concept of *minne*, as the chapter

---

voice of another. In the last chapter of the book, for example, Benno repeats Laura's report of Beatrice's first life in the Middle Ages from chapter 1 of book 1 almost verbatim. He also retells Laura's story, "Café au contraire," which Laura told Beatrice as a story "that is too true," from a male perspective; and he uses the words that Beatrice imagined for the ideal Raimbaut "who does not correspond to reality" in his third information visit in order to introduce himself to Laura (bk 10, ch. 17). In all these passages, Benno speaks in the voice of another character, indicating that he is an imaginary ideal of a new type of man shared by Laura and Beatrice, not necessarily possessing an independent voice of his own. Laura, the character who takes Beatrice's place at the end of the novel, is not a single character but a complex mixture of Beatrice's and Laura's original points of view; she is a voice that incorporates many different perspectives. Repeatedly Morgner creates one single language composed of Laura's and Beatrice's voices in dialogue. For example in bk 4, ch. 17, "Arrival at Laura's and at herself," the two characters finish each other's sentences, complete each other's actions (Laura washes Beatrice's back), and display their identity in their bodily gestures, especially in their embrace at the end of the scene. We see one voice split into two in these scenes.

headings point out. The first poem is called "Roof" [Dach] and forms a chapter with the heading: "Mostly indecent writings by the trobadora, inspired by her base love for the false Alain" (61). The second poem, "Space Suit" [Raumanzug], is framed by the chapter heading: "Mostly decent writings by the trobadora, apparently inspired by her high love for the true Alain" (62). "Roof" is a highly erotic poem that uses sexually explicit language, whereas "Space Suit" is not a love poem at all, instead reflecting upon the lyrical speaker's identity as a poet in the body of a woman. The poem ends with the word "Leibeigenschaft" [bondage], playing with the idea of women owning their bodies, being prisoners of their bodies, and women as chattel. Beatrice's last two poems in Paris continue these reflections, as the representation of women's bodies in their own writing and in the official culture's symbolic system becomes an increasingly important topic in Beatrice's reflections.

After Beatrice has entered the GDR she writes no more poems in the traditional sense of the word, except the ones produced on request for customers in the poetry generator [Versschmiede] (126) she sets up because she cannot find employment as a troubadour. Four of the poems from her poetry machine are included in book 5: "Calling Formula of a Lover's Poem" [Rufformel aynes Liebhaberstücks], "Voices of the Steelworkers" [Stimmen der Stahlgießer], "Provocation for B.D." [Provokation für B.D.], and "Conversation with the Moon over Leuna II" [Gespräch mit dem Mond über Leuna II]. The titles of the poems are followed by rhythmic markers for her verses, but there are no words; the poems do not seem to have any content. On the one hand, these poems might be ironically commenting on the function of art in official doctrine in the GDR, which valued only the party-line content of an artistic text and condemned formal experiments as "decadent" and "formalistic." On the other hand, Beatrice's poems demonstrate Laura's thesis that women have to find new *forms* for their writing. But the titles also show Beatrice beginning to use different forms of genre subversion and parody. The first poem parodies medieval literary language (the archaic spelling conventions of the words strangely contrast with the computers Beatrice uses to manufacture the poems); "Voices of the Steelworkers" parodies socialist-realist literary language; "Provocation for B.D." might be a parody of

Brecht's poems; and the last one again brings science and poetry into dialogue.[37] In different ways, the titles of the poems break with the traditional concept of poetry as self-expression. These "poems" ironically demonstrate that the time for poetry and other orthodox forms of writings seems to be over, as Laura pointed out in the interview with the editor of the *Aufbauverlag*.

From now on, Beatrice begins to write short prose pieces that become increasingly dialogic. Beatrice's first narratives are parodies of fairy tales and legends. Then she writes a story about Laura's great-aunt Berta, entitled "Berta of the Flowering Bed" [Berta vom blühenden Bett], in Laura's name. These stories are followed by three prose pieces that are called first, second, and third "Bitterfeld Fruit," a jest aimed at the literary program established at the Bitterfeld Conference in the GDR in 1959. Finally, Laura reads Valeska's gospel as Beatrice's revelation and last will at her funeral. This is probably the most dialogized text in the novel, mixing biblical styles, diary, autobiography, pamphlet, scientific report, fairy tale, adventure story, and legend.

Encyclopedism

While Beatrice's texts become more and more dialogical, the inclusion of her texts in *Life and Adventures* adds to the encyclopedic nature of the novel. Patricia Herminghouse rightly emphasized in 1979 that this encyclopedism is part of Morgner's strategy to find a new aesthetic suited for women's experiences.[38] It was this feature of *Life and Adventures*, however, that was vehemently criticized in the early reviews. Male critics in particular failed to see the multiple forms of genre subversion as a deliberate political strategy on Morgner's part, accusing her of ignoring traditional genre conventions. The centrality of genre subversion to *Life and Adventures* can be seen in the prevalence of

---

37 Leuna in Merseburg was the GDR's largest chemical plant; at the same time we associate the name of Soviet space probes, which were called Lunik I, II, and III.

38 Herminghouse, "Die Frau und das Phantastische," 248–66.

critical attempts to pin the text down by labeling its genre. Fritz Raddatz, for example, criticized Morgner for having misunderstood the rules of the picaresque novel, and for having become an imitator of voices instead, so that the text turns into a cacophony of "mocking birds of all sizes, colors, and genders in a huge cage"[39] Other attempts to specify the genre of *Life and Adventures* were equally blind to its innovative structure: Gisela Lindemann labeled it a historical novel; Thomas Zenke identified it as the "old humorist novel," a genre "which we have known for a long time"; and Christa Rotzoll called it a "picaresque novel."[40] Gregor-Dellin complained that Morgner did not succeed in writing a *Bildungsroman*, denouncing the novel as an "epic debacle," while Manfred Wolter said its "transitional form" was too complicated for readers.[41] Werner Neubert, on the other hand, attempted to claim the novel as a "socialist novel" to defend it against criticism in the GDR.[42] Only a few critics (Sigrid Damm and Dieter Schiller among them) recognized the experimental nature of *Life and Adventures*.[43] Other scholars, Patricia Herminghouse, for example, praised the novel for its use of fantasy and its subversive attempts to rewrite the medieval quest novel, while Rainer Nägele focused on its oppositional nature as "antistories."[44]

The heterogeneity of responses by different critics confirms that *Life and Adventures* is a true novel in the Bakhtinian sense. *Life and*

39 Raddatz, "Marx Sisters statt Marx," *Die Zeit,* 21 May 1976.

40 Gisela Lindemann, "Des Kaisers alle neue Kleider" *Die Zeit*, 22 July 1983. Reprinted in Marlis Gerhardt (ed.) *Irmtraud Morgner: Texte, Daten, Bilder*, Frankfurt a. M.: Luchterhand, 1990, 159–64; Thomas Zenke, "Aus dem Dornröschenschlaf erwacht" *Frankfurter Allgemeine Zeitung*, 16 November 1976; Christa Rotzoll, "Ein lustiges Klageleid" *Süddeutsche Zeitung*, 13 November 1976.

41 Gregor-Dellin, "Trobadora aus der Retorte"; Wolter, "Leben und Abenteuer der Beatriz …".

42 Neubert, "Aus einem Gutachten," 103–5.

43 Sigrid Damm, "Irmtraud Morgner: Leben und Abenteuer der Trobadora Beatriz nach Zeugnissen ihrer Spielfrau Laura," *Weimarer Beiträge*, 9 (1975), 138–48; Dieter Schiller, "Nahe Spielwelt der Phantasie," *Neues Deutschland*, 4 February 1975.

44 Herminghouse, "Die Frau und das Phantastische"; Nägele, "Trauer, Tropen, und Phantasmen," 193–223.

Adventures absorbs and appropriates other genres in a continual process of evolution, continually engaging in a process of self-criticism and a criticism of language and literary definitions.[45] The basis for a consideration of *Life and Adventures* as a self-consciously Bakhtinian novel lies in Bakhtin's understanding of the social and political implications of this form. The encyclopedism of Morgner's text becomes a source of critical potential because Bakhtin identified encyclopedism with the Menippean satire, a tradition closely linked to the kind of novels that Bakhtin privileged. Bakhtin's argument about how carnival's form-shaping ideology was preserved in the novel's second line of development is part of his broader historical argument.[46] Bakhtin contends that the novel has been influenced by "serious" genres (such as tragedy and epic), on the one hand, and by a second "line of development" shaped by "the carnival sense of the world." Bakhtin's term *carnivalization of literature* refers to the transposition of this carnival spirit into a language of artistic images and eventually into a fully realized literary genre. For Bakhtin, the essence of those forms that preserved and developed the carnivalistic line was their concrete satiric response to *specific* contemporary social, political, and historical moments. The novel that follows this second line of development is a special genre,

45   M. Keith Booker, in his analysis of Virginia Woolf's *Orlando*, points to a similar confusion on the part of critics about its genre. "If it is true that the nineteenth-century society marginalized the novel in such a way as to associate it with the feminine," he argues, "then it is also true that Bakhtin's attempts to recuperate the novel have an interesting feminist potential, despite Bakhtin's own apparent lack of interest in gender issues" (*Techniques of Subversion*, 167).

46   This historical argument is most clearly developed in the new fourth chapter of his *Problems of Dostoevsky's Poetics* (Caryl Emerson (ed. and trans.) (Minneapolis: University of Minnesota Press, 1984)), added to the new edition of the book in 1965. In my own application of Bakhtin's theoretical approach to Morgner's novel, I will be cautious not to overemphasize what Morson and Emerson call the "anarchistic" Bakhtin by trying to use the concept of "carnival" and the "carnivalesque" in a way that corresponds to Bakhtin's ideas before and after the Rabelais book. I am convinced that the Bakhtin that Morson and Emerson describe as the "political" Bakhtin, the Bakhtin for whom ethical questions were always of great importance, serves best to shed light on Morgner's concerns in her novel. The explorations of politically responsible feminist strategies in the light of new – what now might be called postmodern – ideas most interests Morgner.

unique in its contemporaneity, its contact with everyday life, and its close connection with extra literary genres. It can be associated with culturally designated low genres, bearing a potential to resist and relativize official discourses. In this light, Morgner's encyclopedism, her satire of different "high" genres, and her insistence on portraying concrete everyday experiences instead of relying on abstract arguments can be understood as not merely a formal technique, a literary play without a particular reference, but as a specific oppositional attitude toward the world, directed against defined targets. What Raddatz calls her inflationary display of a "cage of mocking birds" is part of Morgner's political strategy of subverting an official discourse by including different perspectives from all walks of life. It attempts to reverse a thinking in terms of abstract, disembodied meaning in favor of the concrete bodily experiences of women.

Carnival: Representing the Body

Carnivalesque subversion, as Bakhtin describes it, is directed against an official, authoritarian language that represses the body, the cyclical nature of human life, and the triumph of the grotesque "laughing death" over the false closure of the absolute death of the individual. For Bakhtin, the carnivalesque is an antiforce not only to a particular dominant discourse, but more generally to a particular form of an abstracted, disembodied concept of meaning favored by the Platonic philosophical tradition. Carnival laughter can thus preserve an "unofficial truth" because it is never an abstract negation; it instead attempts to undermine the official language by mocking it, embodying it, and reconnecting it to the life cycle.[47]

> Negation in popular-festival imagery has never an abstract logical character. It is always something obvious, tangible. That which stands behind negation is by

47 Compare Nancy Glazener, "Dialogic Subversion: Bakhtin, the Novel, and Gertrude Stein," in Ken Hirschkop and David Shepherd (eds), *Bakhtin and Cultural Theory* (Manchester: Manchester University Press, 1989), 109–29.

no means nothingness but the "other side" of that which is denied, the carnivalesque upside down. (*Rabelais and his World*, 410)

The concreteness of women's daily experiences; the messiness of everyday life; the circular nature of women's existence; their close connection to the physical, which Morgner characterizes as an "acceptance of great changes of the body" that women have to deal with at least on a monthly basis; the disruption, disorder, and contradictions women have to face every day – all are aspects of women's lives that Morgner wants included in literature. By simply inserting descriptions of the ordinary, concrete experiences of women (childbirth, problems with clothing, sexual encounters, food preparation, the problem of managing at least two jobs at once, and much more) into highly philosophical and theoretical discussions, Morgner creates a carnivalesque narrative that breaks with a unitary concept of writing.

While the critical potential of carnival transgression holds obvious attractions for Morgner, she does not use the concept in an essentialist manner. For Morgner, carnival itself is not intrinsically radical or conservative. Actual carnivals, as Morgner makes clear in *Amanda,* can be both: they can support the status quo and they can threaten ossified hierarchies. As said before, carnivals form shifting configurations of symbolic practices whose political valence changes with each context and situation.

Feminist critics have therefore embraced the notion of carnival as a celebration of difference and plurality, but they have also warned against the easy appropriation of carnival as an essentially subversive feminist strategy. Mary Russo, for example, points out that real historical carnivals have often been the sites not of emancipation, but of brutal violence directed against women, Jews, and other marginalized groups, because "in the everyday world, women and their bodies" "are always already transgressive – dangerous and in danger."[48] In fact, the critical potential of carnival is often subsumed under the official culture as something of a "licensed affair," as Terry Eagleton has pointed

---

48   Mary Russo, "Female Grotesques: Carnival and Theory," in Teresa de Lauretis (ed.), *Feminist Studies, Critical Studies* (Bloomington: Indiana University Press, 1986), 213–29.

out. Peter Stallybrass and Allon White formulate this dilemma in the following way:

> Most politically thoughtful commentators wonder, like Eagleton, whether the 'licensed release' of carnival is not simply a form of social control of the low by the high and therefore serves the interests of that very official culture which it apparently opposes.[49]

Stallybrass and White therefore warn against a "false essentializing of carnival transgression" and plead for a close historical analysis of the politics of carnival as either transgressive and revolutionary acts of resistance, or as a means to preserve and strengthen the established order by channeling the anger of the marginalized groups into authorized forms of temporary transgressions.

Morgner seems to be acutely aware of the ambivalent nature of carnival. In *Amanda*, the second book of the trilogy, Morgner carefully constructs a series of scenes that makes this ambivalence visible. Both the chief-angel Zacharias and the chief-devil Kolbuk attempt to blackmail Laura into marrying one of them to prevent her from a successful and – for the preservation of their own power – dangerous reunification with her second half, the witch Amanda, who is kept a prisoner at Hörselberg. To pressure Laura into marrying him instead of contacting Amanda, Kolbuk visits Laura and shows her a videotape of the yearly carnival celebration at Blocksberg. The witches, who during the rest of the year are prisoners of the devils and have to work as prostitutes at Hörselberg for their amusement, are shown as they celebrate a carnival festival, which includes the cursing of the ravens and devils, the display of feminist slogans, dramatic performances showing the witches' victory over Satan, and the decapitation and burning of Prince Redbeard (whom Kolbuk offers to the witches as a sacrifice for this day). Like the carnival celebration itself, the tape's production and commentary are authorized by Kolbuk.

Because Laura refuses to marry Kolbuk, Pater Maccotino, who is supposed to force Laura into marrying Zacharias, visits her a few days later. He shows her the same tape but with a different commentary, this

---

49   Peter Stallybrass and Allon White, *The Politics of Transgression* (Ithaca: Cornell University Press, 1986), 13.

216

time authorized by "Deo." This second, "Godly" commentary not only includes organ music instead of the marching bands of the devil's tape, but it also explains the reason for the devil's generous authorization of the witches' subversive behavior. The devil allows this spectacle "to cover up his own tyrannical behavior by granting one pluralistic day of celebration per year" (406). Carnival in this instance channels the aggressions of the oppressed witches by allowing them to identify with the power that oppresses them (the ravens) (409). Moreover, the commentary includes long direct quotes from Bakhtin's *Rabelais* book, which analyzes the function of carnival as "a victory of laughter over fear" that could only take place on special days of celebration, while during the rest of the year fear and oppression returned. Bakhtin in this passage admits that carnival, though transgressive in its nature, does not always succeed in changing a politically oppressive situation. Nevertheless, carnival preserved the survival of a second "unofficial truth" that helped to prepare the consciousness of the Renaissance.

For Morgner, this "unofficial truth" is preserved in the witches' carnival at Hörselberg as well. Laura, after viewing the tape, thinks about the function of this "historical" instance of carnival and comes to the following conclusion:

> At first sight it seems surprising that today not a dummy of the devil symbolizing the medieval hell is burned but a member of the audience from the platform of power. At second sight, one understands that the hatred of the oppressed is already so violent that the regime believes only a naturalistic object, a true execution, could cool the rage of the slaves.[50]

Laura recognizes that the specific form the carnivalesque takes at particular moments in history can reveal something about the inner dynamic of official culture. Although the carnivalesque transgression of the witches is clearly permitted, the particular form, the symbolic shape

50   My translation. "Daß heute keine Teufelspuppe, die etwa der mittelalterlichen 'Hölle' entspräche, symbolisch verbrannt wird, sondern naturalistisch ein Publikumsmitglied der Machttribüne, mag auf den ersten Blick verwundern. Auf den zweiten ahnt man, daß der Haß der Unterdrückten schon als so gewaltig gefürchtet wird, daß das Regime glaubt, nur ein naturalistisches Objekt, eine echte Hinrichtung eines Machtvertreters könne die Sklavenwut kühlen" (*Amanda*, 413).

that it takes, reveals that the agents in power have to make more and more concessions in view of increasing political antagonism. As a result, Laura decides not to marry either of the two powerful men (Kolbuk or Zacharias) to avoid indirectly supporting either one of the oppressive regimes. She begins to understand that she needs to find allies among the witches instead. In this perspective the carnivalesque becomes a resource of possible actions, images, and roles for Laura. While it does not necessarily do away with the official dominant culture, carnival does play a critical role by encouraging Laura to take action.

The notion of carnival transgression is used in other ways in *Life and Adventures*. In Morgner's political and aesthetic analysis of the symbolic values of a dominant patriarchal culture, she often tracks the "grotesque body" and the "low-Other" of the official culture in the GDR to understand its inner dynamic. Her goal is to prove that to secure its identity, the dominant culture is dependent on the exclusion of the low-Other, which is often projected onto women.

The body becomes the focus of Morgner's subversive tactics. I have already discussed Morgner's parody of the objectification of the body in male ideology, for example in the "Letter to Her Male Readers," which criticizes the reduction of the female body to an abstract ideal of beauty based on its physical appearance. In the story of Valeska's sex change, Morgner also criticizes the reduction of the body to its objectified parts in patriarchal discourse. Valeska's reaction to her new position of power as a man, which comes about through an addition of "a small piece of skin" to her body, shows how reductive this ideology really is. She criticizes a male conception of the body whose status is determined by the possession or lack of a penis, misconstrued as the Phallus, a signifier of privilege rather than a bodily organ among others. Morgner's criticism of a male rationality that tries to suppress the physical concreteness of the body on behalf of a disembodied abstraction and idealization displays her more general oppositional and subversive attitude.

Bakhtin had noticed the compelling difference between the human body as represented in the popular festivity of the carnival and the human body as represented in the classical sculptures and paintings of the Renaissance. He saw how the two forms of iconography "embodied" utterly contrary registers of being, and he posited that the body

218

plays a mediating role. He suggested that the shape and plasticity of the human body is indissociable from that of discursive material and social norms in a collectivity. Bakhtin discusses two types of bodies (most emphatically in *Rabelais and His World*), the opposition of which denotes the inherent form of official culture. First, the classical statue of "high" culture is always placed on a pedestal, raised above the viewer and the communality, requiring passive admiration from below. The classical body keeps its distance; the spectator is placed before the statue in an instant of frozen yet apparently universal time. The classical statue has no opening or orifices; it is closed, homogeneous, monumental, centered, and symmetrical:

> [The classical body] presents an entirely finished, completed, strictly limited body, which is shown from the outside as something individual. That which protrudes, bulges, sprouts, or branches off (when a body transgresses its limits and a new one begins) is eliminated, hidden or moderated. All orifices of the body are closed. The basis of the image is the individual, strictly limited mass, the impenetrable façade. The opaque surface and the body's "valleys" acquire an essential meaning as the border of a closed individuality that does not merge with other bodies and with the world. All attributes of the unfinished world are carefully removed, as well as all the signs of inner life. [...]
>
> The grotesque body of carnival, by contrast, is represented as a mobile, split, multiple self; it is seen as a subject of pleasure in the process of exchange; it is never closed off from either its social or ecosystemic context:
>
> Such a body, composed of fertile depths and procreative convexities is never clearly differentiated from the world but is transferred, merged, and fused with it. It contains, like Pantagruel's mouth, new unknown spheres. It acquires cosmic dimensions, while the cosmos acquires a bodily nature. Cosmic elements are transformed into the body that grows, procreates, and is victorious.[51]

In these characteristics the grotesque unites two qualities or orientations in the world that Bakhtin deeply respected: the interdependence of bodies and the messiness of life. Whereas socialist realist art emphasized the clean, closed-off, narcissistic body, the art of the grotesque stresses exchange, mediation, and the ability to surprise. The grotesque restores "the ever uncompleted whole of being," as Bakhtin says.[52] The classical body, on the other hand, keeps its distance; it is

51   Bakhtin, *Rabelais and His World*, 320 and 339.
52   Ibid., 379 n. 3, quoted in Morson and Emerson, *Mikhail Bakhtin*, 449.

the center of transcendent individualism, a figure at which we gaze up and wonder. As Stallybrass and White explain, "[I]n a sense, it is disembodied, because it appears indifferent to a body which is 'beautiful,' but which is taken for granted."[53]

In *Life and Adventures* Morgner engages in a similar analysis of iconographies of the body, contrasting the representation of the body in the GDR's dominant culture of the 1970s with the grotesque body of women's discourse. The images of bodies analyzed and discussed by Beatrice and Laura in *Life and Adventures* include Beatrice's idealized description of her lover's body during the act of lovemaking, her description of Lutz's body when he is occupied with analysis, and a description of a Greek bronze statuette from a GDR art book. These representations of bodies, all in book 7, are part of the discussions between Laura and Beatrice about the best strategies for women "to enter history as subjects." The discussions between Laura and Beatrice are triggered by Laura's discovery of one of Beatrice's poems to her lover Lutz in the chapter "Scandalous Verses and Sleeves for Lutz." This poem celebrates the bodies of the lovers during the act of lovemaking; it emphasizes the body's physical and erotic functions and shows it as uncompleted, multiple, and fluid. Like Bakhtin's concept of the grotesque body of carnival, Beatrice's representation of the body clearly transgresses the conventions of the classical body of official culture:

> Beautiful
> defiled by time and women
> are you
> most beautiful resting
> on your back
> when the column of air presses your skin
> onto innards and bones
> and your flesh is intensely
> revealed.
> Hard on thighs and breast
> gentle around the hollow of the navel
> a pull
> that I follow
> under the words of my tongue

53   Stallybrass and White, *The Politics of Transgression*, 22.

under its strokes
suddenly
just now you age
first among the kings
the last
whose tyranny I sanction
I exist in the prison of your body
world is made of your flesh.
From this sex
no prettier one seen
may it make
its teardrops: pre-secretions of desire.
My mouth awaits the burning of semen
baptismal cry
and I kiss the telltale hands. (144–5)

Beatrice's verses are "scandalous" because the body represented is in radical opposition to the bourgeois individualist conception of the body, the ideal in "official" discourse, even the socialist realist norms of the GDR. The body Beatrice describes is a subject of pleasure in a process of exchange, shown in the physical act of making love. The two bodies of the lovers merge: the one exists in the realm of the other ("in the prison of your body"), the one devours the other ("a pull / that I follow / under the words of my tongue"). There is an emphasis on the material aspects of the body, on physical needs and pleasures of the lower body, for example in the phrases "defiled by time and women," "innards," "bones," "flesh," "tongue," "breast," "mouth," "the burning of semen," and so forth. It is a body that shows impurity, both in the sense of symbolic dirt (the ejaculation and swallowing of semen, and a different consciousness of the body when she speaks of the "pillars of air" that press on the skin and innards letting the flesh appear "shrill," the atmospheric pressure of which we are usually not conscious) as well as "moral filth" (the physical side of lovemaking displayed openly in the poem, something of a taboo in socialist-realist literature).[54] The poem mixes categories in the combination of "high" and "low" expressions (e.g. "flesh," "innards," or "pre-secretions" to-

---

54   In fact, Morgner has emphasized that none of her texts was ever translated into Russian or published in the Soviet Union because they were held to be pornographic. See Berger, "Gespräch mit Irmtraud Morgner."

gether with "king," "baptism," "beautiful"). Beatrice describes a grotesque body that grows and procreates and then lets it acquire cosmic
and biblical dimensions ("world is made of your flesh"). Her language
of desire turns the body into the "grotesque body" that Bakhtin celebrated for its subversive potential.

Beatrice's depiction of the body is scandalous because the norms
of socialist-realist art made the classical body the form of official high
culture. The classical body, which is harmonious, proportionate, and
monumental, represents a disembodied rationality. The grosser, more
material aspects of the body were traditionally displaced onto the
grotesque body. Women – along with other marginalized groups – were
constructed by the dominant culture as the grotesque body, the low
Other, whose discursive norms included heterogeneity, disproportion,
and a focus on gaps, orifices, and symbolic filth. Laura, for example,
explains to Beatrice that her lover Lutz views Beatrice as "a non-linear
system," just like the "doomsday machine, the atomic bomb" (145).
Lutz seeks to understand Beatrice, as Laura points out, to control her,
because in his mind "what one understands, one can control" (145). He
perceives her as the dangerous "Other," one who would threaten his
own identity unless he could exclude it. In this sense, Beatrice's verses
are scandalous not only because her language violates the norms of
official high culture, but also because she speaks as a woman about the
body of a man. Her transgression consists of transforming the male
body into the "grotesque body," a position reserved for women in
official discourse.

Beatrice, who at this point in her journey still believes that the
patriarchal structures of the Middle Ages are no longer operative in
the "promised land" of the GDR, does not understand why her verses
are designated as scandalous.[55] Only in dialogue with her minstrel
Laura is Beatrice able to grasp the extent to which the discursive

55   In fact, Beatrice believes her friend to be jealous of her relationship with Lutz
     because of Laura's long sexual abstinence. When Laura realizes that Beatrice
     has misunderstood her point, the two women make up. "Beatrice took Laura's
     overly sensitive reaction for an effect of abstinence and offered to give Lutz
     back. Not even passionate relations could ever have moved her to quarrel with a
     woman over a man. Laura said no thanks. Reconciliation over Hungarian beef
     soup from a can" (145).

222

structures of the two antithetical representations of the body continue to operate. Morgner uses Beatrice's naïveté to let Laura explain how the opposition of the two types of bodies structures the official discourse of the GDR. To make the trobadora see why her poem violates the norms of the official culture, Laura shows her friend the description of a Greek bronze statuette, which she designates as "full of meaning when talking about Lutz":

> The bronze statuette of a seated man from the Alpheus Valley was created between the ninth and eighth centuries B.C. Its limbs are as fine as wire, symmetrical when seen from the front; viewed from the side, they are constructively united in geometric angles into an abstract figure. Yet it is impossible to view it as an ornamental figure, like a piece of jewelry. Rather, all the elements of a Greek sculpture organically emphasizing the pose find clear and pure expression in this wire figure: the nakedness, which reveals the limbs; the relaxed attitude of each limb, and – despite the symmetry – in the frontal view a powerfully reaching, contrasting movement of above and below that firmly anchors the person. As a particular and most sublime effect of this geometrical abstraction, there emerges an equivalence and thus a relationship of all the limbs to one another, which, owing to the absence of facial features, manifests the dynamism of the figure very purely and powerfully. It is a scaffolding style that foreshadows the facade of an architectonic scaffold in the figure, constituted by the arms and lower thighs. (147)

The bronze statuette thus complies in all its details with the norms of the classical body. It displays the typical "disembodiedness." In its abstraction, its geometry, its symmetry, its static nature, and its finished quality, the statue is removed from the passive observer and keeps its distance. The "real" person and his individual corporeality are unimportant; that is, they are literally not represented. The figure becomes a pure abstraction.

The contrast between this representation of the body and that in Beatrice's poem is significant, not only because we now understand how Beatrice's verses violate the conventions of the official theory of art, but also because we understand from the context of the scene that the classical body that Bakhtin described was far more than an aesthetic standard or model. The classical discursive body encoded systems that were closed, homogeneous, monumental, centered, and symmetrical. From the Renaissance onward, the classical body structured the inner principles of "high" discourses of philosophy, statecraft, theology, and law, as well as literature. Gradually, the protocols of the classical body came to mark the identity of progressive rationalism itself.[56] And, as we learn from the discussions between Laura and Beatrice, the codes of the classical body are still operative in the discursive norms of progressive rationalism in the GDR. This becomes strikingly obvious in the descriptions both women give of Lutz's personality. Laura explains:

> He [Lutz] raised the art of definition to a magic discipline. He calls you a "nonlinear system," the atom bomb a "doomsday machine"; what you understand you can also control, he says. With his explanations he tidies up his head just like his desk, where he won't tolerate any unfinished tasks. He doesn't marvel at anything anymore. […] He has systematically trained himself not to marvel at anything, in order to do more work. (149)

Lutz's ideology, his rationalism, what Laura calls "the art of definition," regulates his whole being. It takes over his personality and his thoughts, his rational explanations literally "clean out his head." In this sense, his rationalism marks out his identity, the structures of which are displayed on his body.

This can be seen in Beatrice's strange observations about Lutz when in particular instances his body literally changes into the classical body of the Greek statuette:

> She [Beatrice] informed Laura that she could observe strange things about Lutz when he was giving definitions, which was his specialty. "As soon as he heads toward a definition, all that is accidental falls away from him," said Beatrice. "The dark blue eyes, the mustache, the thinning hair. His face falls away like a plaster mask; only the scaffold remains standing, an open construction whose parts are fastened together with rivets. During definitions I see the reinforcements under his face and the buttresses and supporting beams of his shoulders, for his sweater is missing too. And the ample ready-to-wear pants are missing too. When he gives definitions, I can look through him." (145)

Like the bronze statuette, Lutz's body has lost its physical materiality. The Greek statuette lacked any individual physiognomic detail, and the observer does not ask for "the Who, When and Where of the person." Likewise, Lutz's face falls off him like a stucco mask, displaying the

---

56   Cf. Stallybrass and White, *The Politics of Transgression*, 22.

geometric, highly abstract figure he has become. The scaffold style of the Greek statuette is fully realized in Lutz's body. Beatrice is the one who can "see through" Lutz, the person who wants to "see through" everything in order to be able to classify and explain the world. Although he is convinced that he can control whatever he understands, the ideology controls him and leaves its traces on his own body. Lutz literally becomes the bronze statuette, he embodies the abstraction that is the essence of his ideology. Ironically, his body directly displays, "embodies," the codes and regulating systems of a specific kind of abstracted, disembodied rationalism.[57]

For Morgner this type of rationality is part of an exclusive and authoritarian patriarchal discourse. The art book's description of the statue itself implies that the statue (and therefore also Lutz's body) partakes in the discursive norms of the official *male* discourse of rationality and reason:

> It is as if a boy who has not yet mastered the language of his fathers and can only stammer, nonetheless represents and gives expression to a way of life that will transcend his fathers and ancestors, signifying the beginning of a new life-form. (148)

The geometric looks forward to the classical ideal. It is a language that takes its norms and conventions from the discourse of the fathers. While this language might eventually lead beyond the language of its fathers, it nevertheless develops in accordance with the official patriarchal discursive norms and gives expression to its ideology.

---

57 Petra Reuffer, in her analysis of this passage points out that Morgner's criticism of patriarchal rationality corresponds to Adorno and Horkheimer's critique of instrumental thinking (cf. *Die unwahrscheinlichen Gewänder der anderen Wahrheit: Zur Wiederentdeckung des Wunderbaren bei G. Grass und I. Morgner* (Essen: Verlag Die Blaue Eule, 1988)). Adorno and Horkheimer's thesis is that Enlightenment rationality developed with the movement from magical thinking of the pre-Homeric world to Enlightenment thinking that can be detected in the Homeric epic. Both the Greek bronze statuette and the Homeric epic date from the eighth century. When Laura says that Lutz has turned the art of definitions into a magical discipline, we hear echoes of Adorno and Horkheimer's analysis of the relationship between myth, magical thinking, and Enlightenment thinking as a dialectical one, with mythical fear being the other side of Enlightenment rationality.

Beatrice's poem, on the other hand, subverts the official language of the "classical body." The author transgresses the neat boundaries between private and public, beautiful and ugly, material body and abstract ideal. Beatrice's own "vocal range," as it can be heard in the poem, subverts and "disunifies" the official language just like the grotesque body in carnival subverts the conventions and limitations imposed by high culture. The norms and conventions that define official discourse are not only made visible, but also rendered absurd, shown to be nothing but rules without a substance. The façade of the body, so important in the classical body, is unveiled as its substance. In fact, there does not exist any substance, but only a façade. Women's vocal range is not the language of the "boy who tries to go beyond the language of the fathers," as in the geometric style of the bronze statuette, but one that is diametrically opposed to the structuring norms of the father's discourse. It does not develop out of the official language of the fathers, but instead is radically opposed to it. The question that Morgner asks again and again and experiments with in her text is how to give expression to this other vocal ranges of women once the norms of official discourse have been rendered absurd. What kind of language remains for women after the father's "tenor, baritone, and bass" have proven inadequate for expressing women's desire? What kind of language would not simply reverse hierarchies, but transcend binary oppositions?

One model for an alternative iconography of the body can be found in Beatrice's description of Split in book 8. This book tells about Beatrice's journey through Europe in search of the miraculous unicorn Anaximander, which could save the world, a quest that becomes necessary because Beatrice finally realizes that the GDR is not the "promised land" for women. Beatrice does not find the unicorn (in its place she brings back a little dog masked as a unicorn with the help of a plastic horn), but she finds the town of Split. Split becomes the metaphor for a new space, an alternative to the male discourse of disembodied rationality. In Split is the palace of Diocletian, whose tyranny has been "subverted" by everyday life in the form of the Salonites; it is inhabited by the Dalmatian women, who wear the pride and sovereignty of having lived a full life in the wrinkles of their skin and their "noble posture" (195); and it displays the messiness and chaotic creativity of life. As Beatrice explains in her travel report, Split resists being turned into a photo opportunity because of its abundance of contradictory images; instead, it makes the American tourists look grotesque. The American wives in their white jersey pants and artificially groomed bodies become the objects for their husbands' cameras because Split, which should be the object of the tourists' gaze, refuses objectification. Instead of Split, the American wives are turned into mere façades (like Lutz); they are reduced to an abstraction by the patriarchal discourse, which is dependent on objects that pose as the subject's other.

Beatrice calls Split an "organism," a "growth" [Gewächs], which is "related to Laura," unlimited and inexhaustible: "one cannot live [in Split] long enough in order to exhaust it" (191). In Beatrice's attempt to find an alternative language of/for the female body, her description of the city of Split turns into a description of Laura's and an/other woman's body:

> In Split, I comprehend a woman's skin. In contrast to her brothers, who sit in university chairs thinking about the world, she tastes of it. That is why Laura is crossed by streets and tracks and rivers which deposit objects in the fabric of her body, animate objects and inanimate ones. The disorder increases with increasing age, the sense for order decreases, as does fear of abundance. Wherein woman knows she is suspended. [...] How many Lauras does the world structure of today need in order to be marbled with Lauras? (202–3)

Beatrice's description of Laura's body is the absolute opposite of the American tourists, the bronze statuette, and Lutz. While Lutz's body has lost everything that might be spontaneous and accidental – he is the "body without organs" (Deleuze and Guattari) – Laura's body is part of a living "organism." In Beatrice's description, Laura's body represents abundance and disorder, since the material world has left organically grown "deposits" of experiences in it. Laura's body has no limits. It is in exchange with the world, since the borders between her and the surrounding world are fluid. She tastes from the world and the world leaves its traces in the fabric of her body. She is dissolved as an individual separate identity but at the same time she is "at home" in the world and "elevated" in this process of exchange (*aufgehoben* means dissolved, at home, and elevated at the same time). While Lutz, who is one of Laura/Beatrice's "brothers, who sit in university chairs thinking about the world," exists in separation from the world representing reduction, abstraction, and order, Laura represents abundance, materiality, disorder, and synthesis. Thus, the iconography of Laura's body displays a utopian potential, which might be realizable if all dogma were cleared away. Not the unicorn Anaximander, some exterior miracle, but the kind of consciousness of the incompleteness of life represented in Beatrice's description of Laura/Split can save the world.

This new female body, this new female subject Beatrice discovers in Laura/Split, is structurally different from the male subject. The new female subject is open-ended, boundless, and dialogic. Absent and excluded from the official patriarchal discourse, "she" embodies the possibility of a different subjectivity, based on the recognition of the other (person or material world) not as an object, but as "an/other" subject. This new subject represented by the open-ended female body does not displace everything that is other in order to guarantee its own wholeness (as with the classical body), but, on the contrary, it embraces difference and alterity. The dialogic represented in this new body stands for the discursive relation between two subjects, in which the subject constitutes itself without the annihilation or assimilation of the other. Such a subject does not need to mirror *itself* in the other, but instead embraces and includes the other. It is not afraid of "disorder" and "abundance," as Morgner says. In the dialogue between Laura and Beatrice, the reader understands that it is the dialogic that might be a strategy for women to gain subject status.

Thus Morgner uses the notion of the dialogic for her own definition of a positive feminist political strategy. For Morson and Emerson, the dialogic is the principle that remains from Bakhtin's works as the most important ethical and political idea. Bakhtin himself came back to the dialogic in his late work as part of a return to the earlier ethical themes, making it part of a positive definition of political strategy:

> The dialogic nature of consciousness. The dialogic nature of human life itself. The single adequate form for *verbally expressing* authentic human life is the *open-ended dialogue*. Life by its very nature is dialogic. To live means to participate in dialogue: to ask questions, to heed, to respond, to agree, and so forth. In this dialogue a person participates wholly and throughout his whole

life: with his eyes, lips, hand, soul, spirit, with his whole body and deeds. He invests his entire self in discourse, and this discourse enters into the dialogic fabric of human life, into the world symposium.[58]

Dialogue, in this sense, is a special sort of interaction, not interaction itself. It depends on the knowledge and acknowledgment that all social and psychological entities are processual in nature. Dialogue is an unfinalizable activity; existence cannot be separated from the ongoing process of communication. Neither individuals nor social entities are ever monads; reality is much looser, messier, and more open than that. The unfinalizable aspects of any interaction and the relative disorder of the participants show that neither individuals nor social entities are locked within their boundaries: the participants in this dialogue are constantly redefined; they develop and create numerous potentials "in" each of them "separately" and between them "interactively" and "dialogically."[59]

Bakhtin himself admitted, however, that existing forms of knowledge inevitably monologize the world by turning an open-ended dialogue into a statement "summarizing" its contents but misrepresenting its unfinalizable spirit. So far, in Bakhtin's view, only literary works have approached this more adequate representation. In *Life and Adventures*, Morgner takes Bakhtin's concept of the dialogic as a starting point and interprets it from a feminist perspective. She identifies the "unifying force" that suppresses the heterogeneity in discourse as the language of a dominant male culture. It functions by repressing difference and alterity, the precondition for any true dialogue, in order to fit all discourse under its norms.

Women's first task, then, is to subvert the monologic discourse of the dominant male culture to make room for dialogue. Morgner suggests a series of strategies: she creates figures that unveil gender definitions as absurd, she parodies a male literary canon, introduces different literary styles and genre definitions, and finally, she criticizes an ideology of disembodied rationality in an attempt to break open a monologic discourse unable to include women or other "marginal"

---

58 Bakhtin, *Toward a Reworking of the Dostoevsky Book*, quoted in Gary Saul Morson and Caryl Emerson, *Mikhail Bakhtin: Creation of a Prosaics* (Stanford: Stanford University Press, 1990), 60.

59 Morson and Emerson, *Mikhail Bakhtin*, 52.

figures. The carnivalesque is an important part in this process. In making the other and repressed side of the official culture visible by taking on the role of the grotesque, the clown, or the buffoon, the structuring dynamics of official culture become visible as authoritarian and exclusive. It is Beatrice as a female picaro who transgresses not only the patriarchal norms of the official GDR culture, but also the literary norms of the socialist-realist novel. This figure makes clear that the available roles for women in patriarchal society and in "orthodox" literary discourse do not allow them the possibility of acting as subjects or taking up their voice and speaking. In the figure of Beatrice, Morgner illustrates the need for women "to exit history." In "Forms of Time and Chronotope in the Novel," Bakhtin says the following:

> In the struggle against conventions, and against the inadequacy of all available life-slots to fit an authentic human being, these masks [the rogue, the clown, the fool, the picaro] take on an extraordinary significance. They grant the right *not* to understand, the right to confuse, to tease, to hyperbolize life; the right to parody others while talking, the right to not be taken literally, not "to be oneself"; the right to live a life in the chronotope of the entr'acte, the chronotope of theatrical space, the right to act life as a comedy and to treat others as actors, the right to rip off masks, the right to rage at others with a primeval (almost cultic) rage – and finally, the right to betray to the public a personal life, down to its most private and prurient little secrets.[60]

In this sense, the function of the figure of Beatrice corresponds to a deconstructive, negative impulse in feminist critical theory.

But for Morgner, a second step needs to follow the first one. Women also need to work for positive definitions, develop an effective political practice, and formulate utopian models of women's true "vocal range." Morgner's fantastic representations of the new positive feminist subject include the antipodean artist, the tightrope walkers, the female picaros, the female Faust figures and prophets, and the 800-year-old trobadoras. The excavation of women's literary talents is dependent on women's efforts to create a "legendary histori-cal consciousness" by inventing fantastic predecessors, as well as searching for realistic female precursors such as Judith Shakespeare, Beatrice de Dia, Orlando, Valeska, Hrotsvith, and Virginia Woolf.

60   Bakhtin, *The Dialogic Imagination*, 163.

The second utopian step involves efforts to create different forms of writing that would be truly dialogic: the fictional experiment conducted "in collaboration with the reader," the operative montage novel of the future, the encyclopedic novel, or a poem that can embrace a multiplicity of other texts and voices. In addition, this second step also calls for a different way of thinking, illustrated metaphorically by Anaximander and Split. It is a thought process that is not dependent on binary opposites, that does not reduce material reality and women's bodies to abstract disembodied concepts. The second step necessarily has to be a utopian goal, one that literally does not have a place yet. It is a step that defines the *process* necessary to reach the goal as more important than the goal and endpoint itself. Only with this second step would women be able to "re-enter history as subjects."

Here is where, to my mind, Morgner's textual practice differs from other contemporary modes of radical, critical, or creative thinking – postmodernism and philosophical antihumanism on the one hand, and the essentialist and/or separatist feminism of the 1970s on the other. The twofold process Morgner promotes in *Life and Adventures* connects the novel to discussions among feminists today: Morgner defines her feminism as a theoretical *and* political force, not merely as a simple grassroots movement, nor merely as a sexual politics. She insists on theoretical analysis *together* with a politics of experience and everyday life. In entering the public sphere, such a creative practice can displace aesthetic hierarchies and generic categories and work to establish a semiotic ground for a different production of reference and meaning. Morgner's critical/fictional texts are examples of this theory and practice. The rereading against the grain of the "master works" of Western culture *and* the textual construction of discursive spaces in which not Woman, but women are represented and addressed as subjects in a dialogue, possessing both a specificity (gender) and a history, is Morgner's participation in an original "cultural creation" set into motion by feminism. More, perhaps, than a new genre of critical/fictional creative expression, it can be thought of as part of a new aesthetic, a rewriting of culture.

Bibliography

Adelson, Leslie A., *Making Bodies, Making History: Feminism and German Identity*, Lincoln: University of Nebraska Press, 1993.

Adorno, Theodor W., *Aesthetic Theory*, C. Lenhardt (trans.), Gretel Adorno and Rolf Tiedemann (eds), London and New York: Routledge & Kegan Paul, 1984.

——, *Ästhetische Theorie*, Gretel Adorno and Rolf Tiedemann (eds), Frankfurt a. M.: Suhrkamp, 1973.

——, "Engagement," in Shierry Weber Nicholsen (trans.), *Notes to Literature*, New York: Columbia University Press, 1991.

——, *Minima Moralia: Reflections from Damaged Life*, E. F. N. Jephcott (trans.), London: NLB, 1978.

——, *Notes to Literature*, Shierry Weber Nicholsen (trans.), New York: Columbia University Press, 1991.

——, "The Position of the Narrator in the Contemporary Novel," in Shierry Weber Nicholsen (trans.), *Notes to Literature*, New York: Columbia University Press, 1991, 30–6.

——, *Prisms*, Samuel Weber and Shierry Weber (trans.), Cambridge: MIT Press, 1981.

——, "Rückblickend auf den Surrealismus," in Shierry Weber Nicholsen (trans.), *Notes to Literature*, New York: Columbia University Press, 1991.

Adorno, Theodor W. and Horkheimer, Max, *Dialectic of Enlightenment*, John Cumming (trans.), New York: Continuum, 1972.

Altbach, Edith Hoshino, Jeanette Clausen, Dagmar Schulz and Naomi Stephan (eds), *German Feminism: Readings in Politics and Literature*, Albany: State University of New York Press, 1984.

Anz, Thomas (ed.), *"Es geht nicht um Christa Wolf": Der Literaturstreit im vereinten Deutschland*, Munich: edition spangenberg, 1991.

Arnold, Heinz Ludwig (ed.), *Die andere Sprache: Neue DDR-Literatur der 80er Jahre*, Munich: text und kritik, 1990.

Auer, Annemarie, "Trobadora unterwegs oder Schulung in Realismus," *Sinn und Form*, 5 (1976), 1067–107. Reprinted in Marlis Gerhardt (ed.), *Irmtraud Morgner: Texte, Daten, Bilder*, 117–49. Frankfurt a. M.: Luchterhand, 1990.

Bakhtin, M. M. *The Dialogic Imagination: Four Essays*. Michael Holquist (ed.), Caryl Emerson and Michael Holquist (trans.), Austin: University of Texas Press, 1987.

——, *Problems of Dostoevsky's Poetics*, Caryl Emerson (ed. and (trans.)), Minneapolis: University of Minnesota Press, 1984.

——, *Rabelais and His World*, Hélène Iswolsky (trans.), Bloomington: Indiana University Press, 1984.

Bammer, Angelika, "The American Feminist Reception of GDR Literature (With a Glance at West Germany)," *GDR Bulletin*, 16:2 (1990), 18–24.

——, *Partial Visions: Feminism and Utopianism in the 1970s*, New York: Routledge, 1991.

——, "Trobadora in Amerika," in Marlis Gerhardt (ed.), *Irmtraud Morgner: Texte, Daten, Bilder*, Frankfurt a. M.: Luchterhand, 1990, 196–209.

Barthes, Roland, *The Pleasure of the Text*, Richard Miller (trans.), New York: Hill & Wang, 1975.

——, *S/Z*, Richard Miller (trans.), New York: Hill & Wang, 1974.

Bathrick, David, "The End of the Wall before the End of the Wall," *German Studies Review*, 14:2 (1991), 297–311.

——, *The Powers of Speech: The Politics of Culture in the GDR*, Lincoln: University of Nebraska Press, 1995.

——, "Productive Mis-Reading: GDR Literature in the USA," *GDR Bulletin*, 16:2 (1990), 1–6.

Benhabib, Seyla, *Critique, Norm, and Utopia: A Study of the Foundations of Critical Theory*, New York: Columbia University Press, 1986.

Bennett, Tony, *Formalism and Marxism*, London: Methuen, 1979.

Berger, Doris, "Gespräch mit Irmtraud Morgner," *GDR Monitor*, 12 (Winter 1984/85), 29–37.

Berman, Russell, "Adorno, Marxism, and Art," *Telos*, 34 (Winter 1977–78), 157–66.

Bogin, Meg, *The Women Troubadours*, New York: Paddington Press, 1976.

Booker, M. Keith, *Techniques of Subversion in Modern Literature: Transgression, Abjection, and the Carnivalesque*, Gainesville: University of Florida Press, 1991.

Booth, Wayne C., "Freedom of Interpretation: Bakhtin and the Challenge of Feminist Criticism," *Critical Inquiry*, 9 (1982), 45–76.

Bovenschen, Silvia, "The Contemporary Witch, the Historical Witch and the Witch Myth: The Witch, Subject of the Appropriation of Nature and Object of the Domination of Nature," *New German Critique*, 15 (Fall 1978), 83–119.

Brandes, Ute (ed.), *Zwischen gestern und morgen: Schriftstellerinnen der DDR aus amerikanischer Sicht*, Berlin: Peter Lang, 1992.

Brandt, Sabine, "Thema Frau: Zum Tode der Schriftstellerin Irmtraud Morgner," *Frankfurter Allgemeine Zeitung*, 8 May 1990.

Brinkler-Gabler, Gisela (ed.), *Deutsche Literatur von Frauen*, 2 vols, Munich: Beck, 1988.

Bürger, Peter, *Theorie der Avantgarde*, Frankfurt a. M.: Suhrkamp, 1974.

——, *Theory of the Avant-Garde*, Michael Shaw (trans.), Minneapolis: University of Minnesota Press, 1984.

Burri, Peter, "Der zweite Schritt: Ein Roman von Irmtraud Morgner über die Alltagswirklichkeit in der DDR," *Nationalzeitung (Basel)*, 2 October 1976.

Butler, Judith, "Contingent Foundations: Feminism and the Question of 'Postmodernism,'" in Judith Butler and Joan W. Scott (eds), *Feminists Theorize the Political*, New York: Routledge, 1992, 3–21.

234

——— and Scott, Joan W. (eds), *Feminists Theorize the Political*, New York: Routledge, 1992.

Calinescu, Matei, *Five Faces of Modernity: Modernism, Avant-Garde, Decadence, Kitsch, Postmodernism*, Durham: Duke University Press, 1987.

Cardinal, Agnès, "'Be Realistic: Demand the Impossible.' On Irmtraud Morgner's Salman Trilogy," in Martin Kane (ed.), *Socialism and the Literary Imagination: Essays on East German Writers*, 147–61, New York: Berg, 1991.

Castein, Hanne, "Wundersame Reisen im gelobten Land: Zur Romantikrezeption im Werk Irmtraud Morgners," in Howard Gaskill, Karen McPerson, and Andrew Barker (eds), *Neue Ansichten: The Reception of Romanticism in the Literature of the GDR*, Amsterdam: Rodopi, 1990, 114–25.

Clark, Katerina and Holquist, Michael, *Mikhail Bakhtin*, Cambridge: Harvard University Press, 1984.

Clason, Synnöve, "Am Ende bleibt das eigene Leben. Ost-Berlin, 1990: Ein Gespräch mit Irmtraud Morgner – kurz vor ihrem Tod," *Die Zeit*, 6 November 1992, 6.

———, "'Mit dieser Handschrift wünschte sie in die Historie einzutreten': Aspekte der Erberezeption in Irmtraud Morgner's Roman *Leben und Abenteuer der Trobadora Beatriz*," *Weimarer Beiträge*, 36:7 (1990), 1128–45.

Damm, Sigrid, "Irmtraud Morgner: Leben und Abenteuer der Trobadora Beatriz nach Zeugnissen ihrer Spielfrau Laura," *Weimarer Beiträge* 9 (1975), 138–48.

Deiritz, Karl and Krauss, Hannes (eds), *Der deutsch-deutsche Literaturstreit oder "Freunde, es spricht sich schlecht mit gebundener Zunge": Analysen und Materialien*, Hamburg: Luchterhand, 1991.

———, *Verrat an der Kunst? Rückblicke auf die DDR-Literatur*, Berlin: Aufbau Taschenbuch, 1993.

De Lauretis, Teresa, *Alice Doesn't: Feminism, Semiotics, Cinema*, Bloomington: Indiana University Press, 1984.

———, *Technologies of Gender: Essays on Theory, Film, and Fiction*, Bloomington: Indiana University Press, 1987.

——— (ed.), *Feminist Studies, Critical Studies*, Bloomington: Indiana University Press, 1986.

Deleuze, Gilles and Guattari, Félix, *Anti-Oedipus: Capitalism and Schizophrenia*, Robert Hurley, Mark Seem and Helen R. Lane (trans.), New York: Viking, 1977.

Delius, F. C., "Ich habe gelesen," *konkret*, 5 (1975), 43.

Doane, Mary Ann, *The Desire to Desire: The Woman's Film of the 1940s*. Bloomington: Indiana University Press, 1987.

———, "Film and Masquerade: Theorising the Female Spectator," *Screen*, 23 (September–October 1982), 74–87.

Drewitz, Ingeborg, "Sprung in die Gegenwart: Irmtraud Morgners neuer Roman," *Der Tagesspiegel*, 8 August 1976.

Eagleton, Terry, *Marxism and Literary Criticism*, London: Methuen, 1976.

———, *Walter Benjamin, or Towards a Revolutionary Criticism*, London: Verso and NLB, 1981.

Eigler, Friederike and Pfeiffer, Peter C. (eds), *Cultural Transformations in the New Germany: American and German Perspectives*, Columbia: Camden House, 1993.

Emmerich, Wolfgang, "Do We Need to Rewrite German Literary History Since 1945? A German Perspective," Peter C. Pfeiffer (trans.), in Friederike Eigler and Peter C. Pfeiffer (eds), *Cultural Transformations in the New Germany: American and German Perspectives*, Columbia: Camden House, 1993, 117–31.

——, "Gleichzeitigkeit: Vormoderne, Moderne und Postmoderne in der Literatur der DDR," in Heinz Ludwig Arnold (ed.), *Bestandsaufnahme Gegenwartsliteratur*, Munich: edition text und kritik, 1988, 193–211.

——, *Kleine Literaturgeschichte der DDR: 1945–1988. Erweiterte Ausgabe*, Frankfurt a. M.: Luchterhand, 1989.

—— (ed.), *Sarah Kirsch/Irmtraud Morgner/Christa Wolf, Geschlechtertausch: Drei Geschichten über die Umwandlung der Verhältnisse*, Frankfurt a. M.: Luchterhand, 1980.

Fehervary, Helen, "Christa Wolf's Prose: A Landscape of Masks," in Marilyn Sibley Fries (ed.), *Responses to Christa Wolf: Critical Essays*, Detroit: Wayne State University Press, 1989, 162–85.

——, "The Gender of Authorship: Heiner Müller and Christa Wolf," *Studies in Twentieth Century Literature*, 5:1 (Fall 1980), 41–59.

Fehervary, Helen, Harrigan, Renny and Vedder-Shuts, Nancy (eds), *New German Critique: Special Feminist Issue* 13 (winter 1978).

Foster, Hal (ed.), *The Anti-Aesthetic: Essays on Postmodern Culture*, Seattle: Bay, 1983.

Foucault, Michel, *The Archeology of Knowledge*, S. Smith (trans.), New York: Harper & Row, 1976.

Fox, Thomas C., "Germanistik and GDR Studies: (Re)Reading a Censored Literature," *Monatshefte*, 85:3 (1993), 284–94.

Gallas, Helga. *Marxistische Literaturtheorie: Kontroversen im Bund proletarisch-revolutionärer Schriftsteller*, Neuwied: Luchterhand, 1971.

Gaskill, Howard, McPherson, Karin and Barker, Andrew (eds), *Neue Ansichten: The Reception of Romanticism in the Literature of the GDR* (GDR Monitor Special Series, No. 6), Amsterdam: Rodopi, 1990.

Geisel, Beatrix, "Unsere 'schöne' Frauenhalter-Kultur," *Mannheimer Morgen*, 25 November 1976.

Genette, Gérard, *Palimpsestes*, Paris: Seuil, 1982.

Gerhardt, Marlis (ed.), *Irmtraud Morgner: Texte, Daten, Bilder*, Frankfurt a. M.: Luchterhand, 1990.

Gilbert, Sandra and Gubar, Susan, *Sexchanges. No Man's Land*, vol. 2, New Haven: Yale University Press, 1989.

Glazener, Nancy, "Dialogic Subversion: Bakhtin, the Novel, and Gertrude Stein," in Ken Hirschkop and David Shepherd (eds), *Bakhtin and Cultural Theory*. Manchester: Manchester University Press, 1989, 109–29.

236

Gregor-Dellin, Martin, "Trobadora aus der Retorte: Was die Speilfrau Laura der DDR-Autorin Irmtraud Morgner verriet," *Frankfurter Allgemeine Zeitung*, 10 March 1975.

Grobbel, Michaela, "Kreativität und Re-Vision in den Werken Irmtraud Morgners von 1968 bis 1972," *New German Review*, 3 (1987), 1–16.

Habermas, Jürgen, "Adorno-Preisrede," Reprinted as "Modernity vs. Postmodernity," *New German Critique* 22 (1981), 3–14.

——, "Modernity Versus Postmodernity," *New German Critique*, 22 (1981), 3–14.

Haraway, Donna, "A Manifesto for Cyborgs: Science, Technology, and Socialist Feminism in the 1980s," *Socialist Review*, 15:2 (1985), 65–107.

Hauser, Kornelia, "Weiblicher Teiresias oder trojanisches Pferd im Patriarchat? Geschlechtertausch bei Christa Wolf und Irmtraud Morgner," *Das Argument* 3 (1991), 373–82.

Held, David, *Introduction to Critical Theory: Horkheimer to Habermas*, Berkeley and Los Angeles: University of California Press, 1986.

Hell, Julia, *Post-Fascist Fantasies: Psychoanalysis, History, and the Literature of East Germany*, Durham: Duke University Press, 1997.

Herminghouse, Patricia, "'Der Autor nämlich ist ein wichtiger Mensch': Zur Prosa [schreibender Frauen in der Deutschen Demokratischen Republik]," in Hiltrud Gnüg and Renate Möhrmann (eds), *Frauen Literatur Geschichte: Schreibende Frauen vom Mittelalter bis zur Gegenwart*, Frankfurt a. M.: Suhrkamp, 1989, 338–53.

——, "Die Frau und das Phantastische in der neueren DDR-Literatur: Der Fall Irmtraud Morgner," in Wolfgang Paulsen (ed.), *Die Frau als Heldin und Autorin: Neue kritische Ansätze zur deutschen Literatur*, Bern: Francke, 1979, 248–66.

——, "Legal Equality and Women's Reality in the German Democratic Republic," in Edith Hoshino Altbach *et al.* (eds), *German Feminism: Readings in Politics and Literature*, Albany: State University of New York Press, 1984, 41–6.

——, "New Contexts for GDR Literature: An American Perspective," in *Cultural Transformations in the New Germany: American and German Perspectives*, Friederike Eigler and Peter C. Pfeiffer (eds), 93–101, Columbia: Camden House, 1993.

——, "Phantasie oder Fanatismus? Zur feministischen Wissenschaftskritik in der Literatur der DDR," in Ute Brandes (ed.), *Zwischen gestern und morgen: Schriftstellerinnen der DDR aus amerikanischer Sicht*, Berlin: Peter Lang, 1992, 69–94.

Herrmann, Anne, *The Dialogic and Difference: "An/Other Woman" in Virginia Woolf and Christa Wolf*, New York: Columbia University Press, 1989.

Hirschkop, Ken and Shepherd, David (eds), *Bakhtin and Cultural Theory*, Manchester: Manchester University Press, 1989.

Hoesterey, Ingeborg, "Postmodernisms," *Yearbook of Comparative and General Literature*, 37 (1988), 161–5.

—— (ed.), *Zeitgeist in Babel: The Postmodernist Controversy*, Bloomington: Indiana University Press, 1991.

Hohendahl, Peter Uwe, "Ästhetik und Sozialismus: Zur neueren Literaturtheorie der DDR," in Peter Uwe Hohendahl and Patricia Herminghouse (eds), *Literatur und Literaturtheorie in der DDR*, Frankfurt a. M.: Suhrkamp, 1976, 100–62.

——, "Autonomy of Art: Looking Back at Adorno's 'Ästhetische Theorie,'" in Judith Marcus and Zoltan Tar (eds), *Foundations of the Frankfurt School of Social Research*, New Brunswick: Transaction Books, 1984, 207–24.

——, "Theorie und Praxis des Erbens: Untersuchung zum Problem der literarischen Tradition in der DDR," in Peter Uwe Hohendahl and Patricia Herminghouse (eds), *Literatur der DDR in den 70er Jahren*, Frankfurt a. M.: Suhrkamp, 1983, 13–52.

—— and Herminghouse, Patricia (eds), *Literatur der DDR in den 70er Jahren*, Frankfurt a. M.: Suhrkamp, 1983.

—— (eds), *Literatur und Literaturtheroie in der DDR*, Frankfurt a. M.: Suhrkamp, 1976.

Hölzle, Peter, "Der abenteuerliche Umgang der Irmtraud Morgner mit der Trobairitz Beatriz de Dia," in Jürgen Kühnel, Hans-Dieter Muck and Ulrich Müller (eds), *Mittelalter-Rezeption*, Göppingen: Kümmerle, 1979, 430–45.

Honecker, Erich, "Bericht des ZK an den VIII. Parteitag vom 15. Juni 1971," Reprinted in *Neues Deutschland*, 18 December 1971.

Huffzky, Karin, "Produktivkraft Sexualität souverän nutzen: Ein Gespräch mit der DDR-Schriftstellerin Irmtraud Morgner," *Frankfurter Rundschau*, 16 August 1975, 111.

Hutcheon, Linda, *Poetics of Postmodernism: History, Theory, Fiction*, New York: Routledge, 1988.

——, *The Politics of Postmodernism*, London: Routledge, 1991.

Huyssen, Andreas, "After the Wall: The Failure of German Intellectuals," *New German Critique* 52 (Winter 1991), 109–43.

——, "Mapping the Postmodern," *New German Critique*, 33 (Fall 1984), 5–52.

Jameson, Fredric, "Postmodernism, or the Cultural Logic of Late Capitalism," *New Left Review*, 146 (1984), 53–92.

Janhsen, Doris and Meier, Monika, "Spiel-Räume der Phantasie. Irmtraud Morgner: *Leben und Abenteuer der Trobadora Beatriz nach Zeugnissen ihrer Spielfrau Laura*," in Karl Deiritz and Hannes Krauss (eds), *Verrat an der Kunst*, Berlin: Aufbau Taschenbuch, 1993, 209–14.

——, "Trobadora passé? Irmtraud Morgner zum Geburtstag," *Freitag*, 20 August 1993.

Jay, Martin, *Adorno*, Cambridge: Harvard University Press, 1984.

——, *The Dialectical Imagination: A History of the Frankfurt School and the Institute of Social Research, 1923–1950*, Boston: Little, Brown, 1973.

Jens, Walter, "Die Tausendsassa Irmtraud Morgner," in Marlis Gerhardt (ed.), *Irmtraud Morgner: Texte, Daten, Bilder*, Frankfurt a. M.: Luchterhand, 1990, 100–8.

Kaplan, E. Ann, *Women and Film: Both Sides of the Camera*, New York: Methuen, 1983.

238

Kaufmann, Eva, "Der Hölle die Zunge rausstrecken ... Der Weg der Erzählerin Irmtraud Morgner," *Weimarer Beiträge*, 9 (1984), 1515–32. Reprinted in Marlis Gerhardt (ed.), *Irmtraud Morgner: Texte, Daten, Bilder*, Frankfurt a. M.: Luchterhand, 1990, 172–95.

——, "Interview mit Irmtraud Morgner," *Weimarer Beiträge* 9 (1984), 1494–514. Reprinted as "Der weilbliche Ketzer heißt Hexe. Gespräch mit Eva Kaufmann," in Marlis Gerhardt (ed.), *Irmtraud Morgner: Texte, Daten, Bilder*, Frankfurt a. M.: Luchterhand, 1990, 42–69.

——, "Irmtraud Morgner, Christa Wolf und andere: Feminismus in der DDR-Literatur," in Heinz Ludwig Arnold (ed.), *Literatur in der DDR: Rückblicke*, München: text und kritik, Sonderband, 1991, 109–16.

Kirsch, Sarah, *Die Pantherfrau*, Berlin, Weimar: Aufbau Verlag, 1973.

Köhler, Erich, *Ideal und Wirklichkeit in der höfischen Epik*, Tübingen: Niemeyer, 1970.

Kristeva, Julia, *The Kristeva Reader*, Oxford, Blackwell, 1986.

Kuhn, Annette, *Women's Pictures: Feminism and Cinema*, London: Routledge, 1982.

Lennox, Sara, "'Nun ja! Das nächste Leben geht aber heute an.' Prosa von Frauen und Frauenbefreiung in der DDR," in Peter Uwe Hohendahl and Patricia Herminghouse (eds), *Literatur der DDR in den 70er Jahren*, Frankfurt a. M.: Suhrkamp, 1983, 224–58.

——, "Trend in Literary Theory: The Female Aesthetic and German Women's Writing," *German Quarterly*, 54 (January 1981), 63–75.

Lewis, Alison, "'Foiling the Censor': Reading and Transference as Feminist Strategy in the Works of Christa Wolf, Irmtraud Morgner, and Christa Moog," *German Quarterly*, 66 (Summer 1993), 372–86.

——, *Subverting Patriarchy: Feminism and Fantasy in the Works of Irmtraud Morgner*, Washington: Berg, 1995.

Liebs, Elke, "Melusine zum Beispiel: Märchen und Mythenrezeption in der Prosa der DDR," in Howard Gaskill, Karen McPerson and Andrew Barker (eds), *Neue Ansichten: The Reception of Romanticism in the Literature of the GDR*, Amsterdam: Rodopi, 1990, 126–41.

Lindemann, Gisela, "Des Kaisers alte neue Kleider," *Die Zeit*, 22 July 1983. Reprinted in Marlis Gerhardt (ed.), *Irmtraud Morgner: Texte, Daten, Bilder*, Frankfurt a. M.: Luchterhand, 1990, 159–64.

Lyotard, Jean-François, *The Postmodern Condition: A Report on Knowledge*, Geoff Bennington and Brian Massumi (trans.), Minneapolis: University of Minnesota Press, 1984.

Maltzan, Carlotta von, "'Man müßte ein Mann sein': Zur Frage der weiblichen Identität in Erzählungen von Kirsch, Morgner und Wolf," *Acta Germanica*, 20 (1990), 141–55.

Marggraf, Nikolaus (Wolfram Schütte), "Die Feministin der DDR: Irmtraud Morgner's *Leben und Abenteuer der Trobadora Beatriz*," *Frankfurter Rundschau*, 24 May 1975.

Martin, Biddy, "Irmtraud Morgner's *Leben und Abenteuer der Trobadora Beatriz*," in Susan L. Cocalis and Kay Goodman (eds), *Beyond the Eternal Feminine: Critical Essays on Women and German Literature*, Stuttgart: Akademischer Verlag, 1982, 421–39.

——, "Socialist Patriarchy and the Limits of Reform: A Reading of Irmtraud Morgner's *Life and Adventures of Troubadora Beatriz as Chronicled by her Minstrel Laura*," *Studies in Twentieth Century Literature*, 5:1 (Fall 1980), 59–74.

——, "Zwischenbilanz der feministischen Debatten," in Frank Trommler (ed.), *Germanistik in den USA*, Opladen: Westdeutscher Verlag, 1989, 165–95.

McCormick, Richard W., *Politics of the Self: Feminism and the Postmodern in West German Literature and Film*, Princeton: Princeton University Press, 1991.

Meier, Monika, "Konzerte der Redevielfalt: Die Walpurgisnacht-Darstellungen in der 'Amanda' Irmtraud Morgners," *Literatur für Leser*, 4 (1990), 213–27.

Meinhof, Ulrike, *Bambule*, Berlin: Wagenbach, 1971.

Morgner, Irmtraud, *Amanda. Ein Hexenroman*, Berlin: Aufbau, 1983; Darmstadt: Luchterhand, 1983.

——, "Apropos Eisenbahn," in Gerhard Schneider (ed.), *Eröffnungen: Schriftsteller über ihr Erstlingswerk*, Berlin: Aufbau, 1974, 204–10. Reprinted in Marlis Gerhardt (ed.), *Irmtraud Morgner. Texte, Daten, Bilder*, Frankfurt a. M.: Luchterhand, 1990, 17–23.

——, *Das Heroische Testament: Roman in Fragmenten*, Rudolf Bussmann (ed.), München: Luchterhand, 1998.

——, *Das Signal steht auf Fahrt. Erzählung*, Berlin: Aufbau, 1959.

——, *Der Schöne und das Tier: Eine Liebesgeschichte*, Frankfurt a. M.: Luchterhand, 1991.

——, *Die Hexe im Landhaus: Ein Gespräch in Solothurn. Mit einem Beitrag von Erika Pedretti*, Zürich: Rauhreif Verlag, 1984.

——, *Die wundersamen Reisen Gustavs des Weltfahrers: Lügenhafter Roman mit Kommentaren*, Berlin: Aufbau, 1972; Munich: Hanser, 1973; Frankfurt a. M.: Fischer, 1975; Darmstadt: Luchterhand, 1981.

——, *Ein Haus am Rande der Stadt: Roman*, Berlin: Aufbau, 1962.

——, *Gauklerlegende: Eine Spielfrauengeschichte*, Mit sechs Fotographien von Lothar Reher, Berlin/DDR: Eulenspiegelverlag, 1970; Munich: Roger & Bernhard, 1971; Darmstadt: Luchterhand, 1982.

——, *Hochzeit in Konstantinopel: Roman*, Berlin: Aufbau, 1968; Munich: Hanser, 1969; Munich: Dtv, 1972.

——, "Kaffee verkehrt," in Ingrid Krüger (ed.), *Die Heiratsschwindlerin: Erzählerinnen der DDR*, Darmstadt: Luchterhand, 1983, 7–8.

——, *Leben und Abenteuer der Trobadora Beatriz nach Zeugnissen ihrer Spielfrau Laura: Roman in dreizehn Büchern und sieben Intermezzos*, Berlin: Aufbau, 1974; Darmstadt: Luchterhand, 1976; Darmstadt: Luchterhand, 1977.

——, "Life and Adventures of Troubadora Beatriz as Chronicled by Her Minstrel Laura: Twelfth Book," Karen R. Achberger and Friedrich Achberger (trans.), *New German Critique* 15 (Fall 1978), 121–46.

———, *The Life and Adventures of Trobadora Beatrice as Chronicled by Her Minstrel Laura. A Novel in Thirteen Books and Seven Intermezzos*, Jeanette Clausen (trans.), Lincoln: University of Nebraska Press, 2000.

———, "Notturno. Erzählung," in *Neue Texte: Almanach für deutsche Literatur*, Berlin: Aufbau, 1964, 7–36.

———, "Rede auf dem VII. Schriftstellerkongreß der DDR," *Neue deutsche Literatur*, 8 (1978), 27–32. Reprinted in Marlis Gerhardt (ed.), *Irmtraud Morgner: Texte, Daten, Bilder*, Frankfurt a. M.: Luchterhand, 1990, 27–32.

———, *Rumba auf einen Herbst: Roman*, Rudolf Bussmann (ed.), Frankfurt a. M.: Luchterhand, 1992.

———, "Stellungnahmen," (Interviews with 39 GDR Writers), in Richard A. Zipser (ed.), *DDR Literatur im Tauwetter: Wandel – Wunsch – Wirklichkeit*, vol. 3, New York: Peter Lang, 1985.

———, "Zeitgemäß unzeitgemäß Hrosvit," *Neue deutsche Literatur*, 2 (1986), 126–8. Reprinted in Marlis Gerhardt (ed.), *Irmtraud Morgner: Texte, Daten, Bilder*, Frankfurt a.M.: Luchterhand, 1990, 70–2.

Morson, Gary Saul and Emerson, Caryl (eds), *Mikhail Bakhtin: Creation of a Prosaics*, Stanford: Stanford University Press, 1990.

Mulvey, Laura, "Visual Pleasure and Narrative Cinema," *Screen*, 16:3 (Fall 1975), 6–18.

Nägele, Rainer, "Trauer, Tropen und Phantasmen: Ver-rückte Geschichten aus der DDR," in Peter Uwe Hohendahl and Patricia Herminghouse (eds), *Literatur der DDR in den 70er Jahren*, Frankfurt a. M.: Suhrkamp, 1983, 193–223.

Neubert, Werner, "Aus einem Gutachten," *Neue Deutsche Literatur*, 22:8 (8 August 1974), 103–5.

Neumann, Oskar, "Weltspitze sein und sich wundern, was noch nicht ist," *Kürbiskern*, 78:1 (1978), 95–9.

Noeske, Britta, *Liebe Kollegin: Texte zur Emanzipation der Frau in der Bundesrepublik*, Frankfurt a. M.: Fischer Taschenbuch, 1973.

Nordmann, Ingeborg, "Die halbierte Geschichtsfähigkeit der Frau: Zu Irmtraud Morgners Roman *Leben und Abenteuer der Trobadora Beatriz nach Zeugnissen ihrer Spielfrau Laura*," *Amsterdamer Beiträge zur Neueren Germanistik*, 11–12 (1981), 419–62.

Owens, Craig, "The Discourse of Others: Feminists and Postmodernism," in Hal Foster (ed.), *The Anti-Aesthetic: Essays on Postmodern Culture*, Seattle: Bay, 1983, 57–82.

Poiger, Uta G., "Rock 'n' Roll, Female Sexuality, and the Cold War Battle over German Identities," in Robert G. Moeller (ed.), *West Germany under Construction: Politics, Society, and Culture in the Adenauer Era*, Ann Arbor: University of Michigan Press, 1990, 373–410.

Raddatz, Fritz, "Marx-Sisters statt Marx: Neue Bücher von Morgner, Schlesinger, Köhler," *Die Zeit*, 21 May 1976.

Reid, J. H., "From Adolf Hennecke to Star Wars – the Fortunes of 'Faust' in the GDR," in Howard Gaskill, Karen McPerson and Andrew Barker (eds), *Neue*

Ansichten: The Reception of Romanticism in the Literature of the GDR, Amsterdam: Rodopi, 1990, 142–59.

Reinig, Christa, "Ein Einhorn soll die ganze Welt erlösen," *Die Welt am Sonntag*, 8 August 1976.

Reuffer, Petra, *Die unwahrscheinlichen Gewänder der anderen Wahrheit: Zur Wiederentdeckung des Wunderbaren bei G. Grass und I. Morgner*, Essen: Verlag Die Blaue Eule, 1988.

Rotzoll, Christa, "Ein lustiges Klagelied," *Süddeutsche Zeitung*, 13 November 1976.

Runge, Erika, *Frauen: Versuche zur Emanzipation*, Frankfurt a. M.: Suhrkamp, 1969.

Russo, Mary, "Female Grotesques: Carnival and Theory," in Teresa de Lauretis (ed.), *Feminist Studies, Critical Studies*, Bloomington: Indiana University Press, 1986, 213–29.

Sanders, Helke, "Rede des Aktionsrates zur Befreiung der Frauen bei der 23. Delegiertenkonferenz des SDS im September 1968 in Frankfurt," *Frauenjahrbuch* 1 (1975). Reprinted as "Speech by the Action Council for Women's Liberation," in Edith Hoshino Altbach *et al.* (eds), *German Feminism: Readings in Politics and Literature*, Edith Hoshino Altbach (trans.), Albany: State University of New York Press, 1984, 307–10.

Sati, Ulrike, "Figuren im Gespräch: Irmtraud Morgners 'Leben und Abenteuer der Trobadora Beatriz nach Zeugnissen ihrer Spielfrau Laura,'" *Carleton Germanic Papers*, 18 (1990), 75–87.

Scherer, Gabriela, *Zwischen "Bitterfeld" und "Orplid," Zum literarischen Werk Irmtraud Morgners*, Bern: Peter Lang, 1992.

Schiller, Dieter, "Nahe Spielwelt der Phantasie," *Neues Deutschland*, 4 February 1975.

Schmitz, Dorothee, "Wilde Ritte durch die Weltgeschichte oder Schreiben ist Welt machen. Unverdient vergessene Autoren (3): Die Schriftstellerin Irmtraud Morgner (1933–1990)," *Handelsblatt*, 24/25, February 1995.

Schulte-Sasse, Jochen, "Theory of Modernism versus Theory of the Avant-Garde," foreword to Peter Bürger, *Theory of the Avant-Garde*, Michael Shaw (trans.), Minneapolis: University of Minnesota, 1984.

——, "Modernity and Modernism, Postmodernity and Postmodernism: Framing the Issue," *Cultural Critique* 5 (1986–87), 5–21.

Schulz, Genia, "Kein Chorgesang: Neue Schreibweisen bei Autorinnen (aus) der DDR," in Heinz Ludwig Arnold (ed.), *Bestandsaufnahme Gegenwartsliteratur*, Munich: edition text und kritik, 1988, 212–25.

Schwarzer, Alice, *Frauen gegen den $ 218*, Frankfurt a. M.: Suhrkamp, 1971.

——, "Auch Genossen sind nicht automatisch Brüder," *konkret*, 9 (1976), 57–8.

——, "Jetzt oder nie! Die Frauen sind die Hälfte des Volkes," *Emma*, 2 (1990), 32–8.

Silberman, Marc, "German Studies and the GDR: Too Near, Too Far," Editorial introduction, *Monatshefte*, 85:3 (1993), 265–74.

Soden, Kristine von (ed.), *Irmtraud Morgners hexische Weltfahrt: Eine Zeitmontage*, Berlin: Elefanten Press, 1991.

242

Stallybrass, Peter and White, Allon, *The Politics of Transgression*, Ithaca: Cornell University Press, 1986.

Stam, Robert, *Subversive Pleasures: Bakhtin, Cultural Criticism and Film*, Baltimore: The Johns Hopkins University Press, 1989.

Stefan, Verena, *Häutungen*, Munich: Verlag Frauenoffensive, 1975.

Stephan, Inge, "Daß ich Eins und doppelt bin. […]": Geschlechtertausch als literarisches Thema," in Sigrid Weigel and Inge Stephan (eds), *Die verborgene Frau: Sechs Beiträge zu einer feministischen Literaturwissenschaft*, Berlin: Argument Verlag, 1983, 53–175.

Struck, Karin, *Klassenliebe*, Frankfurt a. M.: Suhrkamp, 1973.

Suleiman, Susan Rubin, "Feminism and Postmodernism," in Ingeborg Hoesterey (ed.), *Zeitgeist in Babel: The Postmodern Controversy*, Bloomington: Indiana University Press, 111–30.

Todorov, Tzvetan, *Mikhail Bakhtin: The Dialogic Principle*, Wlad Godzich (trans.), Minneapolis: University of Minnesota Press, 1984.

Vinke, Hermann (ed.), *Akteneinsicht Christa Wolf. Zerrspiegel und Dialog: Eine Dokumentation*, Hamburg: Luchterhand, 1993.

von der Emde, Silke, "Places of Wonder: Fantasy and Utopia in Irmtraud Morgner's *Salman Trilogy*," *New German Critique*, 82 (Winter 2001), 167–92.

Wander, Maxie, *Guten Morgen, du Schöne: Protokolle von Frauen*, Frankfurt a. M.: Luchterhand, 1977.

Weigel, Sigrid, *Die Stimme der Medusa: Schreibweisen in der Gegenwartsliteratur von Frauen*, Dülmen-Hiddingsel: tende, 1987.

—— and Stephan, Inge (eds), *Die verborgene Frau: Sechs Beiträge zu einer feministischen Literaturwissenschaft*, Berlin: Argument Verlag, 1983.

Welsch, Wolfgang, "Subjektsein heute. Überlegungen zur Transformation des Subjekts," *Deutsche Zeitschrift für Philosophie*, 39:4 (1991), 347–65.

Wiggershaus, Rolf, *Die Frankfurter Schule: Geschichte, Theoretische Entwicklung, Politische Bedeutung*, Munich: Hanser, 1986.

Wolf, Christa, *Kindheitsmuster*, Darmstadt: Luchterhand, 1984.

——, *Nachdenken über Christa T*, Neuwied: Luchterhand, 1970.

Wolf, Gerhard, "Abschied von der Harmonie," *Sinn und Form*, 4 (1975), 840–6. Reprinted in Marlis Gerhardt (ed.), *Irmtraud Morgner: Texte, Daten, Bilder*, Frankfurt a. M.: Luchterhand, 1990, 109–16.

Wolter, Manfred, "Leben und Abenteuer der Beatriz …," *Sonntag* 8, 23 February 1975.

Woolf, Virginia, *Orlando. A Biography*, New York: Harvest Book, 1956.

——, *A Room of One's Own*, San Diego: Harvest, 1957.

Zenke, Thomas, "Aus dem Dornröschenschlaf erwacht," *Frankfurter Allgemeine Zeitung*, 16 November 1976.

Further reading

Adorno, Theodor W., *Negative Dialectics*, E. B. Ashton (trans.), New York: Seabury Press, 1973.

Auffermann, Verena, "Der Stammbaum. Im Nachlaß gefunden: Irmtraud Morgners erster Roman 'Rumba auf einen Herbst,'" *Die Zeit*, 6 November 1992.

——, "Sirenengesang. Kostbares von Irmtraud Morgner," *Die Zeit*, 16 August 1991.

Bachtin, Michail M., *Die Ästhetik des Wortes*, Rainer Grübel (ed.), Rainer Grübel and Sabine Reese (trans.), Frankfurt a. M.: Suhrkamp, 1979.

——, *Literatur und Karneval: Zur Romantheorie und Lachkultur*, Alexander Kämpfe (trans.), Frankfurt a. M.: Ullstein, 1985.

Bammer, Angelika, "Options and Interventions: An East German View," in *Partial Visions: Feminism and Utopianism in the 1970s*, 104–18. New York: Routledge, 1991.

——, "Sozialistische Feminismen: Irmtraud Morgner und amerikanische Feministinnen in den siebziger Jahren," in Ute Brandes (ed.), *Zwischen gestern und morgen: Schriftstellerinnen der DDR aus amerikanischer Sicht*, Berlin: Peter Lang, 1992, 237–48.

Bauer, Dale, *Feminist Dialogics: A Theory of Failed Community*, Albany: State University of New York Press, 1988.

Bauer, Dale and McKinstry, Susan Jaret (eds), *Feminism, Bakhtin, and the Dialogic*, Albany: State University of New York Press, 1991.

Berger, Christe, "Amanda," *Sonntag*, 22, 29 May 1983.

Bovenschen, Silvia, "Zu der Frage: Gibt es eine weibliche Ästhetik?" *Ästhetik und Kommunikation*, 25 (September 1976), 66–75.

Brandes, Ute, *Zitat und Montage in der neueren DDR-Prosa*, Frankfurt a. M.: Lang, 1984.

Brandt, Sabine, "Und trotzdem Castro überm Bett. Beigewicht an beflügelten Sohlen. Irmtraud Morgners Roman," *Frankfurter Allgemeine Zeitung*, 2 January 1993.

Broich, Ulrich and Pfister, Manfred (eds), *Intertextualität: Formen, Funktionen, anglistische Fallstudien*, Tübingen: Max Niemeyer, 1985.

Bubser-Wildner, Siegrun, "'Der Traum nach vorwärts': Utopie als funktionaler Prozess in Irmtraud Morgners Roman *Leben und Abenteuer der Trobadora Beatriz*," PhD Dissertation, University of Iowa, 1996.

Bürger, Christa and Bürger, Peter (eds), *Postmoderne: Alltag, Allegorie und Avantgarde*. Frankfurt a. M.: Suhrkamp, 1987.

Butler, Judith, *Gender Trouble: Feminism and the Subversion of Identity*, New York: Routledge, 1990.

——, "Gender Trouble, Feminist Theory, and Psychoanalytic Discourse," in Linda Nicholson (ed.), *Feminism/Postmodernism*, New York: Routledge, 324–40, 1990.

Calinescu, Matei, "From the One to the Many: Pluralism in Today's Thought," in Ingeborg Hoesterey (ed.), *Zeitgeist in Babel: The Postmodernist Controversy*, Bloomington: Indiana Press, 1991, 156–74.

——, "Modernism, Late Modernism, Postmodernism," in Danuta Zadworna-Fjellestad and Lennart Bjork (eds), *Criticism in the Twilight Zone: Postmodern Perspectives on Literature*, Stockholm: Almquist & Wiksell, 1990, 52–61.

——, *Rereading*, New Haven: Yale University Press, 1993.

—— and Fokkema, Douwe (eds), *Exploring Postmodernism*, Amsterdam: Benjamin, 1987.

Cixous, Hélène, "The Laugh of the Medusa," Keith Cohen and Paula Cohen (trans.), *Signs*, 1 (Summer 1976), 875–93.

Clason, Synnöve, "Auf den Zauberbergen der Zukunft: Die Sehnsüchte der Irmtraud Morgner," *Text & Kontext*, 12:2 (1984), 370–86.

Clason, Synnöve, "Uwe und Ilsebill. Zur Darstellung des anderen Geschlechts bei Morgner und Grass," in Inge Stephan and Carl Pietzcker (eds), *"Frauensprache – Frauenliteratur" Für und Wider einer Psychoanalyse literarischer Werke*, 104–7, Tübingen: Max Niemeyer, 1986.

Derrida, Jacques, *Of Grammatology*, Gayatari Spivak (trans.), Baltimore: The Johns Hopkins University Press, 1976.

——, *Spurs/Eperons*, Barbara Harlow (trans.), Chicago: University of Chicago Press, 1979.

——, *Writing and Difference*, Alan Bass (trans.), Chicago: University of Chicago Press, 1978.

Diebold, Ursula, "Zum Tode von Irmtraud Morgner," *Frauen in der Literaturwissenschaft: Rundbrief*, 25/26 (January 1990), 26–7.

Eagleton, Mary (ed.), *Feminist Literary Criticism*, London: Longman, 1991.

EB, "Weibliches Fabulieren," *Kölner Stadtauzeiger*, 7 May 1990.

Ecker, Gisela (ed.), *Feminist Aesthetics*, Harriet Anderson (trans.), Boston: Beacon Press, 1985.

Eco, Umberto, *Nachwort zum Namen der Rose*, Munich: dtv, 1986.

Emmerich, Wolfgang, "Identität und Geschlechtertausch. Notizen zur Darstellung der Frau in der neueren DDR-Literatur," in Reinhold Grimm and Jost Hermand (eds), *Basis, Jahrbuch für deutsche Gegenwartsliteratur*, vol. 8, Frankfurt: Suhrkamp, 1978, 127–54.

Endres, Elisabeth, "Das zweite blaue Klavier. Aus dem Nachlaß der Irmtraud Morgner," *Süddeutsche Zeitung*, 11 November 1992.

Engler, Jürger, "Die wahre Lüge der Kunst," *Neue Deutsche Literatur*, 7 July 1983.

Fehervary, Helen, "Autorschaft, Geschlechtsbewußtsein und Öffentlichkeit: Versuch über Heiner Müllers *Die Hamletmaschine* und Christa Wolfs *Kein Ort Nirgends*," in Irmela von der Lühe (ed.), *Entwürfe von Frauen in der Literatur des 20. Jahrhunderts*, Berlin: Argument, 1982, 132–53.

——, "Die erzählerische Kolonisierung des weiblichen Schweigens: Frau und Arbeit in der DDR-Literatur," in Reinhold Grimm and Jost Hermand (eds) *Arbeit als*

Thema in der deutschen Literatur vom Mittelalter bis Gegenwart, Königstein: Athenäum, 1979, 171–95.

——, "Dokumentation: Wolf Biermann," *The German Quarterly*, 57 (Spring 1984), 269–79.

——, "Enlightenment and Entanglement: History and Aesthetics in Bertolt Brecht and Heiner Müller," *New German Critique*, 8 (Spring 1976), 80–109.

——, "Ingeborg Bachmann: Her Part, Let It Survive," *New German Critique*, 47 (Spring/Summer 1989), 53–7.

——, "Thomas Brasch: A Storyteller after Kafka," *New German Critique*, 12 (Fall 1977), 125–32.

Fehn, Ann, Hoesterey, Ingeborg and Tartar, Maria (eds), *Neverending Stories: Toward a Critical Narratology*, Princeton: Princeton University Press, 1992.

Finke, Laurie A., *Feminist Theory, Women's Writing*, Ithaca: Cornell University Press, 1992.

Fokkema, Douwe and Bertens, Hans (eds), *Approaching Postmodernism*, Amsterdam: John Benjamins, 1986.

"Forum: The Christa Wolf Controversy," *GDR Bulletin*, 17:1 (Spring 1991), 1–18.

Foucault, Michel, *Madness and Civilization*, Richard Howard (trans.), New York: Mentor Books, 1967.

——, *The Order of Things*, New York: Random House, 1970.

Fox, Thomas C., *Border Crossings: An Introduction to East German Prose*, Ann Arbor: University of Michigan Press, 1993.

Frank, Manfred, *Was ist Neostrukturalismus?*, Frankfurt a. M.: Suhrkamp, 1983.

Fraser, Nancy, "What's Critical about Critical Theory? The Case of Habermas and Gender," *New German Critique*, 35 (Spring–Summer 1985), 97–131.

—— and Nicholson, Linda J., "Social Criticism without Philosophy: An Encounter between Feminism and Postmodernism," in Linda Nicholson (ed.), *Feminism/Postmodernism*, New York: Routledge, 1990, 19–38.

Fries, Fritz Rudolf, "Emanzipierte Frauen sind alle potentielle Dissidenten," *Neues Deutschland*, 28 August 1990, 8.

Funke, Christoph, "Flug-Besen im Luftraum," *Morgen*, 23 April 1983.

——, "Leben einer Spielfrau," *Der Morgen*, 1/2 March 1975, 122–3.

Geisel, Sieglinde, "Liebesurlaub in Helios' Wagen. Ein Fund im Nachlaß Irmtraud Morgners: der erste Roman der Autorin von *Trobadora Beatriz*," *Der Tagesspiegel*, 24 January 1993.

Gerhardt, Marlis, "Geschichtsklitterung als weibliches Prinzip," in Marlis Gerhardt (ed.), *Irmtraud Morgner. Texte, Daten, Bilder*, Frankfurt a. M.: Luchterhand, 1990, 93–9.

Gilbert, Sandra and Gubar, Susan, *The Madwoman in the Attic: The Woman Writer and the Nineteenth-Century Literary Imagination*, New Haven: Yale University Press, 1979.

Gnüg, Hiltrud and Möhrmann, Renate (eds), *Frauen – Literatur – Geschichte: Schreibende Frauen vom Mittelalter bis zur Gegenwart*, Frankfurt a. M.: Suhrkamp, 1989.

246

Gugisch, Peter, "Irmtraud Morgners Hexerei," *Die Weltbühne*, 36 (1983).

Habermas, Jürgen, *Der philosophische Diskurs der Moderne*, Frankfurt a. M.: Suhrkamp, 1985.

——, "Die Moderne – ein unvollendetes Projekt," in *Kleine politische Schriften*, vol. 2, Frankfurt a. M.: Suhrkamp, 1981, 444–64.

——, *Die neue Unübersichtlichkeit*, Frankfurt a. M.: Suhrkamp, 1985.

——, "The Entwinement of Myth and Enlightenment: Re-reading 'Dialectic of Enlightenment,'" *New German Critique*, 26 (Spring–Summer 1982), 13–30.

Hähnel, Ingrid and Kaufmann, Hans, "Eine Literatur der achtziger Jahre? Prosawerke der DDR am Beginn des Jahrzents," *Zeitschrift für Germanistik*, 1 (1985), 18–34.

Hähnel, Ingrid, and Siegfried Rönisch (eds), "Irmtraud Morgner," in *Werkstattgespräche mit DDR-Autoren*, Berlin: Aufbau, 1984, 383–407.

Hanke, Irma, "Von Rabenmüttern, Fabrikdirektorinnen und Hexen: Frauen schreiben über Frauen," in Gisela Helwig (ed.), *Die DDR Gesellschaft im Spiegel ihrer Literatur*, Cologne: Verlag Wissenschaft und Politik, 1986, 133–62.

Hartl, Edwin, "Legende, Witz und Mond: Irmtraud Morgners *Rumba auf einen Herbst*," *Die Presse*, 24 October 1992.

Hassan, Ihab, *The Dismemberment of Orpheus: Toward a Postmodern Literature*, New York: Oxford University Press, 1971.

Helwig, Gisela (ed.), *Die DDR Gesellschaft im Spiegel ihrer Literatur*, Cologne: Verlag Wissenschaft und Politik, 1986.

Hensel, Kerstin, "Tanz in gefährdeter Welt. Aus dem Nachlaß: Irmtraud Morgners Roman 'Rumba auf einen Herbst'," *Freitag*, 2 October 1992.

——, "Trobadora passé: Irmtraud Morgners Geschichte 'Der Schöne und das Tier'," *Freitag*, 18 (26 April 1991), 23.

Hermand, Jost and Silberman, Marc (eds), *Contentious Memories: Looking Back at the GDR*, German Life and Civilization 24, New York: Peter Lang, 1998.

Heulenkamp, Ursula, "Reiner Geist der frühen sechziger Jahre. Irmtraud Morgner: 'Rumba auf einen Herbst', herausgegeben von Rudolf Bussmann, Luchterhand Literaturverlag, Hamburg und Zürich," *Neue deutsche Literatur*, 3 (1993).

Hildebrandt, Christel, "Irmtraud Morgner," in *Zwölf Schreibende Frauen in der DDR: Zu den Schreibbedingungen von Schriftstellerinnen in der DDR in den 70er Jahren*, Berlin: Frauenbuchvertrieb, 1984, 87–98.

Hilzinger, Sonja, '*Als ganzer Mensch zu leben … ': Emanzipatorische Tendenzen in der neueren Frauenliteratur der DDR*, Frankfurt a. M.: Peter Lang, 1985.

Hirsch, Helmut, "Scherz, Ironie und tiefere Bedeutung," *Neue Deutsche Literatur*, August 1973.

Hirsch, Marianne and Keller, Evelyn Fox (eds), *Conflicts in Feminism*, New York: Routledge, 1990.

Hoesterey, Ingeborg, "Critical Narratology," *Text and Performance Quarterly*, 11:3 (July 1991), 207–16.

——, "Die Erzählsituation als Roman: Uwe Johnsons *Jahrestage*," *Colloquia Germanica*, 16:1 (1983), 13–26.

——, "Laokoon und Modernität: Eine Rettung," *Lessing Yearbook/Jahrbuch*, 15 (1983), 165–76.

——, "Literatur zur Postmoderne," *The German Quarterly*, 62 (Fall 1989), 505–9.

——, "Postmodern Bricoleurs: The New Syncretism in German Studies," *German Studies Review*, 14:3 (October 1991), 587–96.

——, *Verschlungene Schriftzeichen: Intertextualität von Literatur und Kunst in der Moderne/Postmoderne*, Frankfurt a. M.: Athenäum, 1988.

Holquist, Michael, *Dialogism: Bakhtin and His World*, New York: Routledge, 1990.

Howe, Irving, "Mass Society and Postmodern Fiction," *Partisan Review*, 26 (1959), 420–36.

Humble, Malcolm, "Pandora's Box: The Rehabilitation of the Siren and the Witch in Irmtraud Morgner's *Amanda*," *Forum for Modern Language Studies*, 28:4 (1992), 334–48.

Hurrelmann, Bettina, Kublitz, Maria and Röttger, Brigitte (eds), *Man müßte ein Mann sein ...? Interpretationen und Kontroversen zu Geschlechtertauschgeschichten in der Frauenliteratur*, Düsseldorf: Schwann, 1987.

Huyssen, Andreas, *After the Great Divide: Modernism, Mass-Culture, Postmodernism*, Bloomington: Indiana University Press, 1985.

——, "The Search for Tradition: Avant-garde and Postmodernism in the 1970s," *New German Critique*, 22 (Winter 1981), 23–40.

—— and Bathrick, David (eds), *Modernity and the Text: Revisions of German Modernism*, New York: Columbia University Press, 1989.

—— and Scherpe, Klaus (eds), *Postmoderne. Zeichen eines kulturellen Wandels*, Reinbek bei Hamburg: Rowohlt, 1986.

Irigaray, Luce, "And the One Does Not Stir without the Other," *Signs*, 7 (Fall 1981), 60–7.

——, *Speculum of the Other Woman*, Gilliam C. Gill (trans.), Ithaca: Cornell University Press, 1985.

——, *This Sex Which Is Not One*, Catherine Porter with Carolyn Burke (trans.), Ithaca: Cornell University Press, 1985.

Ivanov, V. V., "The Significance of Bakhtin's Ideas on Sign, Utterance, and Dialogue for Modern Semiotics," *Papers on Poetics and Semiotics*, 4, Tel Aviv: The Israeli Institute for Poetics and Semiotics, Tel Aviv University, 1976.

Jameson, Fredric, *The Political Unconscious: Narrative as a Socially Symbolic Act*, Ithaca: Cornell University Press, 1981.

——, "The Politics of Theory: Ideological Positions in the Postmodernism Debate," *New German Critique*, 33 (1984), 53–65.

Jardine, Alice, *Gynesis: Configurations of Women and Modernity*, Ithaca: Cornell University Press, 1984.

Jencks, Charles, "Postmodern vs. Late-Modern," in Ingeborg Hoesterey (ed.), *Zeitgeist in Babel: The Postmodernist Controvers*, Bloomington: Indiana University Press, 1991, 4–21.

Kamuf, Peggy, "Replacing Feminist Criticism," *Diacritics*, 12 (1982), 42–7.

Kändler, Klaus, "Der Hexenroman 'Amanda' von Irmtraud Morgner," in Siegfried Rönisch (ed.), *DDR-Literatur '83 im Gespräch*, Berlin: Aufbau, 1984.

Kittler, Friedrich A. and Turk, Horst (eds), *Urszenen: Literaturwissenschaft als Diskursanalyse und Diskurskritik*, Frankfurt a. M.: Suhrkamp, 1977.

Krechel, Ursula, "Das eine tun und das andere nicht lassen," *Konkret*, 10 (1976), 43–45. Reprinted as "Die täglichen Zerstückelungen. Gespräch mit Ursula Krechel," in Marlis Gerhardt (ed.), *Irmtraud Morgner: Texte, Daten, Bilder*, Frankfurt a. M.: Luchterhand, 1990, 24–33.

Kristeva, Julia, *Desire in Language: A Semiotic Approach to Literature and Art*, Leon S. Roudiez (ed.), Thomas Fora, Alice Jardine and Leon S. Roudiez (trans.), New York: Columbia University Press, 1982.

——, "Women's Time," Alice Jardine and Harry Blake (trans.), *Signs*, 7 (Fall 1981), 13–35.

Krüger, Ingrid (ed.), *Die Heiratsschwindlerin: Erzählerinnen der DDR*, Darmstadt: Luchterhand, 1983.

Kübler, Gunhild, "Die Liebe der letzten Tage: Zu einem verbotenen Roman von Irmtraud Morgner," *Neue Züricher Zeitung*, 12 November 1992.

Lemmens, Harrie, "Frauenstaat. Interview mit Irmtraud Morgner," *konkret*, 10 (1984), 54–61.

Liersch, Werner, "Erzählen im Ensemble," *Neue Deutsche Literatur*, August 1969.

Lodge, David, *After Bakhtin: Essays on Fiction and Criticism*, New York: Routledge, 1990.

Löffler, Sigrid, "Eine anmutige Spinnerin," *Die Zeit*, 10 June 1983.

Lützeler, Paul Michael (ed.), *Spätmoderne und Postmoderne: Beiträge zur deutschsprachigen Gegenwartsliteratur*, Frankfurt a. M.: Fischer, 1991.

Lyotard, Jean-François, "Adorno as the Devil," *Telos*, 19 (Spring 1974), 127–37.

——, "Beantwortung der Frage: Was ist postmodern?", in Wolfgang Welsch (ed.), *Wege aus der Moderne*, 193–203, Weinheim: VCH, Acta Humanoria, 1988

Marks, Elaine, "Feminist Wake," *Boundary*, 12:2 (special issue on *Feminist Writing*) (Winter 1984), 99–110.

Menschik, Jutta and Leopold, Evelyn, *Gretchens rote Schwestern: Frauen in der DDR*, Frankfurt a. M.: Fischer, 1974.

Metz, Doris, Obituary, *Süddeutsche Zeitung*, 8 May 1990.

Meyer-Gosau, Frauke, "Lady sings the Blues: Irmtraud Morgners nachgelassener Roman *Rumba auf einen Herbst*," *Die Tageszeitung*, 30 September 1992.

Möhrmann, Renate, "Feministische Ansätze in der Germanistik seit 1945," in Magdalena Heuser (ed.), *Frauen – Sprache – Literatur*, Düsseldorf: Schwann, 1982, 91–115.

Moi, Toril, *Sexual/Textual Politics: Feminist Literary Theory*, London: Routledge, 1985.

Morgner, Irmtraud, "Abschied von Pauline," *Neue deutsche Literatur*, 8 (1974), 81–103.

——, "Aus *Amanda*," in Ulla Fix and Horst Nalewski (eds), *Sprichwenndukannst: Schriftsteller über Sprache*, Leipzig: Gustav Kiepenheuer, 1989, 258–60.

249

——, "Aus dem Roman *Leben und Abenteuer der Trobadora Beatriz nach Zeugnissen ihrer Spielfrau Laura.* Zweites Buch: 7. Kapitel, Viertes Buch: 1.– 6. Kapitel," in Richard A. Zipser (ed.), *DDR Literatur im Tauwetter: Wandel – Wunsch – Wirklichkeit*, vol. 2, New York: Peter Lang, 1985, 74–83.

——, "Bis man zu dem Kerne zu gelangen das Glück hat. Zufallsbegünstigte Aufzeichnungen über den Oberbauleiter vom Palast der Republik nebst Adjudanten und Ehefrau," in Alice Uszkoreit (ed.), *Bekanntschaften: Eine Anthologie*, Berlin: Aufbau, 1976, 36–60. Reprinted in *Sonntag*, 29 (1974) and *Frankfurter Rundschau*, 18 January 1975.

——, "Bootskauf," *Neue deutsche Literatur*, 2 (1972), 371–6.

——, "Die Heiratsschwindlerin," *Sinn und Form*, 2 (1982). Reprinted in Ingrid Krüger (ed.), *Die Heiratsschwindlerin: Erzählerinnen der DDR*, Darmstadt: Luchterhand, 1983, 134–42. Reprinted in Gerhard Rothbauer (ed.), *Jetzt. 50 Geschichten vom Alltag*, 326–33. Leipzig: Reclam, 1988.

——, "The Duel," Karin Achberger (trans.), in Edith Hoshino Altbach *et al.* (eds), *German Feminism: Readings in Politics and Literature*, Albany: State University of New York Press, 1984, 209–12.

——, "Gute Botschaft der Valeska in 73 Strophen," in Wolfgang Emmerich (ed.), *Sarah Kirsch/Irmtraud Morgner/Christa Wolf, Geschlechtertausch: Drei Geschichten über die Umwandlung der Verhältnisse*, Darmstadt: Luchterhand, 1980.

——, "The Rope" (Abridged), Karin Achberger (trans.), in Edith Hoshino Altbach *et al.* (eds), *German Feminism: Readings in Politics and Literature*, Albany: State University of New York Press, 1984, 215–19.

——, "Shoes," Karin Achberger (trans.), in Edith Hoshino Altbach *et al.* (eds), *German Feminism: Readings in Politics and Literature*, Frankfurt a. M.: Luchterhand, 1990, 213–14.

——, "Sternstunden," *Almanach für deutsche Literatur*, Berlin: Aufbau, Herbst 1968. Reprinted in Konrad Franke and Wolfgang R. Langenbucher (eds), *Erzähler aus der DDR*, Tübingen: Horst Erdmann Verlag, 1973, 304–9.

——, "Weißes Ostern," *Die Heiratsschwindlerin: Erzählerinnen der DDR*, Ingrid Krüger (ed.), Darmstadt: Luchterhand, 1983, 46–53. Reprinted in Richard Christ and Manfred Wolter (eds), *Erzähler der DDR*, vol. 2, Berlin: Aufbau, 1985, 133–40.

——, "White Easter," Karin Achberger (trans.), in Edith Hoshino Altbach *et al.* (eds), *German Feminism: Readings in Politics and Literature*, Albany: State University of New York Press, 1984, 77–82.

Morson, Gary Saul, *Bakhtin: Essays and Dialogues on His Work*, Chicago: University of Chicago Press, 1986.

Morson, Gary Saul and Emerson, Caryl (eds), *Rethinking Bakhtin: Extensions and Challenges*, Evanston: Northwestern Press, 1989.

Neumann, Nicolaus, "Ein Ritterfräulein hat die Männer satt: Von achthundert Jahren Geschlechterkrieg erzählt ein Bestseller aus der DDR," *Stern*, 24 June 1976, 83.

Nicholson, Linda (ed.), *Feminism/Postmodernism*, New York: Routledge, 1990.

Obermüller, Klara, "Irmtraud Morgner," in Heinz Punkus (ed.), *Neue Literatur der Frauen: Deutschsprachige Autorinnen der Gegenwart*, Munich: Beck, 1980, 178–85.

"Pariser Gespräche über die Prosa der DDR," *Sinn und Form*, 6 (1976), 1164–92.

Patterson, David, *Literature and Spirit: Essays on Bakhtin and his Contemporaries*, Lexington: The University Press of Kentucky, 1988.

Pehnt, Annette, "Aussage steht gegen Aussage. Aus dem Nachlaß Irmtraud Morgners: Der Roman 'Rumba auf einen Herbst'," *Badische Zeitung*, 9 March 1993.

Petri, Walther, "Für Irmtraud Morgner," *Neue Deutsche Literatur*, 38:3 (August 1990), 66–7.

Puknus, Heinz, "Irmtraud Morgner," *Kritisches Lexikon zur Gegenwartsliteratur*, Munich: text und kritik, 1983.

Püschel, Ursula, "'Bei mir wächst ein Buch zusammen, nach und nach': *Rumba auf einen Herbst*, ein Roman aus dem Nachlaß von Irmtraud Morgner," *Neues Deutschland*, 30 September 1992.

Rasboinikowa-Fratewa, Maja Stankowa, "Strukturbildende Funktion des Verhältnisses von Wirklichkeit und dichterischer Phantasie – vorgeführt am Werk von Irmtraud Morgner," *Neophilologus*, 7:1 (January 1992), 101–7.

Ryan, Michael, *Marxism and Deconstruction: A Critical Articulation*, Baltimore: The Johns Hopkins University Press, 1982.

Scherer, Gabriela, "Irmtraud Morgner: *Rumba auf einen Herbst* – oder vom Umgang mit der Schwierigkeit 'ich' zu sagen," *Literatur für Leser*, 1 (1994), 1–10.

——, "Phantastische Erfindungen in erzählerischer Fülle. Zu dem neuen Roman 'Amanda' von Irmtraud Morgner," *Neues Deutschland*, 30 May 1983.

Schlaeger, Hilke, "The West German Women's Movement," *New German Critique*, 13 (1978), 59–67.

Schmitz, Dorothee, *Weibliche Selbstentwürfe und männliche Bilder: Zur Darstellung der Frau im DDR-Roman der siebziger Jahre*, Frankfurt a. M.: Peter Lang, 1983.

——, *Trobadora und Kassandra und [...] Weibliches Schreiben in der DDR*, Cologne: Pahl-Rugenstein, 1989.

Schuhmann, Klaus, "Widerspruchsthematik im Spannungsfeld von Gegenwart und Zukunft," in Siegfried Rönisch (ed.), *DDR-Literatur '84 im Gespräch*, Berlin: Aufbau, 1985, 24–36.

Schwarzer, Alice, "Das schwierige Geschäft mit der Sirene," *Der Spiegel*, 6 June 1983. Reprinted in Marlis Gerhardt (ed.), *Irmtraud Morgner: Texte, Daten, Bilder*, Frankfurt a. M.: Luchterhand, 1990, 165–71.

——, "Eine Aufwieglerin," *Neue Deutsche Literatur*, 38:3 (August 1990), 64–66.

Schwitzke, Werner, "Von A wie Antike bis Z wie Zeitgeschichte – Erbe und Gegenwart in Irmtraud Morgners *Salman*-Romanen," *Deutsch als Fremdsprache: Zeitschrift für Theorie und Praxis des Deutschunterrichts für Ausländer*, 24 (supplement) (1988), 113–18.

251

Secci, Lia, "Von der realen zur romantischen Utopie. Zeitgenössische Entwicklungen in der Erzählprosa der DDR," in Gisela Brinkler-Gabler (ed.), *Deutsche Literatur von Frauen*, vol. 2, Munich: Beck, 1988, 417–31.

Serke, Jürgen (ed.), "Eine Feministin, die die Männer nicht aufgibt," in *Frauen schreiben. Ein neues Kapitel deutschsprachiger Literatur*, Hamburg: Gruner und Jahr, 1979, 292–4.

Showalter, Elaine, "Critical Crossdressing: Male Feminists and the Women of the Year," in Alice Jardine and Paul Smith (eds), *Men in Feminism*, New York: Methuen, 1987, 116–32.

——, "Feminism and Literature," in Peter Colliers and Helga Geyer-Ryan (eds), *Literary Theory Today*, New York: Cornell University Press, 1990, 179–202.

——, "Feminist Criticism in the Wilderness," *Critical Inquiry*, 8 (Winter 1981). Reprinted in Elaine Showalter (ed.), *New Feminist Criticism. Essays on Women, Literature, and Theory*, New York: Pantheon, 1985, 243–70.

——, *A Literature of Their Own: British Women Novelists from Brontë to Lessing*, Princeton: Princeton University Press, 1977.

—— (ed.), *The New Feminist Criticism: Essays on Women, Literature, and Theory*, New York: Pantheon, 1985.

——, "Toward a Feminist Poetics," in Mary Jacobus (ed.), *Women's Writing and Writing About Women*, London: Croon Helm, 1979. Reprinted in Elaine Showalter (ed.), *New Feminist Criticism. Essays on Women, Literature, and Theory*, New York: Pantheon, 1985, 125–43.

Snaider Lanser, Susan. *The Narrative Act: Point of View in Prose Fiction*, Princeton: Princeton University Press, 1981.

Sommerich, Günter, "Den Rahmen gesprengt: Irmtraud Morgners Roman," *Stuttgarter Zeitung*, 22 January 1993.

Sperr, Monika, "Nach erster Ernüchterung wächst zaghaft die Hoffnung," *Basler Nachrichten*, 14 September 1976. Reprinted in Marlis Gerhardt (ed.), *Irmtraud Morgner: Texte, Daten, Bilder*, Frankfurt a. M.: Luchterhand, 1990, 155–9.

Stawström, Anneliese, *Studien zur Menschwerdungsproblematik in Irmtraud Morgner's 'Leben und Abenteuer der Trobadora Beatriz Nach Zeugnissen ihrer Spielfrau Laura.'* Stockholm: Almqvist & Wiksell International, 1987.

Stefan, Verena, *Shedding*, Johanna Moore and Beth Weckmueller (trans.), New York: Daughter's Publishing, 1978.

Stephan, Inge and Carl Pietzcker (eds), *Frauensprache – Frauenliteratur? Für und Wider einer Psychoanalyse literarischer Werke*, Tübingen: Max Niemeyer, 1986.

——, Weigel, Sigrid and Wilhelms, Kerstin (eds), *Wen kümmer's wer spricht: Zur Literatur und Kulturgeschichte von Frauen aus Ost und West*, Cologne: Böhlau, 1991.

Suleiman, Susan Rubin (ed.), *The Female Body in Western Culture: Contemporary Perspectives*, Cambridge: Harvard University Press, 1986.

Thomson, Clive, "Bakhtin's Theory of Genre," *Studies in Twentieth Century Literature*, 9:1 (Fall 1984), 29–40.

252

—— (ed.),"Bakhtin Special Issue," *Studies in Twentieth Century Literature*, 9:1 (Fall 1984).

Todorov, Tzvetan, *Literature and its Theorists: A Personal View of Twentieth-Century Criticism*, Catherine Porter (trans.), Ithaca: Cornell University Press, 1987.

Tsch, "Eine Frau griff nach den Sternen," *Die Welt*, 8 May 1990.

Uhde, Anne, "Minnesang und Maiunruhen," *Die Welt*, 26 June 1976.

von der Emde, Silke, "Irmtraud Morgner's Postmodern Feminism: A Question of Politics," in Jeanette Clausen and Sara Friedrichsmeyer (eds), *Women in German Yearbook: Feminist Studies in German Literature and Culture*, vol. 10, Lincoln: University of Nebraska Press, 1994, 117–42.

Walter, Joachin (ed.), "Irmtraud Morgner," in *Meinetwegen Schmetterlinge*, Berlin/DDR: Buchverlag Der Morgen, 1973, 42–54.

Warhol, Robin, *Gendered Interventions: Narrative Discourse in the Victorian Novel*, New Brunswick: Rutgers University Press, 1989.

Welsch, Wolfgang, *Unsere postmoderne Moderne*, Weinheim: VCH, Acta Humanoria, 1988.

—— (ed.), *Wege aus der Moderne: Schlüsseltexte der Postmoderne-Diskussion*, Weinheim: VCH, Acta Humanoria, 1988.

White, Allon, "Bakhtin, Sociolinguistics and Deconstruction," in Frank Gloversmith (ed.), *The Theory of Reading*, Totowa: Barnes & Noble, 1984, 123–46.

Wiggershaus, Renate, Obituary, *Frankfurter Rundschau*, 9 May 1990.

Wolf, Christa, "Der Mensch ist in zwei Formen ausgebildet: Zum Tode von Irmtraud Morgner," *Die Zeit*, 18 May 1990.

——, *Was bleibt. Erzählung*, Frankfurt a. M.: Luchterhand, 1990.

Wolf, Gerhard, "Scheherezade aus Sachsen – Abschied von Irmtraud Morgner," (Rede bei der Beerdigung Irmtraud Morgners am 11. 5. 1990.) In *Sprachblätter Wortwechsel*, Leipzig: Reclam, 1992, 134–140.

——, "Worte zum Abschied," *Neue Deutsche Literatur*, 38:3 (August 1990), 58–64.

Wolter, Manfred, "Trobadora startbereit: Leserbrief," *Sinn und Form*, 29:1 (1977), 207–9.

Index

German Life and Civilization

German Life and Civilization provides contributions to a critical under-standing of Central European cultural history from medieval times to the present. Culture is here defined in the broadest sense, comprising ex-pressions of high culture in such areas as literature, music, pictorial arts, and intellectual trends as well as political and sociohistorical developments and the texture of everyday life. Both the cultural mainstream and oppos-itional or minority viewpoints lie within the purview of the series. While it is based on specialized investigations of particular topics, the series aims to foster progressive scholarship that aspires to a synthetic view of culture by crossing traditional disciplinary boundaries.

10 Barbara Völkel: Karl Philipp Moritz und Jean-Jacques Rousseau. Außenseiter der Aufklärung. 1991. US-ISBN 0-8204-1689-4.

11 Dagmar C. G. Lorenz: Verfolgung bis zum Massenmord. Holocaust-Diskurse in deutscher Sprache aus der Sicht der Verfolgten. 1992. US-ISBN 0-8204-1751-3.

12 Alexander Mathaes: Der Kalte Krieg in der deutschen Literaturkritik. Der Fall Martin Walser. 1992. US-ISBN 0-8204-1824-2.

13 Amy Stapleton: Utopias for a Dying World. Contemporary German Science Fiction's. Plea for a New Ecological Awareness. 1993. US-ISBN 0-8204-1922-2.

14 K. Schultz, K. Calhoon (eds.): The Idea of the Forest. German and American Perspectives on the Culture and Politics of Trees. 1996. US-ISBN 0-8204-2384-X.

16 Jost Hermand (ed.): Postmodern Pluralism and Concepts of Totality. The Twenty-fourth Wisconsin Workshop. 1995. US-ISBN 0-8204-2658-X.

17 Myra J. Heerspink Scholz: A Merchant's Wife on Knight's Adventure. Permutations of a Medieval Tale in German, Dutch, and English Chapbooks around 1500. 1999. US-ISBN 0-8204-2573-7.

18 H. Adler, J. Hermand (eds.): Günter Grass. Ästhetik des Engagements. 1996. US-ISBN 0-8204-2719-5.

19 Christian Essellen: Babylon. Edited and with an Introduction by Cora Lee Nollendorfs. 1996. US-ISBN 0-8204-3045-5.

20 Klaus Berghahn: The German-Jewish Dialogue Reconsidered. A Symposium in Honor of George L. Mosse. 1996. US-ISBN 0-8204-3107-9.

21 Andréa Staskowski: Conversations with Experience. Feminist Hermeneutics and the Autobiographical Films of German Women. Forthcoming.

22 J. Hermand, J. Steakley (eds.): "Heimat", Nation, Fatherland. The German Sense of Belonging. 1996. US-ISBN 0-8204-3373-X.

23 Jörg Bernig: Eingekesselt. Die Schlacht um Stalingrad im deutschsprachigen Roman nach 1945. 1997. US-ISBN 0-8204-3667-4.

24 J. Hermand, M. Silberman (eds.): Contentious Memories. Looking Back at the GDR. 251 pp. 1998, 2000. US-ISBN 0-8204-5254-8.

25 Franziska Meyer: Avantgarde im Hinterland. Caroline Schlegel-Schelling in der DDR-Literatur. 1999. US-ISBN 0-8204-3924-X.

26 J. Hermand, R. Holub (eds.): Heinrich Heine's Contested Identities. Politics, Religion, and Nationalism in Nineteenth-Century Germany. 1999. US-ISBN 0-8204-4105-8.

27 Linda F. McGreevy: Bitter Witness. Otto Dix and the Great War. 467 pp. 2001. US-ISBN 0-8204-4106-6.

28 H. Adler, J. Hermand (eds.): Concepts of Culture. 1999. US-ISBN 0-8204-4141-4.

29 Hannu Salmi: Imagined Germany. Richard Wagner's National Utopia. 1999. US-ISBN 0-8204-4416-2.

30 Dennis Brain: Johann Karl Wezel. From Religious Pessimism to Anthropological Skepticism. 1999. US-ISBN 0-8204-4464-2.

31 Karoline von Oppen: The Role of the Writer and the Press in the Unification of Germany, 1989–1990. 277 pp. 2000. US-ISBN 0-8204-4488-X.

32 J. Hermand, M. Silberman (eds.): Rethinking Peter Weiss. 199 pp. 2000, 2001. US-ISBN 0-8204-5819-8.

33 Peter Morris-Keitel, Michael Niedermeier (eds.): Ökologie und Literatur. 224 pp. 2000. US-ISBN 0-8204-4872-9.

34 Helmut Peitsch: Georg Forster. A History of His Critical Reception. 333 pp. 2001. US-ISBN 0-8204-4925-3.

35 Martin Travers: Critics of Modernity. The Literature of the Conservative Revolution in Germany, 1890–1933. 256 pp. 2001. US-ISBN 0-8204-4927-X.

36 Susan C. Anderson: Water, Culture and Politics in Germany and the American West. 310 pp. 2001. US-ISBN 0-8204-4946-6.

37 Katherine Arens: Empire in Decline. Fritz Mauthner's Critique of Wilhelminian Germany. 222 pp. 2001. US-ISBN 0-8204-5038-3.

38 K. Berghahn, J. Fohrmann, H. Schneider (eds.): Kulturelle Repräsentationen des Holocaust in Deutschland und den Vereinigten Staaten. 253 pp. 2002. US-ISBN 0-8204-5208-4.

39 Hans Adler: Aesthetics and Aisthesis. New Perspectives and (Re)Discoveries. 170 pp. 2002. ISBN 3-906768-40-6, US-ISBN 0-8204-5852-X.

40 Silke von der Emde: Entering History. Feminist Dialogues in Irmtraud Morgner's Prose. 260 pp. 2004. ISBN 3-03910-158-7, US-ISBN 0-8204-6968-8.